ELDERLY CRIMINALS

Elderly
Criminals

Evelyn S. Newman
Donald J. Newman
Mindy L. Gewirtz
  and Associates

State University of New York at Albany

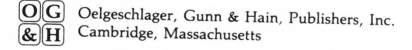 Oelgeschlager, Gunn & Hain, Publishers, Inc.
Cambridge, Massachusetts

International Standard Book Number: 0-89946-203-0

Library of Congress Catalog Card Number: 83-8227

Printed in the U.S.A.

Library of Congress Cataloging in Publication Data

Main entry under title:

Elderly Criminals

   Bibliography: p.
   Includes index.
   1. Aged offenders—United States—Addresses, essays, lectures. I. Newman, Evelyn S. II. Newman, Donald J. III. Gewirtz, Mindy L.
HV6791.E38 1984   364.3'7   83-8227
ISBN 0-89946-203-0

Contents

v

List of Tables and Figures

Tables

Foreword

Albert J. Abrams

In later life, crime may be committed because of a sense of lack of power, a lack of self-esteem, and self-preservation. Little research has been done in this area, and no research has been done on the impact of age on strong cultural values of honesty that may have been present at an earlier age. Are the aged shoplifters, for example, those who earlier in life cut corners on integrity, and had a philosophy that the end justifies the means? Not until longitudinal studies are done will we have more than our own biases to go on.

To understand criminality among the elderly, it is necessary to lay a broad foundation for inquiries by setting forth some of the demoraphic characteristics of old age, presenting some insights into the characteristics of old age, and making a brief foray into the uncharted field of senior offenders, as well as making one or two constructive recommendations for future action.

WHO IS THE CRIMINAL—
THE ELDERLY OR SOCIETY?

To set a tone for the discussion that follows, let us keep in mind that senility is no crime and senesence no sin. Even though brain damage or the fury and frustration of old age may precipitate an offense, gerontologists understand that society commits far more crimes against the elderly than the elderly commit against society. For example, such crimes may be those of neglect, impoverishment, ridicule, imposed loneliness, or nonuse of the aged.

In the movie *Going in Style*, the octogenarian actor, George Burns (whose only crime insofar as I know is leering at slim girls and smoking fat cigars), depicts the lonely oldster who, in desperation to give spirit to his later years, joins a few other lonesome seniors in a major exciting project: robbing a bank! This is to be the ultimate macho victory. And yet, in every older person, burns a desire for recognition and, in an uncaring society, some find it only in acts of defiance.

Biochemical changes in old age, such as reduced libido and physical changes affecting muscular strength, may play an important part in decreasing assaultive crimes in later years. But these generalities need to be analyzed with caution, for gerontologists know that *the aged differ from each other as much as they differ from younger age groups.*

Consider an 87-year-old male recovering from a stroke in a rehabilitation nursing home. Even though the man was nonaggressive all his life, he picks up his cane and assaults his blind roommate, probably due to the agony of frustration and the fear of his new environment. Or could the precipitating factor have been the new medicine he was prescribed?

In our studies of the elderly offender, we need to understand the complex physical and psychological factors involved in causing the aged to commit offenses. These factors include the inability to live up to the youthful standards society demands, the fear of poverty and dying, and the high frustration levels caused by loneliness and societal isolation. They can produce explosive results.

DEMOGRAPHY

Let us take a quick look at the demographics. The 1980 census counted 25.5 million persons in the 65-and-over age bracket in the United States—a growth of 50 percent in twenty years. That is why people speak about the *graying* of America. More startling is the *whitening* of those gray hairs. The highest percentage of increase among the elderly is in those eighty and over. In contrast to previous generations, when aged people declined slowly and steadily in their sixties and seventies, today's elderly are staying vigorous, active, and healthy into their seventies and eighties and declining precipitously and rapidly in their late eighties and nineties.

Table 1. Percentage of 65 and Over of Total Population, 1950–2020

1950	8.5
1960	9.4
1970	10.0
1980	11.1
1990	12.2
2000	12.4
2010	13.0
2020	15.5

As shown in Table 1, those 65-and-over consitute about 11 percent of all Americans. Thus, Congress now wrestles with an economic problem, since this 11 percent gets 25 percent of the nation's annual budgetary expenditure for Medicare, Medicaid, Social Security, and a variety of old age programs.

The elderly white population is quite different in makeup from the elderly of other racial and ethnic origins. About 12 percent of all whites are senior citizens, while only 8 percent of blacks and 5 percent of Hispanics are senior citizens. This suggests that in too many cases blacks and Hispanics don't live long enough to collect their social security!

As we all know, many elderly head south at the delivery of the first pension check, so the northern states have witnessed one of the greatest exoduses since Moses led the Israelites out of Egypt. The result is that our southern states have witnessed tremendous increases in the elderly, and this has imposed enormous strains on the service delivery systems of these states. In the decade between 1970 and 1980, net migration to the West and South increased by 3.3 million and 4.1 million, while the northeastern and north central states lost 1.8 million and 1.6 million, respectively.

Table 2 shows the dramatic extension of life in modern times. In the past seventy years there has been an increase of a quarter of a century in life expectation. In 1910, the average life expectancy was 50 years, while in 1980 it is 73.8 years.

Table 2. Life Expectancy at 65

1946	13.8
1950	14.2
1955	14.3
1960	14.3
1965	14.5
1970	15.0
1975	16.0
1980	16.3

Another example of the amazing extension of life is shown by the fact that of every 100,000 live births in the United States, 76,550 of them will live to age 65, and at that age will have an average life expectancy of 16.7 years. A typical profile of the older American is the elderly *woman* who lives alone and is widowed or divorced.

ECONOMIC FACTORS

Why do elderly people turn to crime? There are many factors, including loss of prestige upon retirement, boredom, feelings of helplessness as life's end draws nearer, and others. Economics seems to be one source of the problem. Although the median household income for all Americans in 1981 was $20,000, it was only $8,000 for the elderly. Single older people fare far worse if they are black, and single black women have median annual incomes of only $5,000.

In the past few years, poverty among old people has been on the rise. There had been a decline after Social Security was instituted, but that decline has now halted, and poverty is on the upswing. Absolute poverty among the aged has dropped in twenty years from 35 percent to 11 percent, but is now moving up to 13 percent. Today, one-third of elderly black people are poor, and 22 percent of elderly Hispanics are living below the poverty line.

Inflation is crippling efforts by those in the lower to middle income brackets to keep up their quality of life. A man who retired at 65 just five years ago has seen his buying power reduced by half. It is not surprising that at 70 he is insecure and frightened.

Since 1900, the number of older people in the labor force has gone down steadily, and now four out of five are either retired or otherwise out of the labor market. However, today increasing numbers of older people are postponing their retirements. The reason is that inflation frightens them. This temporary increase in the number of elderly who are employed, brought on in the past only by wars, will now be repeated at a time of dire inflation.

Fully 63 percent of the elderly rely on Social Security as their biggest source of income, 88 percent have some savings, two out of three own their own homes, and most of them have paid off their mortgage.

With more Americans reaching old age, we can expect a concomitant rise in criminal offenses committed by the elderly. However, while the numbers may increase, there is no reason to believe that the *rate* of offenses will increase in proportion to the number of elderly people. We have such poor statistics about crime among the aged that a good deal of guesswork is involved.

TYPES OF ELDERLY CRIME

As do their younger counterparts, the elderly engage in many types of crime, but not in the same number or proportions. Some crimes are particularly common among the elderly, such as larceny, a form of which is shoplifting, and driving while intoxicated.

In Albany, New York, a police captain reported that in 1979 only six older persons—all males—were arrested on larceny charges. However, out of a total of nine in the 60-and-over age group in 1980, there were two females 60 to 64, and three females 65 and over arrested for larceny. Out of thirteen arrested for larceny in 1981, there were four females 60 and over. Since we are dealing with small numbers, we need be careful not to exaggerate, but from 1979 to 1981, there was an increase of 101 percent in larceny arrests in Albany in the 60-and-over age group.

Statewide, in the upper age brackets, we find a decline in larceny arrests of older persons from 1,340 to 1,214. This represents a 10 percent drop from 1978 to 1980. No one is sure why. There is not much larceny in the hearts of the elderly if only 1,214 of 2,500,000 of them in New York state were arrested.

DRIVING WHILE INTOXICATED

Let us look at the driving while intoxicated figures. In 1980, 860 elderly people were arrested for driving while drunk in New York State. It might seem on viewing the figures that senior citizens are in their cups. However, the 860 number constitutes only about 1.5 percent of all DWI arrestees.

On convictions for all moving violations, the State Department of Motor Vehicles informs us that "it can be concluded that older motorists have significantly fewer convictions than those younger." But there are no scientific data on number of miles driven. From the few data that are available, in considering crimes by older people it becomes clear that DWI is apparently not a serious issue.

THE FBI AND THE MISSING ELDERLY PERSONS

One great crime mystery in the United States not headlined in the media is that of "missing persons over 65"—those who have not been included in FBI and state annual crime reports. Whether out of deference to the elderly or to the age of their computers, FBI and state reports do not separate crimes committed by senior citizens. Thus, while we have a great amount of detail on criminals under 15, under 21, and under 25, the FBI is apparently engaged in a conspiracy of silence on crimes by the elderly.

With an increase in the number of elderly in our society, and with awareness of the need for law enforcement bodies to assemble data on the age of offenders, we can fairly demand that crime-reporting agencies break down data so that we can analyze trends in the field of the aged offender. Only when we have good data can we help society in dealing with this problem.

NEED FOR A SENIOR CITIZEN COURT

Elderly people who fall into the chaotic judicial system today are often victimized by it. It is easy for the aged to become traumatized by the system when they are herded together with pimps, punks, and prostitutes in local holding "tanks" and shoved before overworked judges dealing with life-and-death situations stemming from complex interpersonal relationships.

Today we have family courts, juvenile courts, and a large variety of specialty courts to handle specific problems ranging from admiralty cases to immigration. A special court to handle cases of senior citizens charged with crimes would bring greater justice to bear. We need a court informed on geriatrics and gerontology that can assure the proper counseling service, the proper referral service, the proper family and community support when dealing with the frail elderly caught in the judicial administration system. Today, thousands of elderly arrested on charges ranging from shoplifting to creating a nuisance in Social Security offices are shunted into courts before judges who have little time, patience, or understanding. There is no inquiry into the impact of arterial blockage on cerebral functioning; the frustrations, fears, and confusion of elderly who may not be able to hear or see well; or undetected "mini-strokes" which cause distortions in the elderly perceptions of right and wrong.

Here is a recent case in point. An 84-year-old dentist taking care of his octogenarian, senile wife bruised her by pushing her upstairs. On another occasion he left her in an unattended car in the middle of winter while he went on an errand. The social agency brought charges against him and demanded he be separated from his wife for her safety. What is a judge to do? In this case, the judge was lucky. The judge demurred because he feared that separation of the woman from her husband would kill her. The next day the elderly woman died a natural death. If the judge had separated the two, imagine the abuse that would have been brought upon the judge by a screaming press and outraged social agencies.

A special senior citizens' court could provide insight into the problems of the aged offender, could provide referral and counseling service for the arrested aged, and could segregate mentally infirm elderly from hardened old criminals. In a time when judicial administrators are calling for assembly-line, high-disposal rates of cases, these courts could provide society's final mark of respect for the aged.

A few of the causes of crime for elderly first offenders, may be *hypoxia*—interference with oxygen supply to the brain; *ischemia*—interference of blood supply to the brain, drugs in conflict, or the hyperfunction of the pituitary or other endocrine organs. Between age 30 and 60, 1.2 billion neurons are lost from the normal cerebral cortex, which previously contained about 10 billion neurons. In most elderly people, this irreversible loss of nervous tissue is compensated for in ways we little understand. A court that understands the physical and emotional changes in the aging process can help take many elderly people out of the high-cost law enforcement system and mete out a more humane justice for society and the aged. If need be, facilities geared to lower-cost care should be established.

RESEARCH NEEDED

The field of geronto-crimes is one that has not been scientifically studied. Therefore, creative minds are needed to open up our understanding of elderly criminal behavior.

Some of the research needed includes:
1. Relation of mobility to crimes by the elderly. (When they are separated from their families, do crimes increase?)
2. Relation of aging to the decrease in traditional religious-ethical values. (If there is an increase in religiosity as we age, is there also a decrease in "thou shalt not steal" strictures?)
3. Correlation between economic recession and crimes among the elderly. (Does elderly crime increase when inflation rises, or when unemployment rises?)
4. Longitudinal studies of the elderly repeater—the life-long criminal in old age—and the one-time aged offender. (Psychosocial studies of elderly criminals who keep repeating crimes, compared with first time or one-time aged criminals.)
5. Drugs and crime. (Study of the prescriptions used by elderly criminals to determine whether drugs may have precipitated criminal activity by causing rage, hallucinations, or personality changes.)

These research needs represent only the tip of the iceberg. For example, we do not know whether the elderly shoplift only in impersonal institutions (such as chain stores and shopping centers), and how this compares with neighborhood ma-and-pa stores. The list of "unknowns" in this field is enormous.

Elderly crime will undoubtedly increase in the years ahead as the elderly population grows. There is no way now of predicting whether the rate of crime within the elderly population itself will increase or decrease. However, crimes committed by the elderly are of sufficient importance to warrant increased research in this field, better reporting of the age of offenders, and inquiries into the feasibility of special courts for senior citizens. This book begins to raise some of these very important questions.

Albert J. Abrams

PREFACE

Of all the problems and dilemmas created by the graying of America, one that has received little professional attention is the involvement of greater numbers of elderly persons with the criminal justice system. Over the past decade or so there has been concern about the elderly as victims of predatory crime. This has sparked a good deal of research and, in some jurisdictions, has led to legislative changes that provide more severe penalties for criminals convicted of preying on elderly victims. Actually, the proportion of elderly who are criminally victimized is small. However, because the impact on the elderly victim is often greater than on other victims and since the number of elderly is increasing, the problem assumes larger dimensions.

At the other end, some elderly persons are involved with the criminal justice network as offenders rather than victims. Yet this side of the criminal-victim equation has been relatively neglected in research. This book is an attempt to counteract that neglect by examining the phenomenon of crimes committed by elderly persons and by raising questions about whether our criminal justice system can cope appropriately with aged offenders.

The idea of the elderly criminal strikes many people at first as such a rare occurrence as to be unimportant. Indeed, newspaper accounts of 80-year-olds growing marijuana; 75-year-old bank robbers, or elderly shoplifters seem somehow incongruous and even humorous. Plays and movies about elderly criminals have tended to be comedic. For example, *Arsenic and Old Lace, Going in Style,* and *Mister '88* (the elderly counterfeiter) have won the hearts of audiences. Actually, such portrayals are no more accurate about elderly crime than are Woody Allen's antics about crime committed by younger persons. Elderly persons do commit crimes, and some of these crimes are quite serious.

The number of elderly offenders is small compared to the number of younger criminals. For both gerontologists and those in criminal justice, however, it may be wise to pay less attention to the amount of elderly crime than to the types of offenders and the underlying causes. In this way we may be able to identify etiological conditions about which something can be done to prevent these crimes. If they cannot be prevented, then at least we should be able to assess the effectiveness of alternative methods of enforcement and control.

It may be that in some places elderly persons are so infrequently arrested that, when a case does occur, the incongruity is magnified. Elderly persons, however, are not distributed equally within or across the towns and cities of our country, but tend to cluster in certain neighborhoods and in retirement communities, many located in the Sun Belt from Florida to California. In many of these places crimes committed by the elderly are not at all rare and are certainly not humorous. The number of elderly violators and the types of offenses they commit in age-clustered precincts and retirement communities put unique strains on the criminal justice network. This raises a very fundamental question of the appropriateness of our crime control system, which is designed to deal more with youthful offenders than to deal with the aged.

Crimes committed by elderly persons run the gamut from disorderly conduct to homicide. A major current concern involves larceny (especially shoplifting), which is common in some neighborhoods with dense elderly populations. But the elderly also commit more serious crimes, including assault and murder. Depending upon the type of crimes included, between 23 and 47 percent of elderly arrests are for violent crimes. The difference lies in the definition of violence. If violent crime is limited to murder, aggravated assault, forcible rape, and robbery (the most common list of violent offenses), then 23 percent of arrests of elderly people are for these crimes. If violent crime is expanded to include common assaults, however, then approximately 47 percent of all elderly offender arrests are for these crimes. As will be seen in subsequent chapters, arrests of elderly persons for crimes of violence, no matter how defined, are increasing, while arrests for minor offenses, such as those ranging from vagrancy to burglary, are declining. Violent crimes committed by the elderly differ from those committed by more youthful offenders, with few exceptions, even though legal classifications may be the same. An important difference is that, with the exception of an occasional robbery and some sex crimes, aged criminals are not predatory in the way youthful muggers and rapists are. It is rare for an elderly person to commit a crime against a random victim. Elderly assaults and homicides are perpetrated most frequently on elderly victims and are often the result of the cumulative frustrations of marriages grown old, the narrowing of sexual outlets, the irritations and boredom of retirement living, and the feelings of despair and hopelessness—all of which are only too common in elderly populations.

Are aged offenders primarily a criminological or a gerontological problem? While it is easy to answer "both," we think it is fair to state that the major policy issues which must be addressed in order to deal with this phenomenon can be labeled "gerontological" rather than "criminological." This is probably no different than with crimes committed by younger persons, for the root causes of most criminal behavior are to be found in strains in the social fabric of the society as a whole. Elderly crime cannot really be understood without viewing the aging of America, the trauma of retirement, the loss of status, and the reduced economic self-sufficiency that so often characterize later years. If elderly crime is to be successfully addressed, aging and retirement must be examined from the broadest base. To modify or change the arrest practices of police, the charging practices of prosecutors, or the sentencing provisions of judges is to deal with symptoms, not root causes. Therefore, it strikes us that the heart of the matter lies in gerontological research and in making social and political decisions about how our elderly population is treated.

This is not to say that there is not a criminological interest in elderly crime. Indeed, there is. Older persons caught in the criminal justice network challenge some basic jurisprudential assumptions and pose heretofore unrecognized dilemmas for criminal justice processing. The police taking an elderly suspect into custody raises the question of arrest for what purpose. Are the elderly to be rehabilitated? They seem unlikely candidates to be taught new trades. Likewise, the use of force in apprehending suspects seems almost obscene in dealing with elderly criminals. There may be an occasional dangerous elderly criminal, but by and large the full force of the law is unnecessary when dealing with this population. Elderly offenders challenge our basic sentencing structures. A three-year prison term to a 20-year-old offender is simply a three-year term. To a 75-year-old offender, three years may be a life sentence. Should we change our sentencing structure to reflect probable years remaining in the offender's life and thus sentence to a proportion of these years rather than to a flat term? Are jails and prisons appropriate for older criminals? These institutions are designed to hold the dangerous and the mobile—those likely to escape and flee. Is such costly restraint necessary for an elderly offender population? Perhaps more than any other segment of our population, except the very young, elderly offenders challenge the boundaries, assumptions, and necessities of traditional methods of crime control processing. The basic dilemma is whether the rights of the elderly should properly be considered apart from the rights of others. Should there be unique policies and a separate set of procedures for processing elderly criminals? These are matters of central concern to criminal justice, and in this book we bring together the two fields of gerontology and criminal justice in order to examine a common problem.

This book is an exciting and challenging coalescence of two academic and action fields, both of which are devoted to one of the most serious domestic concerns of our society. Crime and old age are worthy of the most detailed attention and the most sophisticated research. When they come together, as they do with elderly criminals, the two fields find themselves inextricably linked and necessarily cooperative.

It is rare that social scientists have an opportunity to see a problem emerging and can, from the beginning, study, evaluate, and suggest policies. We are at this stage with elderly crime. This book is a first attempt to look at some of the dimensions of this problem.

This work is divided into four major sections: the first looks at the nationwide extent of elderly crime, the second looks at particular types of offenses committed by elderly criminals, and the third and fourth parts devote themselves to issues concerning the ability of our criminal justice system to appropriately deal with elderly criminal populations and suggests some alternative methods of processing. The authors of the chapters represent a mixture of criminal justice scholars and gerontologists as well as a mixture of academic researchers and field practitioners. This is not an exhaustive treatment of all issues relating to elderly criminals, and it is our hope that we will raise more questions than we answer. However, it is a first cut at exploring some dimensions of an emerging social problem that represents the overlapping area between two of our largest social issues—old age and criminal justice.

Because each of these chapters was written in isolation from the others, a note of caution is necessary about comparability of the data and about generalization of any conclusions from one chapter to the next. One problem is definitional. Where "elderly" begins is really the researcher's choice. There is no consensus and no conformity, so that in some studies elderly is defined as persons over 55, in others over 60, and still others over 65. Any conclusions about the frequency of elderly crime or its rate increases or decreases must be considered against population size determined by the entry age at which one is considered elderly. Additionally, the length of time over which rate changes are calculated varies from one study to another. Also, while some studies use national arrest rates, most other studies rely on data from much smaller and more localized populations. So while the data bases are not always comparable from one chapter to the next, it should be remembered that the major emphasis of this book is not on data consensus but on designating the growing problem of elderly crime and the appropriateness of the system we use to control it.

The purpose of this book is not to create the impression of a crime wave, for the number of crimes committed by elderly is comparatively small. There is also no intent to sensationalize this issue. However, although the number of crimes committed by elderly persons is currently small, the problem is bound to increase simply because our population is getting older. And, unless our economy markedly improves, elderly crime may increase much faster than simple demographic changes would suggest.

The elderly, no matter what problems they exhibit, deserve both compassion and dignity in research as in life. This book, which examines the factors of elderly crime, expects to make a contribution to dignity in both these areas.

Evelyn S. Newman
Donald J. Newman
Mindy L. Gewirtz
Albany, New York

Acknowledgments

We wish to thank the many individuals who played important parts in producing this book as well as organizations that helped support our research into elderly crime. First, of course, we wish to thank our coauthors. Their pioneering efforts begin to cast light on a new area. They raise some new questions and force us to begin to look for solutions. We also wish to thank the original advisory group that met with us during the winter of 1982 and helped put together what we bravely called the "First Annual" Conference on Elderly Criminals. This conference was held in Albany, New York, in March of 1982.

At the time we were contemplating the first conference, many people thought the problem of elderly criminals was not serious enough to warrant research nor of sufficient magnitude to cause concern among human services personnel. However, one important person who had the foresight to appreciate and acknowledge the problem was Earnestine Kiano, who was then a project officer with the Alcohol, Drug Abuse, and Mental Health Administration (ADAMHA) of the National Institute of Mental Health. She encouraged us to apply for a grant, which was to serve two purposes. She felt it was most important not only to continue to explore what she saw as a growing problem but also to sensitize personnel who were already encountering older offenders. Subsequently, we did receive a small

grant from ADAMHA to call together the few people, both academi-
cians and practitioners, working in this area. Simultaneously, the
gerontology and criminal justice programs of Florida International
University in Miami joined as cosponsors of the conference, as did
the New York State Defenders Association. There were people from
both FIU and the Defenders Association acting as instructors and
workshop leaders at the conference.

We also wish to thank the Golub Corporation, the parent company
of Price Chopper Stores, for contributing funds to help underwrite
our efforts. The Golub Corporation, sensitive to issues of loss prevention, sent its security director to participate in the conference and
made a financial contribution. Mr. Irving Kirsch also assisted us
financially. Blue Cross and Blue Shield of Northeastern New York
provided conference folders and materials.

The First Annual Conference on Elderly Offenders proved to be of
more interest than even we suspected. It attracted speakers and
workshop leaders from the far reaches of the United States and from
Canada as well. It received a great deal of positive publicity both
nationally and internationally, and media interest in this problem
continues to this day. This extensive media coverage, which included
NBC's "Today" and CBS's "60 Minutes," was primarily the result of
the work of Matthew Maguire of the News Bureau at the State University of New York at Albany. Matt worked with us from the early
days of developing the conference through the production of this
book. His efforts have helped bring the issue of elderly criminals to
the attention of the public.

Graduate students in the SUNYA School of Criminal Justice and
the SUNYA Ringel Institute of Gerontology assisted in developing
the bibliography for this book and in making sure that our references
are accurate. We wish to thank Edmund McGarrell, a doctoral student
in criminal justice, and Michael LaSala, a graduate student in social
welfare. Karl Oelgeschlager was encouraging and supportive from
the beginning of the project. Betsy Smith gave us fine editorial help.
We thank them both.

Most of all, we wish to express our appreciation to Carol Ann Wise
in The School of Criminal Justice and Barbara Rogers in The School
of Social Welfare for their patience in assisting in the conference,
typing the manuscript, and managing the several drafts of this book
as it moved toward publication.

PART I

Incidence and Types of Crimes Committed by the Elderly

This section deals with the nationwide extent of crimes by the elderly. The material deals with the involvement of elderly persons in *all* types of crime—organized, white-collar, professional, and ordinary (sometimes called "conventional," or "street")—crime.

Chapter 1 defines these types of crimes, and a case is made that although the elderly have a much smaller role in ordinary crime, they play a significant part in the first three types (as gangsters, embezzlers, con-artists, and the like). Thus, when viewed broadly, the common notion that crime is solely a product (and problem) of the young is a misconception. Having made this point, we will not further pursue the topic of elderly involvement in organized, white-collar, and professional crime, either here or in subsequent sections. Instead, the major themes of this book are played out against senior citizen involvement in ordinary "street" crime, which ranges from murder to shoplifting and which traditionally has been committed by the young. It is precisely because of this incongruity and the "non-fit" of the older offender in the American criminal justice system that this book focuses on ordinary crimes committed by senior citizens.

In Chapter 2, David Shichor delineates the involvement of elderly persons in ordinary crimes. Of course, all crime data document only the offenders who are apprehended (and tried and convicted) rather than the amount of true involvement in any type of crime. Thus, while Shichor's analysis is based on arrest data gathered annually by the FBI from local and state police departments, he points out that members of the elderly population are often not arrested. He does use these data, however, to document changes in arrests of this population over a fifteen-year period, comparing the number of elderly offender arrests and those of non-elderly offenders involved in various types of ordinary crimes. Shichor then calculates the percentage of increase or decrease in arrests for these crimes, both for elderly suspects and for the entire arrested population. From this we can see that while it is true that the real number of elderly persons arrested for ordinary crimes is small, it seems to be growing at a faster rate than comparable arrests of younger persons. One issue remains, however: whether the increase is in the *rate* of these crimes committed by elderly offenders or whether it is simply a reflection of an increase in the number and proportion of elderly persons in our society.

Shichor makes the point that whether or not the rate is changing, the increase in absolute numbers coupled with the newly felt political power of the elderly and the way they are viewed by the rest of society will, indeed, affect the entire criminal justice system.

Chapter 1

Elderly Criminals and American Crime Patterns

Donald J. Newman

To the uninitiated, the very idea of elderly offenders seems incongruous. Are old people really criminals? Is there a serious and growing problem or is the phenomenon simply an oddity, interesting but rare? Certainly linking the terms *elderly* and *criminal* does not fit the common stereotype of either. Strange as it may seem, however, elderly criminals do exist, and the problem of elderly crime is growing.

Before we can address this phenomenon systematically, it is necessary to define the two terms: who is elderly, and what is criminal? The way these terms are defined affects the measurement of the magnitude of the elderly crime problem and also affects the manner it is approached for amelioration or control. Thus, when does youth end, and when does old age begin in our society? The answers to these questions set the boundaries of the elderly crime problem.

YOUNG, MATURE, AND ELDERLY OFFENDERS

There is no uniform, fully agreed-upon, chronological age at which one becomes "elderly." The most frequent cutoff point between middle age and elderly is 65. This is the usual retirement age, the age for Social Security eligibility, and a lower point of old age for census and other demographic purposes. Some persons, however, retire earlier (at 62, 60, or 55), and others do not retire at all or retire at ages above 65, commonly 70. But although the day of retirement is a passage, a change in lifestyle, it doesn't signify the day middle age ends, with old age beginning the next. Indeed, "old age" is not an entity. Gerontologists often distinguish "young old" from "old old,"[1] and many elderly people will claim that old age is a subjective state, that one is only as old as one feels.

For purposes other than retirement or Social Security or even self-conception, old age begins whenever a classifier defines it as beginning, for whatever purpose. In national statistics about crime and the elderly, the cutoff point is variable. The FBI, for instance, uses "65 and over" as the top age category for arrest data.[2] In some prison systems, including the federal system, the cutoff point on age distribution is 45,[3] but some state prison systems use 60. It is ridiculous, of course, to talk of 45 as the entrance to old age. And many people who are working at 55 or 60 do not consider themselves aged, nor are they commonly thought so by others. When lower ages are treated as elderly in prisons and arrest data, it may seem arbitrary but it is not fully capricious. In the past, so few elderly people were arrested that it was not worthwhile to carry the age breakdown up into the sixties and seventies. The same is true for prisons. There are so few inmates over 45 that it is not worthwhile to disaggregate above these ages. This may well change, however, as our aged population grows.

Thus the definition of who is elderly depends on the data one uses. The criminal justice system often classifies those "55 and over" as elderly, although many research studies draw the line at higher ages if enough data are available about people of those ages. This is why it is often difficult to compare information about elderly criminals from one research project to the next.

The definition of middle age is just as murky, arbitrary, and variable, depending on the purposes to which the category will be put. Many criminal justice observers tend to categorize offenders as "middle aged" or "mature" beginning at about age 30, but not always. In criminal justice research it would perhaps be more significant to relate age categories to the type of criminal conduct involved. For example, auto theft for "joyriding" purposes tends to be a teenage phenomenon. If a 35-year-old is apprehended for joyriding for statistical analyses he or she could well be defined as an elderly offender because this age is so unusual compared to the youth of the typical auto thief. And if a 25-year-old vandalizes a high school, once again the incongruous behavior for someone that old might well cause him to be categorized as elderly.

Categorization of age by type of crime, however, is hard to do systematically, so most researchers fall back on some chronological age to distinguish categories. Various terms are used to distinguish old-age groups, but again they are really arbitrary, depending on the purpose of classification and the availability of data. Some years ago Glueck and Glueck did a follow-up study of a cohort of juvenile delinquents, and found their "burnout" age to be 36.[4] This is the age when, in the careers of ordinary criminals, there tends to be a dropoff in crime.[5] Johnson suggests four levels: "Youth" (under 21), "Young Adults" (21–34), "MiddleAged" (35–49), and "Senior Adults" (over 49).[6] This categorization is unusual, in that the top cutoff point is 49 years and the lowest point, youth, continues to age 21. More commonly, teenagers to 30-year-olds are youthful offenders, 30- to 55-year-olds are mature offenders, and offenders over 55 are elderly. This, then, is a working definition of half of the label "elderly criminal"; the other half, "criminal," also needs to be defined.

TYPES OF CRIME

Crime is a collective noun, encompassing many different types of behavior, many different motives, and various consequences. In this sense *crime,* like *disease,* is a term so broad as to be of little help in studying, treating, or preventing the phenomenon. Just as disease comprises multiple yet distinct syndromes, symptoms, and causes, so crime is neither a legal nor a behavioral entity. In motive, consequences, and amenability to deterrence, murder is quite distinct from larceny. In fact, the two crimes are related only in that both are law violations. The processing of murderers or the prevention of homicide requires quite different techniques than treatment of thieves or prevention of larceny.

Crime can be, and often is, subdivided into smaller categories for different purposes. In all states (and the federal jurisdiction), crimes are divided into two major legal categories: felonies and misdemeanors. In the opinion of legislatures that have identified and distinguished the two categories, felonies are more serious crimes, including most crimes of violence. They are punished by sentences to state prisons rather than local jails, and in some states murder is punished by the death penalty. Misdemeanors, on the other hand, are less serious types of crime usually punished by fines or short jail terms. The distinction between felonies and misdemeanors rests on the maximum punishment that can be imposed and not on differences between specific crimes such as larceny or assault. Whether larceny is a felony or misdemeanor ordinarily depends on the value of property stolen.[7] For example, grand larceny is theft of property valued over a certain amount, and petit larceny is theft of property worth a lesser amount. Grand larceny is a felony, petit larceny a misdemeanor. The same is true with assault: it ranges from very serious knifings and gunshot wounds, which are felonies (aggravated assault), to common fistfights, which are misdemeanors (simple assault).

Crimes are often categorized in other ways. In law (and in common usage), a distinction usually is made between violent crimes against persons and property crimes in which no one was injured or no injury threatened. Today many legislatures are enacting more severe penalties for any crime in which violence is used or threatened.[8]

Classifying crimes in these ways is essentially drawing legal dichotomies, which have implications not only for sentencing but also pertain to different standards for arrest and for the degree of force that may be used in taking a suspect into custody. By statute police officers, under certain conditions, can use greater force, including deadly force, in the apprehension of felons and violent criminals but cannot use this same force with offenders observed to be committing lesser crimes or fleeing from the crime site.[9]

Criminologists, who are social science researchers dedicated to seeking the causes of crime and to making suggestions for its prevention or control, have found these legal classifications inadequate for their purposes. It is clear, for example, that intrafamily homicides committed after extended periods of aggravation and in the heat of passion are quite different from murders committed by hired killers to support the organized crime system. And the teenage mugger, although in fact a robber, differs in many ways from the calculating bank robber who disdains stickups that are likely to net less than $50,000. Criminologists argue that the classification of crimes by offense (larceny and so on) does not accurately describe all criminals nor suggest feasible ways to curb or prevent crime. Instead, they have isolated certain "behavior systems" in crime that depend less on the legal definition of crime than on the motives, skills, career patterns, self-concepts, and similar behavioral traits of the criminals.[10] This has led to the identification of four major (and some minor) behavior systems as a way of approaching and understanding crime: (1) ordinary crime and criminals, (2) professional crime and criminals, (3) organized crime and criminals, and (4) white-collar crime and criminals. Other categories include violent personal offenders, sex offenders, political criminals (terrorists), and public-order violators like vagrants and chronic down-and-out inebriates.[11]

To the extent that these *types* of criminal behavior—indicated by similar offense patterns, common criminal career pathways, and similar environmental histories—can be identified, appropriate forms of intervention for control or prevention can be tailored to cope with each. For example, many murders spring from a subculture of violence and are products of deep-seated emotional patterns in offenders.[12] Murders committed under these conditions are almost impossible to deter. Yet stringent sentences for murder, rape, and other violent crimes are expected not only to provide just punishment for the perpetrators, but to deter other potential violators. Because of the nature of causal problems, severe punishment, including the death sentence, simply does not deter violent criminals. However, if similar punishments were used with profesional thieves and other more rational and calculating offenders, deterrence might prove more successful. Furthermore, ordinary offenders who are personally inadequate, educationally and vocationally deprived, unskilled, even inept at committing crimes, might be appropriate candidates for rehabilitation. Similar techniques of rehabilitation, though, would prove fruitless with professional, hardened offenders for whom crime is a way of life.

It is hard to say—indeed, it is controversial—which type of criminal behavior is the most serious threat to our social order. We apply most of our enforcement efforts to ordinary crime, which involves some violent behavior, sex offenses, and property crimes from robbery to larceny. Ordinary crime is the business of the police, prosecutors, courts, jails, and prisons in our society. Public concern about crime as well as public pressure for "get-tough" sentences and enforcement techniques usually apply to ordinary crime. Yet it can be argued that organized crime, involving gangsters and racketeers operating illicit vice-enterprise systems, is really more serious and more threatening to our social order than "snatch-and-grab" thieves, teenage muggers, and the like. The same applies to white-collar crime. The smallest embezzlement may be equivalent in monetary loss to scores, or even hundreds, of larcenies: "fixing" the price of a commonly used product may affect almost every citizen in the nation. A burglary is tiny and isolated in comparison.

The general point here is that the crime problem in our society is much too large and much too complex to be limited to ordinary crime. Behavior systems differ on a number of dimensions, not the least of which is the typical age of the perpetrators. In general, when the point is made that crime is a young man's game it applies with accuracy only to ordinary crime, not to other behavior systems.

AGE AND ORDINARY CRIME

That ordinary crime is a young man's game (by and large, women and girls do not fit the stereotype) is supported by the FBI's official crime statistics. The annual *Uniform Crime Reports* (UCRs) tabulate arrest information sent to the FBI by local police agencies and cover eight Index crimes: murder and non-negligent homicide, aggravated assault, forcible rape, arson, robbery, burglary, larceny, and auto theft.[13] The two basic statistics in the UCRs are "crimes known to the police" (reported) and "crimes cleared by arrest" (crimes for which a suspect has been taken into custody). And with almost monotonous regularity, the UCRs demonstrate that young people, mostly men between the ages of 16 and 24, are arrested for these Index crimes.[14]

Not only does the 16- to 24-year-old "at-risk" population dominate arrest data, but most offenders appear to "burn out" in their early thirties. Among suspects arrested for Index crimes, a high number are recidivists, that is, they have committed prior crimes and will likely commit more crimes after serving their sentences on the present charge—but only up to about age 30. After this, whether because of moral maturity or slowed juices, recidivism stops and the crime rate drops off.

Not only are "ordinary" criminals young adults on the average, but so are their victims. The young tend to prey on the young.[15] This does not mean, of course, that elderly persons do not commit ordinary crimes or find themselves victims. They do, but their numbers in both categories (offender and victim) are small. Now that our population tends to live longer, however, the number of elderly perpetrators and victims of ordinary crime is bound to increase. More about this later.

AGE AND PROFESSIONAL CRIMINALS

Professional criminals are ordinarily men and women who have been recruited into a life of crime by other professionals. The kinds of crimes they engage in take a good deal of planning and great skill. There are two general subtypes of professional criminals: "hustlers"—including confidence men, professional shoplifters ("boosters"), pickpockets, and various flim-flam artists—and "heavies", who commit crimes of the same category as ordinary criminals but bigger, more sophisticated, and usually more lucrative. Heavies include big-time armored car and bank robbers, safecrackers, jewelry and fur thieves, operators of massive auto theft rings, and the like. The determining characteristics of professional criminals are that crime is their principal occupation, that they are recruited by other professionals into small gangs (professional crime is always group behavior), that they are recognized by each other and by the police as professionals, and that many requirements of other professions also apply.[16] For example, professional thieves serve long apprenticeships, become highly skilled, and are even governed by a code of ethics relating to each other and to their victims (no violence, no larceny from poor boxes, etc.). Most large municipal police departments have specialized units, commonly called "bunco squads," devoted to gathering intelligence on professional criminals who operate in the city or float through from time to time.

There is no accurate way of knowing how many professional criminals there are in our society, how many crimes they commit in any given period, nor how effective the criminal justice system is in apprehending them or preventing their offenses. Even if arrest or conviction data were available it would likely be erroneous, for professional thieves are particularly skilled at "fixing" arrests or trials and discouraging complaints (called "cooling the mark"). Inciardi comments, "The professional criminal accumulates sufficient money from illegal activities and is able to thus avoid incarceration when caught. The money is used to arrange a fix with anybody who is fixable (cop, victim, court personnel, witnesses, judges and/or prosecutor)."[17]

Many professional offenses—swindling and pickpocketing, for example—are not contained in FBI statistics; the others, robbery and auto theft, are not differentiated from amateur robberies and thefts. It is reasonably evident, however, that the bulk of professional criminals do not fall into that 16–24 age category characteristic of ordinary criminals. Most professional thieves are recruited at a young age and begin their life's career in crime in their teens or twenties. By and large, the successful operators fall into the category of mature or middle-aged (roughly from age 30 to 55), and many of the top thieves have successfully pursued their careers well into old age by any definition. Indeed, the longevity of some professional thieves is astounding. Joseph ("Yellow Kid") Weil, a notorious confidence man and one of the prototypes for Paul Newman's role in *The Sting*, lived to be over 100 years old and was last arrested at 72.[18] The Gondorf brothers (additional models for Newman's role, including his movie name) were well into old age when last apprehended.[19] "Count" Victor Lustig, an international con man who was most notorious for having sold the Eiffel Tower several times, went from middle age to old age during his career.[20] So did Patrick H. ("Packy") Lennon, one of the slickest stock hustlers in the nation, who practiced his business for thirty years.[21] Willie Sutton, a professional bank robber and escape artist, spent his entire life robbing banks and in and out of prison. Sutton was nearly into his eighties and still on parole when he died in Florida.

While summary demographic data about professional criminals do not exist, it is clear that this type of crime is not a young man's game. Professional thieves may begin young, but in order to become really successful in their profession they must mature and age. Indeed, the older the con man, the more likely he is to be successful simply because the stereotype of "criminal" is youth. Lemert comments:

> The con man begins his special career at a much older age than other criminals, or perhaps it is better said that he continues his criminal career at a time when others may be relinquishing theirs. Unemployment occasioned by old age does not seem to be a problem of con men; age ripens their skills, insight, and wit, and it also increases the confidence they inspire in their victims. With age the con man may give up the position of the roper and shift to being an inside man, but even this may not be absolutely necessary . . . . We know of one con man who is seventy years of age and has a bad heart, but he is still as effective as he ever was.[22]

In career paths (not in honesty), professional thieves are no different from members of other professions. All professionals require extensive training and apprenticeship in their youth but reach full stride only in middle age and beyond.

AGE AND ORGANIZED CRIME

Most of the leaders of organized crime, while they may have embarked on their criminal careers in their youth, are in the upper registers of the age scale. Only the lower echelons of organized crime families are young. The young carry out the dictates of the old men (as far as can be determined, there are no women in the higher echelons of organized crime), which range from selling narcotics to "shakedowns" of business establishments for protection money, and murder. According to Clinard and Quinney, "Many organized criminals, especially those lower in the hierarchy, have careers similar to the conventional offender, in which there is association with young gang members and a long series of delinquencies and crimes. Instead of ending their careers in their early twenties, however, they continue their criminal activities in association with organized criminals."[23]

While organized crime is said to be divided into "families" (with a "godfather" at the head of each), actually these illicit enterprise structures are organized like corporations, complete with a hierarchic management system, administrative officers, and even boards of directors.[24] Organized crime is age-stratified. The heads of families, counselors (*consigliore*) and managers of various operational units (gambling, narcotics, loan sharking, and the like), and their advisors and assistants are all mature, if not elderly. Important operational decisions in organized crime, ranging from the takeover of a legitimate business to murder, are made by the older leaders in the crime hierarchy, not by the youngsters, who are simply employees (soldiers) of the corporation.

Organized crime, then, is not a young man's game, but an old man's game. The godfather is also likely to be a grandfather. Frank Costello, whom the Kefauver Committee labeled the "Prime Minister" of organized crime, lived to be 80. He was 58 years old when he was subpoenaed to testify before the committee.[25] Likewise, Vito Genovese, who died in prison at age 71, but who was still in command of his organization from his prison cell, was 59 years old when he chaired the notorious Apalachin meeting of the dons, which attracted more than a hundred syndicate leaders. Charles ("Lucky") Luciano died in Italy at age 65, still very active and influential in organized crime matters. And Meyer Lansky was still on the run to avoid prosecution for tax evasion when he died, in Florida, at age 81.[26]

The policy decisions—the orders that the soldiers carry out—are made by mature and aged syndicate leaders. We ordinarily do not think of gangsters and racketeers as elderly, but this is precisely what they are.

AGE AND WHITE-COLLAR CRIME

White-collar crime, a violation of the law (and of trust) in the course of one's occupation or profession,[27] ranges from embezzlement to corporate price fixing and from accepting a bribe to systematic tax evasion. The higher-echelon business and professional people who violate the law and the trust placed in their positions are likely to be mature and elderly, just like the bosses of organized crime. Indeed, it takes age and maturity to get into a position to commit white-collar crime. "To embezzle, one has to be in a position of trust over valuables," say Bittner and Messinger. "To defraud a customer, one has to be a purveyor of goods or services. To accept a bribe, one has to be in office."[28]

The determination of the age of white-collar violators is complicated by the fact that some of the offenders are not individuals at all, but corporations.[29] Sometimes officers of a violating corporation can be prosecuted, convicted, and sentenced for white collar crimes, but many times it is difficult to lay individual responsibility. Does blame lie with the corporate board of directors, the president of the firm, stockholders? With minor exceptions, membership on corporate boards, presidencies of large companies, and stockholders in commercial firms tend not to be young but well into middle age and beyond.[30]

Some observers argue that white-collar crime is at least as serious as conventional or organized crime. Not only does white-collar crime hurt the economy and defraud and cheat large segments of our population, but because of the high prestige and status of violators—who are commonly treated leniently—it provides an easy rationalization for ordinary criminals and for gangsters and racketeers to defend their illegal actions. Gibbons comments, "It is not unlikely that the existence of white-collar criminals, along with differential handling of the individuals involved in it, provides run-of-the-mill offenders with powerful rationalization for their own conduct. The latter can argue that 'everyone is crooked' and that they are the 'little fish' who are victims of a corrupt and hypocritical society."[31]

In recent years enforcement against white-collar criminals has been stepped up, particularly in the federal jurisdiction. Sparked by increasing evidence of wrongdoing during the Watergate hearings and then by Abscam, federal officials have given new priority to the enforcement of laws regulating commerce, professions, and public office. Once again, we see that elderly offenders play an important, and sometimes dominant, role in white-collar types of crime.[32]

THE ELDERLY OFFENDER AND AMERICAN CRIME PATTERNS

The involvement of elderly persons in professional, organized, and white-collar crime is significant, giving lie to the myth that crime is a young man's game. Only if the reference point is ordinary street crime does the stereotype of young criminal accurately apply.

Even here the picture is changing. While the degree of involvement of elderly persons in most forms of ordinary crime is likely to remain tiny for many years, the frequency will increase as our population ages. The elderly now account for no more than 3 or 4 percent of annual arrests for ordinary crime; the small number of elderly involved in this type of crime certainly does not indicate a crime wave. All arrest data about elderly offenders should be taken cautiously, however. Many experienced people believe that the elderly may be the most underarrested category of offenders except for the very young. The significance of the problem is not its size, but the challenge it presents to our criminal justice system. The kind of ordinary offenses committed by elderly offenders, from murder to auto theft, make *any* involvement of the elderly incongruous. The very idea of 70-year-old burglars, 65-year-old murderers, and 80-year-old shoplifters seem aberrant, capricious exceptions to the rule, and therefore not in need of careful attention. Yet crimes committed by the elderly are not flukes, and although numbers are presently small they represent a growing social problem.

THE ELDERLY OFFENDER AND THE CRIMINAL JUSTICE SYSTEM

The involvement of the elderly in all types of crime challenges the common assumption that American crime is solely a product of youth and, more particularly, of young, poor members of minorities. Even so it can fairly be asked why elderly criminals deserve our attention, particularly those involved in ordinary crime, where they account for such a small percentage of offenses.

More than other types of crime, ordinary crime is the target of enforcement of municipal police, local prosecutors, trial courts, probation services, prison systems, and parole boards. This system is geared for the young, for predatory and mobile people (who will likely flee)—none of which describes the ordinary elderly offender. The existence of elderly criminals raises some basic questions about the appropriateness of our crime control system. Is police hardware (handcuffs, leg irons) necessary for elderly offenders? Are common booking procedures—including fingerprinting, photographing, and lineups—necessary and appropriate for 70-year-old suspects? Is monetary bail the only way elderly offenders can be released awaiting trial? Are they likely to flee? Do many or most elderly offenders really need to be jailed and imprisoned? How well do the purposes of our crime control system—punishment, restraint, deterrence, and rehabilitation—fit an elderly offender population? In short, can our criminal justice system effectively address the problems of elderly offenders? Might elderly offenders be more effectively and more humanely processed from arrest through sentencing in a distinct geriatric crime control system much as we provide a special system for juvenile delinquents in all states and the federal jurisdiction?

This dilemma of whether it is appropriate and necessary to use traditional crime control methods with elderly criminals will be examined closely in subsequent chapters of this book. At this point, it is necessary only to conclude that the elderly play a more prominent role in major American crime patterns than is commonly believed.

NOTES

1. Bernice L. Neugarten, "Age Groups in American Society and the Rise of the Young-Old," in Frederick R. Eisele (ed.), *Political Consequences of Aging* (Philadelphia: Annals of the American Society of Political and Social Sciences, 1974), pp. 184–198.
2. Federal Bureau of Investigation, *Uniform Crime Reports for the United States, 1980* (Washington, D.C.: U.S. Government Printing Office, 1981).
3. Kenneth Carlson, *American Prisons and Jails, Volume II: Population Trends and Projections,* U.S. Department of Justice, National Institute of Justice (Washington, D.C.: U.S. Government Printing Office, 1980).
4. Sheldon Glueck and Eleanor T. Glueck, *Juvenile Delinquents Grown Up* (New York: Commonwealth Fund, 1940), pp. 103–106.
5. Marshall B. Clinard, *Sociology of Deviant Behavior,* 4th ed. (New York: Holt, Rinehart and Winston, 1974).
6. Elmer H. Johnson, *Crime, Corrections and Society,* rev. ed. (Homewood, Ill.: The Dorsey Press, 1968), pp. 70–71.
7. See Donald J. Newman, *Introduction to Criminal Justice,* 2nd ed. (Philadelphia: J. B. Lippincott, 1978), pp. 26–34.
8. See, for example, American Law Institute, *Model Penal Code,* Proposed Official Draft (Philadelphia: American Law Institute, 1967); Advisory Council of Judges of the National Council on Crime and Delinquency, *Model Sentencing Act,* (New York: National Council on Crime and Delinquency, 1963); and also American Bar Association Project on Minimum Standards for Criminal Justice, *Sentencing Alternatives and Procedures* (New York: Institute of Judicial Administration, 1967).
9. See Lawrence W. Sherman, "Execution Without Trial: Police Homicide and the Constitution," *Vanderbilt Law Review 33,* (1980): 71–100; and Steven C. Day, "Shooting the Fleeing Felon: State of the Law," in *Criminal Law Bulletin 4* (July–August 1978): 285–310.
10. Marshall B. Clinard and Richard Quinney, *Criminal Behavior Systems: A Typology,* 2nd ed. (New York: Holt, Rinehart and Winston, 1973).
11. Ibid., pp. 16–21.
12. See Marvin Wolfgang and Franco Ferracuti, *The Subculture of Violence: Towards an Integrated Theory of Criminology* (London: Tavistock, 1967). See also Marvin Wolfgang, *Patterns in Criminal Homicide* (Philadelphia: University of Pennsylvania Press, 1958).
13. FBI, *Uniform Crime Reports, 1980.*
14. The same holds for ordinary offenders not included in the UCR. See Timothy

Flanagan, David J. Van Alstyne, and Michael Gottfredson (eds.), *Sourcebook of Criminal Justice Statistics, 1981,* U.S. Department of Justice, Bureau of Justice Statistics (Washington, D.C.: U.S. Government Printing Office, 1982).

15. Michael Hindelang, *Criminal Victimization in Eight American Cities* (Cambridge, Mass.: Ballinger Publishing Company, 1976), p. 171.

16. For a classic study of the professional criminal, see Edwin H. Sutherland, *The Professional Thief* (Chicago: University of Chicago Press, 1937). See also David W. Maurer, *The Big Con* (New York: Signet Press, 1962), Jay R. Nash, *Hustlers and Con Men* (New York: M. Evans and Co., 1976), and Mary Owen Cameron, *The Booster and the Snitch* (New York: Macmillan, 1964).

17. James Inciardi, *Careers in Crime* (Chicago: Rand McNally, 1975), pp. 62–67.

18. Joseph Weil (told to W. T. Brannon), *Yellow Kid Weil* (Chicago: Ziff-Davis Publishing Co., 1948). See also "The Yellow Kid Returns," *Newsweek,* December 24, 1956.

19. Nash, *Hustlers and Con Men,* pp. 257–265.

20. Ibid., pp. 233–236.

21. Ibid., pp. 227–232.

22. Edwin M. Lemert, *Social Pathology* (New York: McGraw-Hill Book Company, 1951), pp. 323–324.

23. Clinard and Quinney, *Criminal Behavior Systems,* p. 229.

24. See President's Commission on Law Enforcement and the Administration of Justice, *Task Force Report: Organized Crime* (Washington, D.C.: U.S. Government Printing Office, 1967). See also Donald R. Cressey, *Theft of a Nation: The Structure and Operations of Organized Crime in America* (New York: Harper & Row, 1969).

25. Jay Robert Nash, *Bloodletters and Badmen* (New York: M. Evans and Co., 1973), pp. 134–136.

26. Ibid., pp. 213–216, 311–316, 335–342.

27. Edwin H. Sutherland, *White Collar Crime* (New York: Dryden Press, 1949).

28. Egon Bittner and Sheldon L. Messinger, *Criminology Review Yearbook, Vol. 2* (Beverly Hills, Calif.: Sage Publications, 1980), p. 157.

29. Marshall B. Clinard and Peter C. Yeager, *Corporate Crime* (New York: The Free Press, 1980).

30. Ibid., pp. 280–298.

31. Don C. Gibbons, *Changing the Lawbreaker* (Englewood Cliffs, N.J.: Prentice-Hall, 1965), p. 271.

32. John C. Spencer, "A Study of Incarcerated White Collar Offenders," in Tadeusz Grygier, Howard Jones, and John C. Spencer (eds.), *Criminology in Transition* (London: Tavistock Publications, 1965), p. 255.

Chapter 2

The Extent and Nature of Lawbreaking by the Elderly: A Review of Arrest Statistics

David Shichor

Since the early 1970s an increasing amount of attention has been paid to crime and the elderly. The majority of this research has dealt with victimization. Seemingly, the public consensus is that the elderly constitute the most victimized age group in the population. Even the fact that victimization surveys indicate that the elderly consistently report the lowest rate of actual victimization among various age groups does not change the situation. This issue is complex, however, since the great extent of "fear of crime" experienced by the elderly can be perceived as serious victimization in itself. In addition, the consequences of actual victimization seem to be more severe for the elderly than for other victims because of their increased physical vulnerability and their reduced financial capacity to absorb material losses.[1] The helplessness and often diminished physical and psychological capacity of the elderly provide convenient rationale to cast them into the victim role, while not much attention has been paid to their lawbreaking behavior.

The relatively few professional works that touch on connections between age and crime tend to indicate the existence of a pattern of gradual decline of criminal involvement from about the age of 30 onward, without too much effort toward accounting for this fact, and without analyzing the extent and nature of the criminal behavior of the members of the older age groups.[2] Recent research also indicates that not only actual criminal involvement but also criminal propensity (a desire to commit crimes) tends to decline with age; this may be partly the result of life-cycle changes in terms of the development of higher stakes in conformity.[3]

However, the extent and nature of criminal activity by the elderly warrant more attention than they have received so far, especially because the elderly population of the United States is increasing rapidly in absolute numbers and in relative terms as well. As is known, in most industrial countries, including the United States, the population is gradually aging as a result of declining birth rates and an increasing life span. For instance, it is estimated that in 1979, 11.2 percent of the U.S. population (about 24,658,000) was 65 years old and older while five years earlier, in 1974, the percentage of this age group was only 10.3 percent (about 21,815,000).[4]

This chapter is designed to review and analyze the extent and nature of involvement in lawbreaking behavior by the elderly. Analysis is based on the arrest statistics of the FBI's *Uniform Crime Reports* (UCRs) at five-year intervals between 1964 and 1979, a fifteen-year span that provides a description of general trends. Unfortunately, official statistics on crime are neither accurate nor complete. The UCRs have been criticized by many researchers.[5] Criticism generally has focused on (1) the victims' and witnesses' decision to report or not to report crimes to law enforcement agencies, (2) the organizational factors that impede accurate law enforcement recording, and (3) the role of the individual police officer in arresting for crime.[6]

In all arrest statistics, selectivity also becomes a problem, for not every lawbreaker is arrested and many of those who are are not proved to be criminals. Furthermore, arrest rates and the determination of rare charges are undoubtedly affected by the law enforcement policy decisions of the various police and sheriffs' departments. Nevertheless, because they are the best available, these statistics can be used as general indicators of long-term trends of lawbreaking activity. For the purposes of this study, "elderly" status was applied to the 55-and-over age group. The share of this age group in the U.S. population was 17.9 percent in 1964 and increased to approximately 20.7 percent in 1979.[7]

The total numbers of arrest in the general population and among the elderly were examined (see Table 2.1). These figures indicate that there was a continuous increase in the number of arrests in the total population during the fifteen-year research period. Arrests of all ages increased 102.9 percent from 1964 to 1979. At the same time the increase in arrests of the elderly was only moderate, 5.7

Table 2.1.   Total Number of Arrests (Including Minor and Major Offenses)

	1964	1969	1974	1979	
55 years old and over	364,381 (7.8)	398,303 (6.8)	298,538 (4.8)	385,107 (4.1)	
Percent change		+ 14.5%	− 25.0%	+ 29.9%	
Percent change, 1964–79					+ 5.7%
Total Population	4,685,080	5,862,264	6,179,406	9,506,347	
Percent change		+ 25.1%	+ 5.4%	+ 53.8%	
Percent change, 1964–79					+ 102.9%

Source: Based on FBI, *Uniform Crime Reports,* 1964, 1969, 1974, 1979 (Washington, D.C.: U.S. Government Printing Office).

Note: Numbers in parentheses are the percent of the total arrests for a given year.

percent for the fifteen-year period. These percentages should be viewed cautiously, however. They indicate a continuous decline in the share of elderly among arrestees for all major *and* minor crimes taken together. Yet, as we shall see in the following analysis, the small overall increase in elderly crimes is the result of a *decline* in arrests of elderly for *minor* crimes; in the same period, there was a marked *increase* in elderly involvement in *serious crimes,* ranging from larceny to homicide. In fact, the number of elderly arrested for FBI Index crimes increased at a greater rate than arrests of the general population for these same offenses.

These increases and decreases in arrest data should not be taken as a true indication of the actual amount of crime, major or minor, committed by the elderly. Arrest data measure police *decisions* to take suspects into custody, not necessarily all who were discovered breaking the law. In all times of a general increase in the crime rate, police arrest practices become more selective. As in prosecutorial decisions to charge suspects, there is an often-expressed rule to "get the worst first." Any group or category that is not violent or intrinsically threatening will find greater on-the-scene forgiveness by police who are busy with more serious matters. What this means is that while arrests of the elderly for serious crimes is more likely to accurately reflect their actual criminal participation in these offenses, the decline of elderly arrests in minor crime may be a deceptive indicator of their actual involvement in larceny, burglary, fraud, and other nonviolent crimes.

ARRESTS FOR SERIOUS OFFENSES

The more serious offenses form the FBI's so-called Crime Index, "which is not an index at all in the usual sense, but simply consist of those crimes described by the F.B.I. as 'serious' or 'the most common local problem.' "[8] This Crime Index provides the summary data for the *Uniform Crime Reports* and usually is taken as an indicator of general crime trends.

Where arrests for these serious offenses are concerned, the picture becomes different. The share of the elderly in arrests for Index crimes has *increased* from 1.5 percent in 1964 to 2.2 percent in 1979.

Table 2.2. Arrests for More Serious Crimes (Index Crimes)

	1964	1969	1974	1979	
55 years old and over	13,575 (1.7)	19,581 (1.8)	24,745 (1.7)	48,418 (2.2)	
Percent change		44.2%	26.4%	95.7%	
Percent change (1964–79)					+ 256.7%
Total population	780,501	1,111,674	1,474,427	2,163,302	
Percent change		42.4%	32.6%	46.7%	
Percent change (1964–79)					+ 177.2%

Source: Based on FBI, *Uniform Crime Reports,* 1964, 1969, 1974, 1979 (Washington, D.C.: U.S. Government Printing Office).

Note: Numbers in parentheses are the percent of the total arrests for a given year.

Arrests for major (Index) crimes have risen continuously in the total population as well as in the elderly population (Table 2.2). In the total population the number of arrests for these crimes increased 177.2 percent between 1964 to 1979. However, the percentage increase in arrests for the elderly population for these crimes was higher than that of the general population, 256.7 percent.

Table 2.3. Proportion of Arrests for Serious (Index) Offenses, 1964, 1969, 1974, 1979

	1964	1969	1974	1979
All ages	16.7	19.9	23.9	22.8
55 and over	3.7	4.9	8.3	12.6

Source: FBI, *Uniform Crime Reports,* 1964, 1969, 1974, 1979 (Washington, D.C.: U.S. Government Printing Office).

The proportion of arrests among the elderly for Index offenses also grew at a faster rate—from 3.7 percent in 1964 to 12.6 percent in 1979—than the general population, where the growth was from 16.7 percent to 22.8 percent respectively (Table 2.3).

ARRESTS FOR VIOLENT CRIMES

When arrests for Index crimes are divided into violent crimes (murder, forcible rape, robbery, and aggravated assault) in contrast to property crimes (burglary, grand larceny, and motor vehicle theft), the data indicate that a higher percentage of elderly people are arrested for violent crimes than is the case for the general population. However, the trend among the elderly shows a decrease in arrests for offenses of violence, from 29.8 percent in 1964 to 22.6 percent in 1979. In contrast, in the general population arrests for violent offenses show an increasing pattern: from 17.3 percent to 20.1 percent for the same period of time (see Tables 2.4, 2.5, and 2.6).

On the whole, arrests for both violent and property Index crimes have increased in the general population as well as in the elderly population, but the increase (in contrast to a percentage of arrests in each subcategory) in the number of arrests for offenses of violence is higher in the general population than in the elderly age group: 222.3 percent versus 176.6 percent. On the other hand, the increase in the number of arrests for property offenses is higher in the elderly group: 166.1 percent versus 296.6 percent (this was especially the case during 1974–1979).

Table 2.4. Percentage Distribution of Arrests for Violent and Property Index Offenses

	55 and over				Total Population			
	1964	*1969*	*1974*	*1979*	*1964*	*1969*	*1974*	*1979*
Violent[a]	29.8	29.5	27.7	22.6	17.3	19.4	20.0	20.1
Property[b]	70.2	70.5	72.3	77.4	82.7	80.6	80.0	79.9

Source: FBI, *Uniform Crime Reports,* 1964, 1969, 1974, 1979 (Washington, D.C.: U.S. Government Printing Office).

[a]Violent index offenses: murder and non-negligent manslaughter, forcible rape, robbery, aggravated assault.

[b]Property index offenses: burglary, larceny, motor vehicle theft.

Table 2.5. Arrests for Violent Index Crimes

	1964	1969	1974	1979	
55 years old and over	3,961	6,843	6,859	10,957	
Percent change		+72.8%	+ 0.02%	+37.4%	
Percent change, 1964–79					+176.6%
Total population	134,891	216,194	294,617	434,778	
Percent change		+60.3%	+36.3%	+47.6%	
Percent change, 1964–79					+222.3%

Source: FBI, *Uniform Crime Reports,* 1964, 1969, 1974, 1979 (Washington, D.C.: U.S. Government Printing Office).

ELDERLY ARRESTS FOR SPECIFIC CRIMES

The analysis of arrests for individual Index offenses indicates the following patterns (see Table 2.7):

Murder. Arrests for this offense among the elderly constitute between 4.6 and 5.7 percent of the total arrests. Figures show an increasing trend in the number of arrests for both the general population and the elderly. The increase is somewhat higher in the elderly group for the entire fifteen-year period: 201.7 percent versus 184.8 percent.

Forcible Rape. Arrests in the elderly group constitute only 1.0 to 1.6 percent of the total arrests. The number of arrests in both groups, however, is increasing markedly. During the entire period this increase was 355.3 percent for the elderly and 208.6 percent for the general population. The small number of actual arrests of

Table 2.6. Arrests for Property Index Crimes

	1964	1969	1974	1979	
55 years old and over	9,365	13,564	17,760	37,140	
Percent change		+44.8%	+30.9%	+109.1%	
Percent change, 1964–79					+296.6%
Total population	642,925	892,283	1,177,584	1,728,524	
Percent change		+38.8%	+32.0%	+ 45.3%	
Percent change, 1964–79					+166.1%

Source: FBI, *Uniform Crime Reports,* 1964, 1969, 1974, 1979 (Washington, D.C.: U.S. Government Printing Office).

Table 2.7. Arrests for Individual Index Crimes

	1964	1969	1974	1979	
Murder					
55 and older	301 (4.7)	652 (5.7)	631 (4.6)	908 (5.0)	
Percent change		+111.6%	−3.2%	+43.9%	
Percent change, 1964–79					+201.7%
Total population	6,412	11,509	13,818	18,264	
Percent change		+79.5%	+20.1%	+32.2%	
Percent change, 1964–79					+184.8%
Forcible rape					
55 and older	103 (1.1)	154 (1.1)	163 (0.9)	469 (1.6)	
Percent change		+49.5%	+5.8%	+187.7%	
Percent change, 1964–79					+355.3%
Total population	9,450	14,428	17,804	29,164	
Percent change		+52.7%	+23.4%	+63.8%	
Percent change, 1964–79					+208.6%
Robbery					
55 and older	198 (0.5)	279 (0.4)	432 (0.4)	653 (0.5)	
Percent change		+40.9%	+54.8%	+51.2%	
Percent change, 1964–79					+229.8%
Total population	39,134	76,533	108,481	130,753	
Percent change		+95.6%	+41.7%	+20.5%	
Percent change, 1964–79					+234.1%
Aggravated Assault					
55 and older	3,359 (4.2)	4,697 (4.1)	5,633 (3.6)	8,927 (3.5)	
Percent change		+39.8%	+19.9%	+58.5%	
Percent change, 1964–79					+165.8%
Total Population	79,895	113,724	154,514	256,597	
Percent change		+42.3	+35.9	+66.1	
Percent change, 1964–79					+221.2%
Burglary					
55 and older	951 (0.5)	1,185 (0.4)	1,162 (0.3)	2,093 (0.4)	
Percent change		+24.6%	−2.9%	+80.1%	
Percent change, 1964–79					+120.1%
Total population	187,000	255,937	340,697	468,085	
Percent change		+36.9%	+33.1%	+37.4%	
Percent change, 1964–79					+150.3%
Larceny					
55 and older	8,209 (2.3)	12,071 (2.4)	16,211 (2.2)	34,317 (3.1)	
Percent change		+47.0%	+34.3%	+111.7%	
Percent change, 1964–79					+318.0%
Total population	358,569	510,660	729,661	1,098,398	
Percent change		+42.4%	+42.9%	+50.5%	
Percent change, 1964–79					+206.3%

Table 2.7. *(continued)*

	1964	1969	1974	1979	
Motor Vehicle Theft					
55 and older	205 (0.2)	308 (0.2)	387 (0.4)	730 (0.5)	
Percent change		+50.2%	+25.6%	+88.6%	
Percent change, 1964–79					+256.1%
Total population	97,356	125,686	107,226	143,654	
Percent change		+29.1%	−14.7%	+34.0%	
Percent change, 1964–79					+47.6%

Source: Based on FBI, *Uniform Crime Reports,* 1964, 1969, 1974, 1979 (Washington, D.C.: U.S. Government Printing Office).
Note: Numbers in parentheses are the percent of the total arrests for a given year.

elderly, however, undoubtedly overemphasizes the steep percentage increase.

Robbery. The 55-and-over age group constituted only about 0.5 percent of the total arrests for this offense. In both groups, however, there was an increase in arrests for robbery. The pattern of growth was almost identical for the two groups during 1964–1979: 229.8 percent for the elderly, and 234.1 percent for the general population. Again this percentage might be unduly influenced by the small absolute number of robbery arrests of elderly suspects.

Aggravated Assault. Arrests among the elderly for this offense account for 3.6 to 4.2 percent of the total. Both in the general population and in the elderly group there has been a constant increase in the number of arrests over the fifteen-year period. The increase is higher in the general population (221.2 percent) than in the 55-and-over age group (165.8 percent).

Table 2.8. Arrests for Minor Offenses

	1964	1969	1974	1979	
55 and older	350,806 (9.0)	378,722 (8.0)	271,175 (5.8)	336,689 (4.6)	
Percent change		+7.9%	−28.4%	+24.2%	
Percent change, 1964–79					−4.0%
Total population	3,904,579	4,750,572	4,704,979	7,343,045	
Percent change		+21.7%	−1.0%	+56.1%	
Percent change, 1964–79					+88.1%

Source: Based on FBI, *Uniform Crime Reports,* 1964, 1969, 1974, 1979 (Washington, D.C.: U.S. Government Printing Office).
Note: Numbers in parentheses are the percent of the total arrests for a given year.

Table 2.9. Arrests for Selected Minor Offenses

	1964	1969	1974	1979
Drunkenness				
55 and older	224,802 (15.4)	237,947 (16.8)	138,111 (15.1)	122,719 (11.3)
Percent change		+5.8%	−42.0%	−11.1%
Percent change, 1964–79				−45.4%
Total population	1,458,821	1,420,161	911,837	1,090,233
Percent change		−2.7%	−37.5%	−19.6%
Percent change, 1964–79				−25.3%
Vagrancy				
55 and older	13,268 (10.0)	10,420 (9.8)	2,798 (8.5)	1,527 (4.4)
Percent change		−21.5%	−73.1%	−45.4%
Percent change, 1964–79				−88.5%
Total population	132,955	102,269	32,802	34,662
Percent change		−20.1%	−69.1%	+5.7%
Percent change, 1964–79				−73.9%
Disorderly conduct				
55 and older	28,851 (6.1)	29,250 (5.1)	21,018 (3.9)	24,673 (3.5)
Percent change		+1.4%	−28.1%	+17.4%
Percent change, 1964–79				−14.5%
Total population	475,756	573,502	544,321	711,730
Percent change		+20.5%	−5.1%	+30.8%
Percent change, 1964–79				+49.6%
Driving under influence				
55 and older	21,172 (9.4)	35,858 (10.3)	57,860 (9.4)	90,548 (7.4)
Percent change		+69.4%	+61.4%	+56.5%
Percent change, 1964–79				+328.5%
Total population	225,672	349,326	616,549	1,231,665
Percent change		+54.8%	+76.5%	+99.8%
Percent change, 1964–79				+445.8%
Liquor Laws				
55 and older	6,132 (4.0)	6,066 (2.3)	4,330 (2.3)	7,283 (1.9)
Percent change		−1.1%	−28.6%	+68.2%
Percent change, 1964–79				+18.8%
Total population	153,829	212,660	191,213	386,957
Percent change		+38.2%	−10.1%	+102.4%
Percent change, 1964–79				+151.6%
Gambling				
55 and older	12,825 (12.4)	13,742 (17.6)	7,215 (15.7)	7,819 (15.3)
Percent change		+7.2%	−47.5%	+8.4%
Percent change, 1964–79				−39.0%
Total population	103,814	78,020	45,900	50,974
Percent change		−24.8%	−41.2%	+11.1%
Percent change, 1964–79				−50.9%

Source: Based on FBI, *Uniform Crime Reports,* 1964, 1969, 1974, 1979 (Washington, D.C.: U.S. Government Printing Office).

Note: Numbers in parentheses are the percent of the total arrests for a given year.

Burglary. Elderly arrestees for this offense accounted for 0.3 to 0.5 percent of the total arrestees. Arrests in the general population rose at a constant rate and through the entire period reached 150.3 percent. Burglary arrests for the 55-and-over age group increased in a less constant pattern than for the general population. In this group the increase during the years 1964–1979 was 120.1 percent.

Larceny (Theft). The share of the elderly for the total arrests in this category is 2.2 to 3.1 percent. This is the Index offense for which the highest number of people in both categories were arrested. The increase of arrests in the 55-and-over group for the entire period was 318.0 percent. During the same time, the general population showed an increase of 206.3 percent.

Motor Vehicle Theft. The 55-and-over age group accounted for only 0.2 to 0.5 percent of the total arrests for this crime. The increase in arrests in this group for the 1964–1979 period was 256.1 percent, versus 47.6 percent for the general population. Again, the generally small number of elderly arrestees influenced the high rate of growth in this group.

A summary of the patterns of arrests for major crimes shows that in four categories—murder, forcible rape, larceny, and motor vehicle theft—the rate of growth was higher among the elderly than in the general population. The rate of increase in robbery arrests was almost equal in the two groups, whereas for aggravated assault and burglary the increase in the general population was higher.[9]

ARRESTS FOR MINOR CRIMES

To present a more complete picture, we also examined patterns of arrests for certain minor offenses (see Table 2.8).

Generally, it is clear that the number of arrests of people 55 years old and older constitutes a considerably higher percentage of the total number of arrests for minor offenses than is the case for Index crime arrests. However, there is a continuous decline in the percentage of arrests for minor crimes from 1964 (9.0 percent) to 1979 (4.6 percent).

Shichor and Kobrin found that five minor offenses were prominent in the arrest statistics pertaining to the elderly population: gambling, driving under the influence of alcohol or drugs, drunkenness, disorderly conduct, and vagrancy (see Table 2.9).[10]

Arrests for drunkenness constituted the highest absolute number

Table 2.10. Arrests for Selected Offenses (Percent of the Total)

	55 and Older				General Population			
	1964	1969	1974	1979	1964	1969	1974	1979
Driving under the influence	5.8	9.2	20.9	23.7	4.8	6.0	10.0	13.0
Liquor laws	1.7	1.5	1.5	1.9	3.3	3.6	3.1	4.1
Drunkenness	61.7	59.7	46.7	31.9	31.1	24.2	14.8	11.5
Disorderly conduct	7.9	7.3	7.1	6.4	10.2	9.8	8.8	7.5
Vagrancy	3.6	2.6	0.9	0.4	2.8	1.8	0.5	0.4
Gambling	3.5	3.5	2.4	2.0	2.2	1.3	0.7	0.5
Total	84.2	83.8	78.6	66.3	54.4	46.7	37.9	37.0

Source: Based on FBI, *Uniform Crime Reports,* 1964, 1969, 1974, 1979 (Washington, D.C.: U.S. Government Printing Office).

of charges against elderly arrestees. Elderly arrests for this offense accounted for between 16.8 percent (1969) and 11.3 percent (1979) of the total arrests. During the period of analysis there was a declining trend in the arrest patterns for this offense both in the general population and in the elderly population. The extent of decline is considerably steeper in the 55-and-over group than in the general population: 45.4 percent versus 25.3 percent.

In the arrest patterns for another offense connected with alcohol, vagrancy, the situation is similar. Arrest figures among the elderly for this offense are relatively high, accounting for 10.0 percent (1964)

Table 2.11. Arrests for Sex Offenses

	1964	1969	1974	1979	
55 and older	2,678 (4.6)	2,404 (4.8)	1,971 (4.4)	3,162 (5.0)	
Percent change		+10.3%	−18.0%	+60.4%	
Percent change, 1964–79					+18.1%
Total population	58,082	50,143	44,375	62,633	
Percent change		−13.7%	−11.5%	+41.4%	
Percent change, 1964–79					+7.8%

Source: Based on FBI, *Uniform Crime Reports,* 1964, 1969, 1974, 1979 (Washington, D.C.: U.S. Government Printing Office).

to 4.4 (1979) percent of the total. The share of the elderly arrestees is declining with time. There is a sizable decrease in the absolute numbers of arrestees in both groups. This decline is somewhat steeper in the 55-and-over group (88.5 percent) than in the general population (73.9 percent).

Disorderly conduct is another minor offense often connected with the consumption of alcohol. The share of the elderly among the total number of arrestees is on the decline: 6.1 percent in 1964 and only 3.5 percent in 1979. The decrease in 55-and-older arrestees for this period of time is 14.5 percent. On the other hand, in the general population there was an increase of 49.6 percent in arrests during the 1964–1979 period.

One of the drinking-related offenses for which the arrest trends show a strong increase for both groups is driving under the influence of alcohol or drugs. There was a 445.8 percent increase in arrests for this charge in the general population during the period of inquiry, while among the elderly the number of arrests rose 328.5 percent. This pattern seems to reflect, at least partially, the increased use of automobiles by large segments of the population.

Arrests for the violation of liquor laws have increased in both the general population and the elderly group. The elderly arrests account for between 4.0 and 1.9 percent of the total arrests. The number of arrests in the older group grew 18.8 percent and, in the general population, 151.6 percent.

For a final offense, gambling, often connected with the consumption of alcohol, arrests were high among the elderly. They accounted for between 17.6 percent (1969) and 12.4 percent (1964) of total arrests for gambling. The trend of gambling arrests shows a declining pattern, however. During the fifteen-year period of investigation there was a 50.9 percent decline in the number of arrests for the general population, and a 39.0 percent decline for the elderly group. It is interesting to note, though, that for the last five years of analysis—1974 through 1979—both groups showed a modest increase in arrests: 11.1 percent for the general population and 8.4 percent in the elderly group.

On the whole, it is clear that the overwhelming majority of arrests among the elderly are alcohol-related offenses (Table 2.10). Between 84.2 percent in 1964 and 66.3 percent of the arrests in 1979 are for charges of such offenses in this group. Arrests for these offenses also constituted a substantial part of the arrests for the total population, ranging from 54.4 percent to 37.0 percent. The substantial decline of the share of the alcohol-related charges for arrest during the years seems to reflect the changes in attitudes and treatment of alcoholics and skid row people by the authorities (i.e., increased use of civil procedures) than an actual decrease in the numbers of people involved in this kind of behavior.

Another offense is often attributed to the elderly: sex crimes other than forcible rape. As shown in Table 2.11, between 4.4 percent (1974) and 5.0 percent (1979) of the total number of arrestees for this offense were elderly. The pattern of arrests indicates an increasing trend both in the general population and in the elderly group as well. The increase among the elderly arrestees is higher: 18.1 percent, versus 7.8 percent in the general population. The real growth in arrests occurred during the 1974—1979 period, when there was a 60.4 percent increase in elderly arrestees and 41.4 percent increase in arrests in the general population.

CONCLUSION

The review of the official statistics of arrests, which were seen as indicators of the extent of the involvement of elderly citizens in lawbreaking behavior, shows that in relative terms (in comparison with the general population) arrests among the elderly constitute only a small part of the total arrests. The share of people 55 and older among the arrestees is considerably smaller than their share in the total population.

In American society, where the total number of yearly arrests reaches into the millions (e.g., over 9.5 million in 1979), even relatively small percentages of arrests can account for considerably large absolute numbers of suspects. For example, in 1979 over 385,000 people in the 55-and-older age group were arrested. This is probably a better indicator of the extent of this problem than simple percentages. In addition, more than 48,000 of these arrests were for major (Index) crimes in 1979, and the number of arrests for these more serious crimes through time rose more rapidly in the elderly group than in the general population. If the claim that the elderly are being handled somewhat more leniently than other people by law enforcement officers is true, then their share in lawbreaking is even greater. It should also be noted that the proportion of the elderly in the total population is constantly increasing. This means that there is a strong likelihood that the absolute numbers of the elderly among all arrestees will increase in the future and, in certain types of crimes, that their relative numbers will increase, too. This is a small but significant problem that should command more attention both among policymakers and the general public.

Patterns of lawbreaking behavior, and of control, are deeply rooted in the social structure of every society. The political process of legislation expresses society's (or, according to some, the politically dominant and powerful segment's) definitions of criminal and deviant behavior and determines the social control policies in accordance with them.[11] In this vein, Shichor and Kobrin suggest that the continuous aging process in the U.S. population will affect the definitions of crime and policies of social control.[12] As mentioned, it is anticipated that the absolute number of elderly arrestees will increase and that in certain offenses their relative share will increase also. Judging from the preceding analysis, the relative growth in the number of elderly arrests will occur primarily in the more serious (Index) crimes. This increase might affect the total number of victims as well, since there seems to be a correlation between the overall rate at which the members of an age group are arrested for crime and the rate at which they are victimized.[13]

The criminal justice system is basically geared to process and work with relatively young males. (Roughly, the median age of arrestees for all crimes is below 25). We do not have a comprehensive knowledge of the ways in which the elderly are handled by the agencies of the criminal justice system. There are some indications that the elderly are handled more leniently by the police and other agencies both in this country and elsewhere.[14] However, the exact details and extent of this differential handling are not completely known. Research into this area would be useful and important for a better understanding of the working of the social control system and also for purposes of public policy formulation in dealing with elderly offenders.

It was mentioned also that certain changes in social control policies might affect the elderly differently than they affect other age groups. For instance, the sharp decline in arrests for drunkenness, probably because of the use of alternative methods to lock-up in dealing with drunks, is considerably steeper among the elderly than in the general population. On the other hand, arrests for "driving under the influence" (which showed the highest increase in arrests in the general population—445.8 percent) rose to a somewhat lesser degree among the elderly (328.5 percent).

Another dimension of social control concerning the elderly is connected with the rising political activity of the aged. Some segments among the elderly, no doubt because of their continuous increase in numbers, have developed a sense of group consciousness. This in turn has led to the creation of a more or less effective political bloc focused on social and economic problems and issues common to the elderly. This political consciousness is demonstrated by the

"Gray Panthers" movement and also by the public debates of issues in the 1981 White House Conference on Aging and the current public campaign opposing cuts in Medicare, Social Security benefits, and other programs that mainly concern the elderly. It is likely that increased group consciousness and activity will result in increased political influence and ultimately will affect the status of the elderly in American society. The image of the elderly as helpless, powerless, and in need of support will thus undoubtedly change to one that depicts them as more influential, a powerful group that fights for its interests, rights, and privileges. This change in image, actual power, and social status will also affect public and official attitudes toward the aged and the ways in which they are handled by the agencies of the criminal justice system.[15] According to this point of view, it is expected that gradually the same standards will apply to the elderly as to the rest of the population. Thus the more lenient treatment accorded to the elderly, if it really exists, might diminish. (This is what happened with juveniles.) Usually, a set of expectations is attached to the social role of the powerless and dependent; if these expectations are violated, both the public and the officers of various public agencies often respond negatively.[16]

While the study of various aspects of the aging process and problems of the aging population is currently expanding by leaps and bounds, there is still only a relatively small volume of studies dedicated to issues connected with elderly crime, criminality, and criminal behavior. It is important for the enhancement of our knowledge and for the formulation of adequate and effective social control policies to gain a deeper insight into the phenomenon.

NOTES

1. See, for instance, Jack Goldsmith and Sharon S. Goldsmith (eds.), *Crime and the Elderly* (Lexington, Mass: D. C. Heath, 1976).
2. Edwin H. Sutherland and Donald R. Cressey, *Criminology* (Philadelphia: J.B. Lippincott, 1978); Hans W. Mattick, "The Contemporary Jails of the United States: The Unknown and Neglected Area of Justice," in Daniel Glaser (ed.), *Handbook of Criminology* (Chicago: Rand McNally, 1974); Norval Morris, *The Future of Imprisonment* (Chicago: The University of Chicago Press, 1974).
3. Alan R. Rowe and Charles R. Tittle, "Life Cycle Changes and Criminal Propensity," *The Sociological Quarterly* 18 (Spring 1977): 223–236.
4. U.S. Bureau of the Census, *Statistical Abstracts of the United States*, for the years 1965, 1970, 1975, and 1980. (Washington, D.C.: U.S. Government Printing Office).
5. See, for instance, Albert D. Biderman and Albert J. Reiss, Jr., "On Exploring the 'Dark Figure' of Crime," *The Annals of the American Academy of Political and*

Social Science, 374 (1967): 1–15; Donald J. Black, "Production of Crime Rates," *American Sociological Review* 35, no. 4 (1970): 733–748; Nigel Walker, *Crimes, Courts and Figures: An Introduction to Criminal Statistics* (Middlesex, England: Penguin Books, 1971); Michael Maltz, "Crime Statistics: A Historical Perspective," *Crime and Delinquency* 23 (January, 1977): 32–40.

6. Robert M. O'Brien, David Shichor, and David L. Decker, "An Empirical Comparison of the Validity of UCR and NCS Crime Reports," *The Sociological Quarterly* 21 (Summer 1980): 391–401.

7. This age grouping follows the work of David Shichor and Solomon Kobrin, "Criminal Behavior Among the Elderly," *The Gerontologist*, 18, no. 2 (1978): 213–218.

8. Gresham M. Sykes, *Criminology* (New York: Harcourt Brace Jovanovich, 1978), p. 77.

9. It is worthwhile to mention that there is no cross-tabulation of age and sex available in the *Uniform Crime Reports.* Arrest data show that among the arrestees in the general population males prevail, accounting for between 80 and 90 percent. The male-to-female sex ratio is considerably higher in the general population than among the elderly; therefore, adjusted arrest rates for the elderly were calculated in order to estimate what the arrest figures in the elderly group would be if there were the same sex ratio as in the general population. Some selected calculations indicated that there would be an increase in arrests among the elderly, for instance:

   in the total arrests—5.4- to 8.4-percent increase

   in index crimes arrests—5.3- to 14.3-percent increase

   in violent index crime arrests—4.2- to 8.5-percent increase

10. Shichor and Kobrin, "Criminal Behavior Among the Elderly."

11. See, for instance, William J. Chambliss, "The State, the Law, and the Definition of Behavior as Criminal or Delinquent," in Glaser, *Handbook of Criminology;* Richard Quinney, *Crime and Justice in Society* (Boston: Little, Brown, 1969); and George Vold, *Theoretical Criminology* (New York: Oxford University Press, 1958).

12. Shichor and Kobrin, "Criminal Behavior Among the Elderly."

13. See, for instance, Lamar T. Empey, *American Delinquency* (Homewood, Ill.: Dorsey, 1978), pp. 178–179.

14. Some works that relate to this issue are John Hagan, "Extra-Legal Attributes and Criminal Sentencing: An Assessment of a Sociological Viewpoint," *Law and Society Review* 8 (1974): 357–383; James Q. Wilson, *Varieties of Police Behavior* (Chicago: The University of Chicago Press, 1968); Menachem Amir and Simon Bergman, "Crime Among the Aged in Israel," unpublished manuscript, 1975; Simon Bergman and Menachem Amir, "Crime and Delinquency Among the Aged in Israel," *Geriatrics* (January 1973): 149–157.

15. Shichor and Kobrin, "Criminal Behavior Among the Elderly."

16. For a more detailed analysis, see Robert A. Scott, *The Making of Blind Men* (New York: Russell Sage Foundation, 1969).

PART II

Varieties of Elderly Crime

Current research into all aspects of ordinary crimes committed by elderly offenders is sparse and fragmented. The reason, perhaps, is the small number of aged criminals and the tiny percentage of crimes committed by them. Depending on how "elderly" is defined (i.e., usually age 55 and over in criminal justice), these persons who make up about 16 percent of the population do not account for more than 4 percent of all arrests. The significance of the elderly crime problem is clearly not its size nor its current threat to our social order. The phenomenon is significant, however, in two other aspects: first, it poses very real dilemmas for our methods of crime control (to be discussed in Parts III and IV); and second, the magnitude of the problem is bound to grow as our society ages and elderly offenders increase with the demographic shift. In Sun Belt communities where elderly populations are congregated, the problem has the potential to become much more serious.

The chapters in this section focus on research into various types of elderly crime, from shoplifting to homicide. These studies provide sufficient information to indicate that there are enough elderly offenders in each of these categories to be worth additional and more sophisticated research and perhaps to begin to examine policy regarding amelioration and treatment. Each chapter stresses the importance of empirical data in the development of theories about the etiology of elderly crime and of public policies regarding its control.

Gary Feinberg's research casts doubt on several popular beliefs about elderly shoplifting. He compares status roles and life situations of juvenile delinquents with those of elderly shoplifters. The extent to which the elderly of Broward County, Florida (where Feinberg's research is based), are representative of shoplifters nationwide is unknown. This research, nevertheless, represents one of the first attempts to study systematically the problem of elderly shoplifters.

Allan R. Meyers examines the incidence of alcoholism among the elderly and the relationship of alcoholism to crime. While Meyers contends that alcohol-related arrests have decreased, perhaps due to the decriminalization of alcohol abuse, he does voice a particular concern about traffic violations committed by aged drivers while under the influence of alcohol. He expresses the necessity for further research on the relationship of alcohol to crime and the elderly.

Stephen J. Hucker examines the problems of violence and sex offenses in a population of elderly Canadians from a psychiatric viewpoint. His analysis of relevant literature concludes that findings are often contradictory about both the frequency and etiology of elderly violence and sex deviation. His study is offered as the first to use comparison groups in investigating violent elderly offenders, a topic that has been dealt with primarily by case histories of aged violent offenders, and not very many of them.

William Wilbanks and Dennis D. Murphy compare old and young murderers on a number of personal and situational variables. They use as their data base the *Special Homicide Reports* (SHRs) issued annually by the FBI. These reports are similar to but more refined and detailed than the *Uniform Crime Reports* (UCRs). The more precise definitions and the details surrounding the crimes in the SHRs may explain some apparent discrepancies from the more gross data compiled in the UCRs, in which the only murder category is "non-negligent manslaughter." One of the authors' findings regarding age of murderers and victims is that it is not always true that "old kills old."

The picture that emerges from this section is one of early attempts in defining and conducting research in an area previously ignored. It is clear that each author has a unique perspective and that there is neither uniformity in concepts nor a common source of data. This creates limitations to any generalizability of the findings and clearly documents the need for further empirical research to build on the beginnings contained here.

Chapter 3

Profile of the Elderly Shoplifter

Gary Feinberg

Emergent within the literature on criminology is a growing concern about shoplifting. Recent research efforts have focused on the sociodemographic characteristics of shoplifters, the cost of shoplifting, the reporting of shoplifting, the prosecution of shoplifters, the prevention of shoplifting, the cause of shoplifting, the meaning of shoplifting, and attitudes toward it.[1] This chapter examines a particular population of shoplifters having one major common characteristic: they are all 60 years of age or older. This effort therefore constitutes an alliance between two otherwise disparate fields of study, namely, criminology and social gerontology.

The invisibility of the elderly offender echoes in the veritable dearth of scientific research about even the more descriptive dimensions of this phenomenon. A computerized search of the literature is likely to reveal only a handful of articles addressing the subject.[2] Systematic research regarding the characteristics of elderly shoplifters, the etiology of this aberrant behavior, their choice of victims, their interpretation of their own acts, and society's response are uncharted intellectual territories. If such inquiries have eluded scholarly conceptualization, one might suspect that shoplifting by the elderly simply does not occur. That this is no mare's nest for which we search is attested to by data from the FBI's *Uniform Crime Reports*.

ELDERLY LARCENY RATES

In 1979, for the United States as a whole, there were 21,138 arrests of individuals 60 years of age or over (60+) for the crime of larceny, the general legal rubric under which shoplifting is categorized. This constitutes a rate of 93 per 100,000 for those 60 to 64 years of age and 50 per 100,000 for those 65 and over. Furthermore, elderly (60+) arrests for larceny account for the vast majority of all elderly felony arrests: 21,138 out of 28,204, or 75 percent.

Larceny by the elderly is definitely increasing, and by an impressive amount. In 1971, for example, the national larceny rate of those aged 60 to 64 was about 50 per 100,000 population. By 1979 it had risen to nearly 93 per 100,000 population, an 80-percent increase. An even more drastic increase is evidenced for the "older elderly," those 65 years of age and over. Their rate of arrest for larceny rose from 25.9 per 100,000 nationally in 1971 to 50 per 100,000 in 1979, nearly double. At the same time, elderly homicide rates, as measured by arrests, remained stable over this same period, and the rate of arrests for aggravated assault increased approximately 40 percent.[3]

In one of the more popular retirement states, Florida, the following demographic patterns can be noted. Approximately 17.5 percent of Florida's population in 1978 was 65 years of age, and as many as one out of four were 60 years of age or older. In all, almost 2 million Floridians fell within the age category generally designating the elderly, that is, 60 and over. As demonstrated in Table 1, there were 9,437 arrests in 1978, including 2,859 for felonies committed by

Table 3.1.   Rate of Arrest per 100,000 of Those 60 Years of Age and Over, State of Florida, 1971 and 1978 by Type of Offense

	1971		1978	
Homicide	2.37	(32)	1.58	(31)
Rape	.30	(4)	.97	(19)
Robbery	.52	(7)	1.07	(21)
Aggravated Assault	23.11	(312)	23.26	(457)
Burglary	2.52	(34)	4.43	(87)
Larceny	91.04	(1,229)	113.54	(2,231)
Motor Vehicle Theft	.52	(7)	.41	(8)
Total Index Crimes	120.81	(1,631)	145.50	(2,859)
Total All Crimes	1,266.81	(17,102)	480.25	(9,437)

Source: State of Florida Uniform Crime Reports, 1971, 1978; *Statistical Abstract of the United States,* 1982–1983; U.S. published population statistics, 1978.

those 60 years of age and over (the FBI "Index" crimes of willful homicide, forcible rape, aggravated assault, robbery, burglary, larceny, and motor vehicle theft). This constitutes a total Index arrest rate of 145 per 100,000. Larceny dominates elderly Index arrests (114 per 100,000) followed by aggravated assault (23 per 100,000), with burglary a poor third (4 per 100,000).[4]

Between 1971 and 1978, elderly arrest rates (60+) for Index crimes rose 20 percent (from approximately 121 to 146 per 100,000). Again larceny dominated the field, with an arrest increase of 25 percent over this period (from 91 to 114 per 100,000). Indeed, so strong is Florida's elderly larceny arrest rate that it outstrips the comparable elderly larceny rate for the nation by two to one. Elderly larceny arrests account for a greater *proportion* of all elderly arrests in Florida than they do for the nation as a whole. Florida contains 6.7 percent of the nation's elderly, but accounts for 13 percent of the nation's elderly larceny arrests.[5]

THE BROWARD COUNTY DIVERSIONARY PROGRAM

Growing cognizant of the elderly crime problem in general, and increasingly burdened by elderly shoplifting cases finding their way into the arrest data and onto already crowded court dockets, at least one Florida county, Broward, has responded by implementing a special diversionary program designed to cope with such elderly offenders. This program, known as the Broward Senior Intervention and Education (BSIE) Program, is designed specifically to rehabilitate the elderly shoplifter.

Established in the spring of 1979, the BSIE is a nonsectarian program operating under the aegis of the Jewish Community Centers of South Florida. Recruitment of clients is done through direct recommendation by the Broward County Court. To be eligible, the client must meet all the following criteria:

1. be 60 years of age or older;
2. be charged with only one count of *misdemeanant* shoplifting;
3. enter a plea of guilty;
4. be a first-time offender;
5. voluntarily agree to participate in the program.

Typically, all clients have appeared as defendants before the presiding judge in open court, have been apprised of the nature of the misdemeanant shoplifting charge against them, and have entered a plea of guilty. The judge has then explained that the court will withhold judgment, thereby avoiding a criminal record, if the defendant agrees to participate in the BSIE program. If affirmative, a representative counselor of the BSIE program is introduced to the defendant and outlines the goals and procedures of the program.

Essentially, the BSIE is a three-dimensional rehabilitation program designed to reduce the likelihood of recidivism among elderly shoplifters. The first dimension of the program emphasizes counseling, including an opportunity to reduce the trauma of the shoplifting event and accompanying pretrial anxieties, as well as addressing more long-standing family, economic, social, and personal woes (e.g., loneliness), especially those regarded as causing or motivating the shoplifting behavior. The second dimension of the program focuses on getting the client involved in certain social activities, including participating in a lecture series, learning new crafts such as painting or ceramics, teaching a skill to others, and so on. The third dimension is an externship with a community service organization, such as a local hospital or a food delivery service for shut-ins. This is especially designed for those diagnosed as overly concerned with their own problems and unable to transcend or see their situation in perspective. From intake to completion the program takes three months. The client's progress is monitored weekly.

Since its inception, the Broward program has handled over a thousand cases. Given the surreptitious nature of the offense, the restrictive eligibility criteria, the myriad difficulties of getting the program known and accepted by members of the judiciary, and the fact that the program is operative in only one county—albeit one densely populated by elderly residents (with approximately one out of four persons over 60 years of age)—this would appear to be a substantial number of cases. Of the approximate thousand cases completed, only nine incidents of recidivism have been observed. Given this brief background of the BSIE program as prologue, the objectives of this preliminary study are: a rough sociodemographic profile of the first-time elderly shoplifter and an exploration of the empirical validity of a number of commonly held beliefs, or myths, that people have about elderly shoplifting behavior.

INTERVIEWING ELDERLY SHOPLIFTERS

An interview study was undertaken with a sample of 191 of the 245 BSIE elderly shoplifter cases handled between January 1981 and February 1982. The representativeness of the sample to the total population of elderly shoplifters cannot be demonstrated. Rather, this was an exploratory effort designed to profile the elderly shoplifter. Requisite control groups are being implemented, including one made up of elderly shoplifters who refuse to participate even though eligible for the program, a second made up of those who refuse to plead guilty, a third made up of nonarrested, self-reported elderly shoplifters, and a fourth composed of elderly nonshoplifters. Although it is difficult to predict the nature of any bias extant in what constitutes little more than a fortuitous sample, it is preferable to take a more conservative, noninferential position with respect to the findings. This is merely a preliminary effort, a testing of the waters, in anticipation of much more rigorous and extensive evaluative studies.

This elderly shoplifter profile is based on data secured by program counselors at the BSIE using a stardardized interview schedule, which doubles as a program intake form. The same counselor remains with each client over a three-month period, and during this time any inconsistencies in responses may become evident and efforts can be made to reconcile conflicting information. For example, a respondent may indicate that his family relationships are excellent when questioned in a more objective manner by the counselor. However, at a later time when discussing problems more informally with the same counselor, he may begin to recount serious family squabbles, the inability to trust a sibling, and the like. Corrections for such disparities are then introduced into the file.

With rare exceptions, external validation has not been undertaken. At this preliminary stage of research, when a response to a question is of uncertain validity, it is simply removed from the data base. However, the program is designed to introduce more sophisticated data validation techniques in the future.

With these limitations and disclaimers in mind, certain findings seem worthy to report, especially as they call into question a number of "commonsense" understandings about shoplifting and the elderly.

ELDERLY SHOPLIFTING: MYTHS AND REALITY

Myth # 1: Shoplifting Is a Female-Dominated Offense

In her now-classic study *The Booster and the Snitch*, Mary Owen Cameron found that females tend to dominate in shoplifting statistics.[6] Several studies since also report a higher proportion of women than men involved in shoplifting, especially among adult shoplifters.[7] Theoretically, such a pattern makes sense in that women are more likely to be shoppers and thereby more likely to find themselves in situations where shoplifting can occur. Others factors—including perhaps that store security personnel believe that women are more likely to shoplift than men and thus pursue them more—might also account for male–female statistical differences. According to data from the present study, however, females only slightly outnumber males in shoplifting, and then only for ages 60 to 64. In all 191 cases studied, 102 were females and 89 were males. The significance of even this slight difference is further reduced when one recognizes that the proportion of women aged 60 to 64 in this community (as in all the older age groups) far outstrips that of men. Furthermore, it would appear that with increasing age there is no difference between the proportion of men and the proportion of women among the elderly shoplifting population. Indeed, for each five-year age category (65 to 69, 70 to 74, 75 to 79, and 80 and over) the absolute number of male shoplifters slightly exceeds the absolute number of females. Again, this is made a more salient difference since with increasing age the proportion of elderly males to elderly females steadily decreases in the population as a whole.

Myth # 2: Where Shoplifting Occurs Among the Elderly, It's More Likely to Occur Among the Young Elderly than Among the Frail Elderly

The 191 persons in the sample ranged in age from 58 to 89. Interestingly, there were fifty-one cases in which the shoplifter was between the ages of 60 and 64, and an equal number in which the shoplifter was between 70 and 74. Indeed, as many as 42 percent of our shoplifters were over 70. We assume that there are more people living in Broward County who are between the ages of 60 and 64 than between 70 and 74. If so, findings would support the rather unexpected conclusion that after age 60, involvement in shoplifting may actually increase for a time rather than decrease.

Myth # 3: Elderly Shoplifters Steal Because They Are Indigent

To test the proposition that the elderly who steal do so because they are indigent, five traditional indices of social class were used: (1) amount of income, (2) source of income, (3) level of education, (4) home ownership, and (5) occupation.

1. Amount of Income. Out of 191 cases, only 149 provide information about income. Of these, sixty, or approximately 40 percent, have incomes in excess of $10,000 per year and twelve report incomes in excess of $20,000. In only two cases do the subjects report incomes of less than $2,500. The median income is about $7,500.

2. Source of Income. Eighty-six cases (45 percent) indicated three or more sources of income. Typically these included "Social Security" and, in addition, "Interest from Savings" and "Stocks and Bonds." Only twenty-five cases (13 percent) have only a single source of income, and in one of these it is listed as "Investments."

3. Level of Education. The educational level of this population of shoplifters appeared relatively high. One hundred and one (52 percent) were at least high school graduates. Only fifty-two (29 percent) of the cases reported only an eighth-grade education or less. Thirty-nine individuals, or about 20 percent of the total, had at least some college education.

4. Home Ownership. One hundred and fifty-six (83 percent) of the respondents own their own residence. One hundred and two of these own condominiums and an additional fifty own their own homes. Four respondents replied that they own mobile homes. In sum, the vast majority are home owners, not renters, and we may assume that the community integration thereby evidenced is more extensive than might have been anticipated.

5. Occupation. White-collar workers, professionals, and administrators outstrip blue-collar, semiskilled, unskilled, or service workers in their involvement as elderly shoplifters.

Taken together, these indices would suggest that the elderly shoplifter tends to be more affluent than otherwise suspected. Admittedly, as per census data, Florida's elderly tend to be wealthier than the elderly in general.[8] Regardless, these data certainly do not support the common myth that elderly shoplifters steal because they are indigent. Furthermore, elderly shoplifters tend to come from the middle rather than lower classes. This is consistent with data secured by other researchers using entirely different samples. Won and Yamamoto, for example, in a comparative study of 493 cases of department store and supermarket shoplifting in Honolulu, report that "supermarket shoplifting is numerically and proportionately more a middle income phenomenon and less a lower stratum phenomenon."[9]

Myth # 4: The Elderly Shoplifter Steals for Subsistence Purposes

Closely akin to the belief that the elderly shoplift because of indigence is the belief that what they steal is necessary for them to survive. To test this more formally, this study focused on the types of items targeted for shoplifting and categorized them as follows: (1) food, (2) drugs, (3) clothing, (4) personal goods (e.g., toothbrush, cosmetics), and (5) household goods (e.g., batteries, detergent).

A frequency distribution of each article was constructed. This was varied to include incidents where only one article was actually taken, where two items were stolen, and where three or more items were taken. It was found that the most frequently purloined item was neither food nor drugs, but clothing. The second most frequently stolen articles were personal goods, especially cosmetics. Although this is obviously a value judgment, it is possible that food and drugs are more significant subsistence items than clothing in a subtropical climate. Given the large number of shirts, blouses, and cosmetics stolen by elderly shoplifters, the subsistence thesis is not supported. Indeed, further justification for rejecting such a thesis is seen in the fact that where two or more items are purloined (fifty-three cases) in no instance was the theft of food (twenty-three instances) accompanied by a theft of drug items (six instances). Moreover, in several instances the food stolen was more a luxury than a necessity, for example, canned hams and packages of veal rather than milk and bread. One woman who stole a wedge of cheese replied, "We often buy cheese, but not such an expensive kind" (value of the purloined cheese: under $4.00). In sum, analysis of the stolen items would suggest they are not targeted out of subsistence need but are more likely to be one of life's "extras."

Myth # 5: The Elderly Who Shoplift Are Victims of Poor Memory, Not Perpetrators with Criminal Intent

Evidence of selective loss of memory with age abounds.[10] Thus the suggestion is often made that elderly shoplifters do not intentionally take objects without paying for them, but rather that they forget that they have selected the items to be purchased.

To walk off with one item mistakenly is not without credibility. Many people, not only the elderly, occasionally do this. However, in fifty-three instances (28 prcent) *two* items were stolen, and in thirty-seven additional instances (20 percent of the total cases) *three* items were taken. Multiple-item theft as a result of forgetfulness is much more questionable.

When asked, "Do you feel you are guilty of shoplifting," 75 percent of the respondents (143 cases) said "Yes." At the same time, when asked, "Do you consider yourself a law violator?" 72 percent of the 191 respondents said "No." How they mentally accept apparently contradictory beliefs about themselves—that they are shoplifters but not law violators—is a conundrum that needs further unraveling. One possibility is that while they admit to shoplifting, the value of the items stolen causes them to reject the act as a law violation. We therefore controlled for the value of goods stolen and then checked to see if there was a significant relationship between the value of the goods stolen and the likelihood of defining one's self as a law violator. In all, only 23 percent of the shoplifters saw themselves as law violators, and no significant relationship was noted between the value of the goods taken and the likelihood of defining one's self as a law violator.

Myth # 6: The Elderly Shoplifter Is More Likely to Be a Recent Resident Rather than a Long-Time Resident of the Community

The underlying rationale behind this myth is that people who are recent arrivals are less likely to feel integrated into and a part of the community. At the same time, they are more likely to feel a sense of strain in having broken ties with previous communities and perhaps, too, have some sense of guilt for leaving their "hometown."[11] On the other hand, according to the myth, those who have resided for many years within a community are more likely to feel a part of it and obliged to obey its laws.

In fact, better than 50 percent of the sample of elderly shoplifters defined themselves as "old-time Floridians." Objective information show that 58 percent have lived in Florida over five years and 12 percent (of the total 191) have actually lived in Florida twenty years or more. Only 7 percent reported having lived in Florida one year or less. The vast majority of shoplifting is done by people who have lived in Florida over two years. Perhaps getting to know the turf is critical. Obviously, controlling for the age at which one moved to Florida, satisfaction with the move, its voluntariness, and the like need to be tested.

Myth # 7: Elderly Shoplifters Steal Because They Are Lonely

One popular suggestion is that the elderly shoplifter steals as a means of seeking attention. Underlying such a rationale is the belief that elderly shoplifters are lonely, isolated, and crave attention. Our data, however, do not support such a description.

Approximately 70 percent do not live alone. One hundred and twenty-five of the 191 elderly shoplifters live with at least one other person. Moreover, 65 percent of the shoplifters are married. Concomitantly, only 25 percent are widowed, and less than 3 percent reported being widowed within the past year. In addition, the vast majority (80 percent) indicated that they have family or close friends living in the area.

Of course, a person may be lonely even when other people are around. We therefore asked, "Do you feel you are really a part of your family?" Respondents answered by selecting from the following four-item scale:

1. Really a part;
2. Included in most ways;
3. Included in some ways but not others;
4. Don't feel I really belong.

Of the 191 cases, 141 (72 percent) responded that they felt "Really a part" of their family. Only 9 cases chose "Don't feel I really belong."

As a furter test of loneliness, the five-item Srole test of anomie was implemented. More specifically, respondents were asked whether or not they agreed or disagreed with each of the following statements:

1. Most public officials (people in public office) are not really interested in the problems of the average man. In general, would you agree with that statement or disagree?
2. These days a person doesn't really know whom he can count on.
3. Nowadays, a person has to live pretty much for today and let tomorrow take care of itself.
4. In spite of what some people say, the lot (situation) (condition) of the average man is getting worse, not better.
5. It's hardly fair to bring a child into the world with the way things look for the future.[12]

A standard six category Likert scale was used ranging from very strongly agree to very strongly disagree. The 191 shoplifters were found to be about equally divided between those who agreed and those who disagreed with each scale item. We noted, however, that approximately twice as many subjects disagreed with all five items (strong anti-alienation) as agreed with all five items (strong alienation). In sum, these data do not support the popular belief that elderly shoplifters are lonely and isolated.

OTHER CHARACTERISTICS OF
ELDERLY SHOPLIFTERS

Some additional information emerges from this study concerning the beliefs and behavior of elderly shoplifters:

1. Asked if they have been hurt by what they have done, 90 percent answered "Yes." However, when asked, "Who else is hurt?" 59 of the 191 respondents (30 percent) said "No one." Fewer than 10 percent mentioned the store and fewer than 1 percent perceived the general public as being in any way harmed. When they do think that someone (other than themselves) might be injured by their behavior, they typically think it would be a spouse or other family member. Although stores often pass on their losses due to shoplifting and related security costs to other patrons, including the elderly, in the form of higher retail prices charged for all merchandise, not one of the 191 respondents named such patrons as the ultimate victims of their shoplifting activity.

2. Approximately 90 percent of those sampled rated their treatment by the police as acceptable, good, or very good. Only 10 percent rated it as unfavorable. This is, of course, consistent with other studies of public attitudes toward law enforcement officers.[13]

3. Interestingly, almost 50 percent of the 191 cases did not tell anyone that they had been arrested for shoplifting. Only 28 percent looked to a spouse for support. Fewer than 7 percent sought advice or assistance from an attorney. Even though the arrest is the first in their lives (and thus likely an especially traumatic event) for whatever reason these elderly shoplifters frequently prefer to bear the burden alone.

4. Elderly shoplifters do not appear motivated by a desire to "get even" for some maltreatment by the store victimized. More specifically, we asked if they were selecting their target victims because of (a) dislike for store personnel; (b) poor service; or (c) being overcharged. One hundred and nine rated personnel in their chosen victim as about the same as in other stores. (Whether they shoplifted in the other stores remains an open question). Somewhat unexpectedly, more subjects rated the personnel in the store they victimized as at least a little more pleasant than at other stores, outstripping those who ranked such personnel as at least "a little less pleasant" by a margin of two to one.

Concomitantly, almost 60 percent rated the level of assistance they received in the victimized store as about the same as the assistance they received in other stores. Again they were twice as likely to rate the quality of assistance as at least "a little more helpful" than in other stores as they were to rate it as at least "a little less helpful."

Finally, better than 50 percent rated the victimized store's prices as being about the same as in other stores. Oddly enough, the remaining respondents were equally divided; half rated the victimized store's prices as higher and half rated them as lower than in other stores at which they shop.

In sum, we unearthed no evidence to support the thesis that these elderly shoplifters were trying somehow to "get even" for negative treatment they may have suffered in past relations with the target victims. (Table 3.2)

GENERAL CONCLUSIONS AND A THEORETICAL NOTE: ELDERLY DELINQUENTS

Despite sampling limitations and the need for more sophisticated statistical analyses beyond percentage comparisons, these initial exploratory efforts cast doubt on several popular beliefs about elderly shoplifters and about the act of elderly shoplifting. Many of these findings are not without empirical precedent, which helps lend credibility to these results.[14]

In seeking to place these empirical descriptions into a theoretical perspective, it should be noted that the status of the elderly in our society, and the accompanying role obligations and expectations, are in many respects reminiscent of those ascribed to youth. For example:

1. exemption from work responsibilities;
2. relatively unstructured time schedules;
3. relative freedom from future life planning;
4. low prestige of status position;
5. limited financial independence;
6. relative freedom from family responsibilities;
7. de-emphasis on production and emphasis on consumption;
8. emphasis on play and leisure as a way of life.

There are, of course, important differences between the status-role of the elderly and that of the juvenile:

1. Juveniles can anticipate future engagement in economic, familial, and political roles; the elderly can anticipate mainly disengagement from such roles.
2. Juveniles expect and are expected to enter mainstream society;

Table 3.2. Perception of Their Target Victims by Elderly Shoplifters

Question: How would you rate prices in this store relative to others at which you shop?

Response:	Frequency
A little higher	29
Much higher	12
A little lower	31
Much lower	10
About the same	109
Don't know	0
No response	0
Total	191

Question: How would you rate the personnel in this store relative to others at which you shop?

Response	Frequency
A little more pleasant	13
Much more pleasant	13
A little less pleasant	4
Much less pleasant	11
About the same	109
Don't know	24
No response	17
Total	191

Question: How would you rate the assistance in this store relative to others where you shop?

Response	Frequency
A little more helpful	13
Much more helpful	12
A little less helpful	5
Much less helpful	7
About the same	112
Don't know	20
No response	22
Total	191

the elderly expect and are expected to leave mainstream society—and not return.

3. In time, the status, financial, and power positions of juveniles become stronger, whereas in time they become weaker for the elderly.

4. Juveniles look up to those currently in power for acceptance, and their reference groups rest within the ongoing social order. The elderly are outside mainstream society, like the youth, but above it. Career concerns, the need to postpone gratification in anticipation of long range goals, the myriad benefits of acquisitional behavior, the lure of certain status passages, and similarly societally tauted ideals which function as the prover-

bial "carrot" leading society's members along prescribed routes have lost their motivational appeal, stripped as they are of their relevance, intrinsic value, and even their pretense by experience and the cool wind of objective reality.

5. Juveniles tend to have close, and intimate role models to follow; the elderly tend to lack such idealized role models.

There are a number of other important differences in interests, values, perspectives, and *weltanschauung* that distinguish the status-role and life situation of juveniles from those of the elderly. Nevertheless, the many significant social dimensions they share suggest that it might be profitable to look to juvenile delinquency theory to interpret or explain elderly involvement in certain forms of crime, including shoplifting. In particular, the elderly can be viewed as involved in an emergent role passage that includes (a) role disengagement, (2) role transition, and (3) role acquisition.[15] In terms of emergent role passage, the elderly must create, discover, and shape their own roles as they disengage from the work force. In this passage, they lack certain critical supportive systems: there are (a) few institutionalized rules to follow; (b) few timetables; (c) only nominal strategies of change; (d) limited agreement on new definitions of status; (e) few guidelines or models to follow; and (f) asynchronous transitions (e.g., widowhood, followed by retirement, followed by change in residence to a Sunbelt community). The elderly are thus set adrift and society has provided them with neither map, itinerary, nor friendly shore. They are on their own, captain and mate, actor and agent of their own destiny. Making matters more difficult, they must often transit several roles at once: retirement, death of a spouse, physical disabilities, change in residence, and the like. Moreover, a good deal of role relinquishment is not accompanied by the acquisition of new roles.

Separated from mainstream society, the elderly must try out different selves and different meanings, often revaluating past experience in light of current life situations, changing moralities, and so on. For example, had she become widowed in the 1950s, an elderly woman might never have thought about living with another man outside of marriage. Indeed, she probably would have disowned a granddaughter who took on such an arrangement, for at that time such behavior was anathema. Widowhood in the early 1980s, however, would find that same elderly woman having to revaluate such past attitudes and behavior in light of the growing acceptance of alternative family life styles and concomitant increased likelihood for her to seek out such companionship through cohabitation. Certain inner and outer containments, freed from traditional social bonds, are especially likely to suffer disintegration, at least until their status-role becomes crystallized for the elderly. Walter Reckless conceives of inner containment as consisting of the following: (a) a favorable self-image, (b) an awareness of being innerdirected, (c) a high level of status frustration, (d) a strong set of internalized morals and ethics, and (e) a well-developed superego.[16] Comparing these elements of social control with extant empirical data about the elderly, it is clear that they evidence weaknesses in each of these areas.[17] Concomitantly, the elderly may score poorly with respect to Reckless's conceptualization of outer containment. Specifically, they tend to lack the following constraining influences: (a) a broad role structure; (b) a set of reasonable limits and responsibilities (we contend that the elderly aren't overwhelmed as much as underwhelmed with responsibilities); (c) opportunities for status achievement; (d) cohension and *esprit de corps*, including joint activity with other elderly and non elderly in society; (e) a strong sense of belonging; and so on.[18]

Breakdowns in inner and outer containment are then viewed as either causing or facilitating elderly persons to become involved in shoplifting, at least insofar as they free them from bonds that normally prevent such deviance. Why shoplifting is the form of the deviance the elderly choose is a much more difficult question to answer. That it does not require an apprenticeship or the acquisition of new skills, that it can be integrated with one's normal daily activities (i.e., shopping), that it may not be defined as a crime, and that there may be some economic motive related to financial insecurity are at this stage only hypothesized possibilities for a causal model that needs to be formally tested.

NOTES

1. Andre Normandeau, "Quelques Faits sur de Vol dans les Grandes Magasins a Montreal, *Canadian Journal of Criminology and Corrections* 13 (1971): 251–265; G. Fournier, et al., "Les Aspects du Vol dans les Grandes Magasins," *International Annals of Criminology* 9 (1920): 455–564; Jean Sohier, "A Rather Ordinary Crime: Shoplifting," *International Criminal Police Review* 229 (1969): 161–165; Mary Margaret Hughes, "Shoplifting Statistics," *Security World* 11 (1974): 58–62; Edward M. Shapson, "The 4 Billion Retail Ripoff," *Public Relations Journal* (July 1973): 12–15; Mary Owen Cameron, *The Booster and the Snitch: Department Store Shoplifting* (New York: The Free Press, 1964), especially Chapter 1: D.J. Steffensmeier and R.H. Steffensmeier, "Who Reports Shoplifters? Research Contributions and Further Developments," *International Journal of Criminology and Penology* 5 (1977): 79–89; Max C. Dertke, Louis A. Penner, et al., "Observer's Reporting of Shoplifting as a Function of Thief's Race and Sex,"

The Journal of Social Psychology, 94 (1974): 213–221; Lawrence E. Cohen and Rodney Stark, "Discriminatory Labeling and the Five Finger Discount: An Empirical Analysis of Differential Shoplifting Dispositions," Journal of Research in Crime and Delinquency 1 (1974): 25–39; Lee Casey and John L. Shuman, "Police/Probation Shoplifting Reduction Program in San Jose, California: A Synergetic Approach," Crime Prevention Review 6 (1979): 1–9; Lloyd W. Klemke, "Does Apprehension For Shoplifting Amplify or Terminate Shoplifting Activity," Law and Society Review 12 (1978): 391–403; Robert E. Kraut, "The Deterrent and Definitional Influences on Shoplifting," Social Problems 23 (1976): 358–368; Anthony C. Gaudio, An Assessment and Evaluation of Shoplifters (Richmond, Va.: Advisory Legislative Council, 1968); George Won and Douglas Yamamura, "Social Structure and Deviant Behavior: A Study of Shoplifting," Sociology and Social Research 53 (1968): 44–55; L. Bickman, "Interpersonal Influence and the Reporting of a Crime," Personality and Social Psychology Bulletin 5 (1979): 14–19.

2. M. E. Adams and Clyde Vedder, "Age and Crime: Medical and Sociological Characteristics of Prisoners over 50," Geriatrics 16 (1961): 177–185; S. Hays and Morris Wisotsky, "The Aged Offender," Journal of the American Geriatrics Society 17 (1969): 1064–1073; P.L. Schroeder "Criminal Behavior in the Later Period of Life," American Journal of Psychiatry 92 (1936): 915–920; David Moberg, "Old Age and Crime," Journal of Criminal Law and Criminology 43 (1953): 773–780.

3. U.S. Department of Justice, Federal Bureau of Investigation, Uniform Crime Reports: Crime in the United States, 1979 (Washington, D.C.: U.S. Government Printing Office, 1979).

4. Florida Department of Law Enforcement, Crime in Florida: 1978 Annual Report (Tallahassee, 1978).

5. Ibid.

6. Cameron, The Booster and the Snitch.

7. Guido, Assessment and Evaluation; Normandeau, "Quelques Faits": Hughes, "Shoplifting Statistics." For contradictory evidence, see P. Mayhew, "Crime in a Man's World," New Society 40 (1977): 560; and R.G. Redding, "The Social Evil," Justice of the Peace 140 (1976): 17–18.

8. Florida Department of Community Affairs, Division of Public Safety Planning and Assistance, Florida's Plan to Reduce Crime Against the Elderly, 1980 (Tallahassee, 1980).

9. Won and Yamamura, "Social Structure and Deviant Behavior."

10. Matilda White Riley and Anne Foner, Aging and Society, Volume 1: An Inventory of Research Findings (New York: Russell Sage Foundation, 1968).

11. Irving Rosow, Socialization to Old Age (Berkeley: University of California Press, 1974).

12. Leo, Srole, "Social Integration and Certain Corollaries: An Exploratory Study," American Sociological Review, 21 (December, 1956): 709–716.

13. Richard D. Knudten et al., "The Victim in the Administration of Criminal Justice: Problems and Perceptions," in William F. McDonald (ed.), Criminal Justice and the Victim (Los Angeles: Sage, 1976).

14. Riley and Foner, Aging and Society.

15. B. Glazer and Anselm Strauss, Status Passage (Chicago: Aldine, 1971).

16. Walter C. Reckless, "A Non-Causal Approach: Containment Theory," Excerpta Criminologica 1 (1962): 131–134.

17. Riley and Foner, Aging and Society.

18. Reckless, "A Non-Causal Approach."

Chapter 4

Drinking, Problem Drinking, and Alcohol-Related Crime Among Older People

Allan R. Meyers

There is considerable controversy about the nature and magnitude of the relationship between the use of alcohol and criminal behavior by older people and about trends in drinking, problem drinking, and alcohol-related crime committed by older adults. Although there are too few data and too many methodological problems with those data to justify firm conclusions about alcohol and crime in old age, there are sufficient data to address some of the more important research and policy questions and, in that way, to develop a better-informed agenda for both social policy and social research.

On the basis of national crime statistics, Shichor and Kobrin have shown that alcohol-related arrests, especially drinking and driving and public drunkenness, accounted for the great majority of criminal behavior by people aged 55 or older in the decade 1964–1975.[1] In the same way, Epstein et al. have shown that more than 80 percent of arrests of older people (aged 60 and over) in San Francisco, California, during a four-month period in 1967 and 1968 were for charges

Supported, in part, by Grants # R01-AA02133-03 and R01-AA02133-05 from the National Institute on Alcohol Abuse and Alcoholism and a grant from the Milbank Memorial Fund. I have received ample advice and technical assistance from my colleagues Ralph Hingson, Marc Mucatel, and Tim Herren. Insofar as I have incorporated their advice into this chapter, they have improved it. Insofar as I have failed to do so, they bear no responsibility for its faults.

of drunkenness. In fact, they concluded that "were it not for drunkenness very few older people . . . would be arrested in San Francisco."[2] Moreover, they suggested that alcohol use played at least some part in many of the other arrests.

Although there are few data on the risk factors associated with alcohol-related crime committed by older people, it appears that such crimes are only rarely committed by first-time offenders; the majority of offenders are males with long-term, chronic drinking problems and long histories of alcohol-related crime. For example, Cahalan et al. found that older male problem drinkers (those 60 or older) were more likely to report that they had had "problems with police" than were younger problem drinkers and those without drinking problems.[3] Schuckit and Miller found that among older in-patients in a general medical ward those who were diagnosed as "alcoholics" were significantly more likely to have been imprisoned and to have had "severe problems" with the police than were their nonalcoholic counterparts.[4] In a study of older adults in both institutional and community settings in the Baltimore (Maryland) Standard Metropolitan Statistical Area, Rathbone-McCuan et al. reported that 47 percent of "known" alcoholics and 17 percent of "unknown" alcoholics in their sample reported "problems with the police," a proportion that was significantly higher than the general older adult population.[5] Finally, in a study of older males arrested for driving under the influence of alcohol in Mississippi, Wells-Parker and Spencer found no difference between offenders' and controls' reported levels of drinking, but significantly higher levels of problem drinking and alcohol-related arrests among younger adults arrested than among age-matched controls.[6]

Prevailing theories suggest that many older adults drink excessively and pose alcohol-related law enforcement problems in response to the material and emotional stresses associated with aging and old age: illness, bereavement, impoverishment, and social isolation from family and friends. Others drink at normal levels but react differently to alcohol because of the effects of normal aging, illness, or therapeutic drugs. In either case, there are suggestions that as the U.S. population ages and as older people's levels of material, social, and psychological privation increases, so will alcohol-related crime among older adults.[7]

These are plausible and popular hypotheses. Evidence from a number of sources suggests, however, that they may be unsound. For example, several studies have shown that older people generally drink less than younger ones,[8] and Meyers et al. have shown that neither drinking nor alcohol-related problems among older people are necessarily related to satisfaction, isolation, or material or emotional loss.[9] In fact, their data suggest that older adults who are very old (75 or older), who are widows or widowers with relatively little formal education, and who are less satisfied with their lives are more likely to abstain. Those who report that they are problem drinkers (1 percent of their sample) or that they have alcohol-related problems (3 percent) appeared to have had these problems for many years, and in some cases for all their adult lives.[10] Insofar as they expressed more dissatisfaction than those without problems, it was in reference to human relationships—with spouses, family members, and friends—rather than material ones. Since the study was cross- sectional rather than longitudinal, there is no evidence of temporal sequence, that is, whether dissatisfaction caused drinking or vice versa.

Finally, Shichor and Kobrin have shown that in the decade 1964–1975, while the older population grew dramatically, the levels of alcohol-related arrests of older people declined and the distribution of these crimes changed markedly—for example, arrests for driving under the influence rose sharply while those for drunkenness declined.[11]

A number of biases are associated with all these studies: sampling bias, reporting bias (reflecting problems of both reliability and validity), and inconsistent definitions of alcoholism, problem drinking, and alcohol-related crime. What is more significant, there have been no prospective studies of the relationships among alcohol use, problem drinking, and the incidence of criminal behavior among large community samples of older adults. Even in the absence of ideal data, however, there are a number of indications that neither the relationship nor the trends in alcohol use and criminal behavior by older people are so obvious as prevailing hypotheses predict.

ALCOHOL-RELATED CRIME IN OLD AGE

No data describe the incidence of alcohol-related crime, nor even the total number of alcohol-related arrests. The best approximation is contained in the FBI's *Uniform Crime Reports* (UCRs) for the United States, which are published annually. These data have been reported each year since 1972 in the *Sourcebook of Criminal Justice Statistics*.[12] Although these data are subject to substantial sampling and reporting bias, they represent the most comprehensive picture of alcohol-related crime and trends in such crimes in the United States. They suggest that the trends first noted by Shichor and Kobrin have continued through the past decade.

Table 4.1. Alcohol-Related Crime Committed by Older Persons, 1977–1978

	All Ages	55–59	60–64	65 and Older
OUI (operating motor vehicle under the influence of alcohol)[a]				
1977	1,104,132	46,537	26,099	18,854
1978	1,204,733	48,436	27,047	20,034
Liquor law violations				
1977	321,573	3,391	2,119	1,875
1978	357,450	3,732	2,248	2,084
Public drunkenness				
1977	1,208,525	75,421	45,252	36,257
1978	1,117,349	66,096	39,696	31,106

Sources: Marc Schuckit, "Geriatric Alcoholism and Drug Abuse," The Gerontologist 17 (1977): 168–174; Schuckit, "The Elderly as a Unique Population: Alcoholism," Alcoholism: Clinical and Experimental Research 2 (1978): 31–38.

[a]Sometimes reported as DWI ("driving while intoxicated").

Table 4.1 shows the national incidence figures for the three categories of alcohol-related crime in 1977 and 1978, the two most recent years for which data are available. The data are reported for offenders of all ages, and then separately for the three oldest age groups: 55 to 59 years old, 60 to 64, and 65 and older. As Shichor and Kobrin have demonstrated, this is not an artificial distinction; there appear to be marked age-related differences in the criminal behaviors of the adult population, with the most striking difference between those aged 18 to 54 and those aged 55 and older.[13]

The table shows, first, that OUI ("operating under the influence") is by far the most prevalent alcohol-related crime, both among the general population and among older adults. Public drunkenness is also relatively common. There are, in contrast, relatively few liquor law offenses, since these include mainly commercial violations (sale of alcohol to minors, sales after hours, or sales on Sundays). Other offenses, such as procuring alcohol for minors, are relatively rare among older people.

Second, the data show that older adults account for a small proportion of alcohol-related crime, though for a much larger proportion of these offenses than they do for all crime. In 1978, when adults aged 55 or older accounted about 20 percent of the total population,[14] they accounted for 4 percent of all reported arrests in the United States. By comparison, they accounted for 3 percent of all liquor law violations, 8 percent of all OUI violations, and 12 percent of all drunkenness arrests. Finally, the data show that alcohol-related crimes account for the great majority of reported criminal behavior by older people. Approximately 58 percent of arrests of people aged 55 or older were for alcohol-related crimes, a rate more than three times higher than that among the population-at-large.

Trends in alcohol-related offenses are much more elusive. The absolute numbers of operating under the influence and liquor law violations have increased consistently and markedly since 1972.[15] The number of arrests for drunkenness increased from 1972 until 1975, fell in 1976, rose in 1977, and fell again in 1978. These data, however, do not necessarily reflect changes in criminal behavior nor even in levels of arrests. In the first case, there has been a growing tendency to "decriminalize" alcoholism and public drunkenness since the enactment of the federal Uniform Alcoholism and Intoxication Treatment Act of 1971. In response to that act, various states passed laws that define alcoholism and alcohol-related problems as disease rather than criminal behavior, and there has been a corresponding tendency toward fewer arrests for drunkenness, although not necessarily fewer alcohol-related arrests.[16]

Moreover, there is substantial reporting bias in the *Uniform Crime Reports* statistics. Since 1972 there has been a 92 percent increase in the number of jurisdictions providing data to the UCRs (from 6,195 units to 11,872). There has been a corresponding 29- percent increase in the population covered by these reports.[17] Since older people are not evenly distributed throughout the country, and since there are no data on the age compositions of the populations covered by each report,[18] neither the magnitude nor the direction of this reporting bias is clear.

Other trends that are less sensitive to these biases are the proportion of older offenders within each class of criminal behavior, and the proportion of all older offenders who are arrested for alcohol-related crimes. These two data provide some insight into the dynamics of alcohol-related crime committed by older people between 1972 and 1978.

In general, the proportion of older offenders within each category has remained remarkably stable over time. The proportion of older OUI offenders has decreased over time, but not by any great amount. People aged 55 to 59 have accounted for between 4.0 percent and 5.1 percent of all OUI offenders; the proportion was stable between 1972 and 1975 and has declined since 1976. Offenders aged 60 to 64 have accounted for between 2.2 percent and 2.9 percent of offenders, and those aged 65 or older, between 1.7 percent and 1.9 percent of all offenders; in both cases the proportion has consistently declined since 1973.

In reference to liquor law violations, the proportion of "young old" offenders (55 to 59 years old) has decreased consistently since 1972, from 1.4 percent to 1.0 percent. The proportion of offenders aged 60 to 64 has stayed constant at about 1 percent of all offenders. The proportion aged 65 and older has also stayed at about 1 percent. The proportions of OUI offenders aged 55 or older has declined steadily and consistently since 1972: among those aged 55 to 59, the decrease has been from 7.3 percent to 5.9 percent; among those aged 60 to 64, from 4.7 percent to 3.6 percent; and among those aged 65 and older, from 3.8 percent to 2.8 percent.

Tables 4.2 through 4.4 show the proportions of all older offenders who have been charged with each type of alcohol-related crime. Table 4.2 shows that the frequency with which older offenders have been charged with liquor law violations, which have never accounted for a significant proportion, has declined since 1972; following a slight increase between 1972 and 1976, there was a decline between 1976 and 1978. The trend was similar for all three cohorts of older adults.

Table 4.3 shows the trends for arrests for drunkenness. In all cases, these, too, have declined steadily and markedly between 1972 and 1978. There were declines of 37 percent for those aged 55 to 59, 36 percent for those aged 60 to 64, and 40 percent for those aged 65 or older. By comparison, there was an overall decrease of 42 percent among offenders of all ages. Therefore, while arrests for drunkenness have become considerably less frequent in the United

Table 4.2. Liquor Law Violation Arrests as a Percentage of All Arrests, by Age

	All Ages	55–59	60–64	65 and Older
1972	3.0%	1.5%	1.6%	1.6%
1973	2.8	1.4	1.5	1.5
1974	3.1	1.4	1.5	1.6
1975	3.3	1.7	1.7	1.8
1976	3.8	2.1	2.3	2.4
1977	3.6	1.7	1.9	1.9
1978	3.7	1.9	2.0	2.1

Sources: Eloise Rathbone-McCuan and J. Bland, "A Treatment Typology for the Elderly Alcohol Abuser," Journal of the American Geriatric Society 23 (1975): 553–557; National Institute on Alcoholism and Alcohol Abuse, Third Special Report to Congress on Alcoholism and Health (Washington, D.C., 1978); Alexander Simon, "The Neuroses, Personality Disorders, Alcoholism, Drug Use and Misuse and Crime in the Aged," in James Birren and R. Bruce Sloane (eds.), Handbook of Mental Health and Aging (Englewood Cliffs, N.J.: Prentice-Hall, 1980), pp. 653–670; Marc Schuckit, "Geriatric Alcoholism and Drug Abuse," The Gerontologist 17 (1977): 168–174; and Marc Schuckit, "The Elderly as a Unique Population: Alcoholism," Alcoholism: Clinical and Experimental Research 2 (1978): 31–38.

Table 4.3. Drunkenness Arrests as a Percentage of All Arrests, by Age

	All Ages	55–59	60–64	65 and Older
1972	19.7%	52.7%	54.7%	52.0%
1973	18.3	50.1	52.3	50.8
1974	14.8	45.7	48.0	45.1
1975	14.7	42.5	44.9	40.9
1976	13.5	40.3	41.8	38.8
1977	13.4	38.1	39.8	37.2
1978	11.4	33.2	35.0	31.2

Sources: See Table 4.2.

States over the past decade, for offenders of all ages, there has been less of a decline among older adults. There is some evidence that police officers have always been less inclined to arrest older offenders for drunkenness, a form of de facto decriminalization.[19] If this is so, it may explain the lesser effect of de jure decriminalization on older people than on the population-at-large.

Table 4.4 shows the trends in OUI offenses, which, in contrast to the other two classes of offenses, have grown steadily among older offenders, in excess of the general growth in the relative frequency of OUI arrests. The proportion of OUI arrests among offenders of all ages increased 43 percent between 1972 and 1978. By comparison, the increase among older offenders was considerably higher. The proportion of older offenders who were arrested for OUI increased 51 percent for offenders aged 55 to 59, 60 percent for those between ages 60 and 64, and 78 percent for those aged 65 or older. OUI arrests now account for between 20 and 25 percent of all arrests of older adults.

These data must be interpreted with considerable caution because of several possible sources of substantial biases. There is, above all,

Table 4.4. OUI Arrests as a Percentage of All Arrests, by Age

	All Ages	55–59	60–64	65 and Older
1972	8.6%	16.1%	14.9%	11.3%
1973	10.1	19.9	18.3	14.3
1974	10.9	21.4	20.9	14.9
1975	11.3	23.1	22.1	17.5
1976	10.6	21.6	21.2	17.9
1977	12.0	23.5	21.2	19.3
1978	12.3	24.3	23.9	20.1

Sources: See Table 4.2.

the possibility of sampling bias: the jurisdictions that report to the UCRs may not be representative of the U.S. population and may therefore either underrepresent or overrepresent older people. There may also be age-related reporting biases: many sources suggest that police officers may be more or less inclined to arrest older adults, particularly for drunkenness. Third, arrest data report not levels of criminal behavior, but only numbers of arrests. If older adults commit alcohol-related crimes at different times, in different places, or in different ways from offenders of other age groups, the data may understate or exaggerate their total contribution to alcohol-related crime. Moreover, since the data are aggregate national data, they may disguise local or regional variations or variations between rural, urban, and suburban locales. Finally, the data provide no information on the relationship between alcohol and such other crimes as shoplifting, assault, or other felonies, in which the use of alcohol may play a substantial role.[20]

Nevertheless, their limitations notwithstanding, these national data confirm those presented by Shichor and Kobrin and suggest several conclusions about the relationship between alcohol and crime for older adults. They suggest, first, that there is no evidence of epidemic alcohol-related crime by older people. On the contrary, the proportion of older offenders in all three categories has remained essentially unchanged at a time when the older population has grown at a rapid rate. Second, the data suggest that incidence rates are inversely proportional to age: the youngest cohort (55 to 59 years old) accounts for more offenses than the group aged 60 to 64; the group aged 65 and older accounts for least of all. Third, the data show that if older people are arrested for crimes, they are very likely to be alcohol-related crimes; in fact, the three classes of alcohol-related offenses account for about 60 percent of all reported arrests of older adults. Finally, the data show that one single offense, operating under the influence, has come to play an increasingly prominent role in the criminal behavior of older adults.

Subsequent research should therefore address the more prevalent crimes, particularly OUI. Who commits these offenses? Why? Under what circumstances? How much do they drink? And, finally, how many others who are not arrested commit the same kinds of offenses?

National crime statistics provide only limited data on the demographic risk factors associated with alcohol-related crime. They provide no data on psychological risk factors, nor on offenders' motives, nor on offenses that do not lead to arrests. These are serious limitations, most of which are unavoidable with national-level epidemiological data. However, more intensive local studies of drinking and alcohol-related offesnes can provide additional information about criminal behavior by older people and the relationship between crime and alcohol use in old age.

DRINKING AND DRIVING BY OLDER PEOPLE IN MASSACHUSETTS AND MAINE

The School of Public Health of the Boston University School of Medicine has undertaken such a study, as part of a larger study of the impact of a new law—the so-called OUI Law—to control drinking and driving in Maine. Data derived from this study show not only the relative risk of OUI by older and younger drivers in these two states, but also some of the risk factors associated with OUI by older adults.

In September 1981, prior to the law's enactment, researchers conducted telephone surveys of samples of 1,334 adults (at least 18 years old), selected by random-digit dialing in Maine, and 1,250 in Massachusetts, which was the control state. The Massachusetts sample was stratified to include sufficient numbers of people living outside the densely urban areas (Boston SMSA and the city of Worcester) for separate analyses in those areas. The result of this stratification produced half the interviews in less urbanized areas, which are more similar in population density to Maine.

The interview protocol included questions about respondents' personal characteristics, perceptions of law enforcement and the judicial processing of alcohol-related offenses, alcohol use, driving habits, involvement in accidents, encounters with law enforcement officials, episodes of driving after drinking, and driving after drinking five or more drinks—a surrogate measure of OUI.

The response rate was approximately 75 percent in Maine and 77 percent in Massachusetts. The pooled sample consisted of 1,959 individuals (1,000 in Maine and 959 in Massachusetts). There were complete data for 1,673 individuals who drove during the month preceding the survey; 425 of them (25 percent) were at least 55 years old.

The data show that older adult drivers (those aged 55 or older) were significantly more likely to report that they abstain from alcohol than younger ones (41 percent versus 21 percent, $p < .001$) and significantly less likely to report that they drink two or more drinks[21] per day (9 percent versus 16 percent $p < .001$). (In reference to continuous data, tests of statistical significance are based on Tau-B or Tau-C. In reference to interval data—e.g., occupational status or ethnicity—they are based on chi-squared.) They are also significantly less likely to drive—45 percent estimated that they drove 5,000 miles or less each year, compared to 34 percent of younger drivers (p <.001) —and to drive after drinking.

Sixteen percent of older drivers reported that they had ever driven after drinking during the month before the survey, compared to 45 percent of younger drivers. Of these, 4 percent had done so on seven or more occasions, compared to 9 percent of their younger counterparts (p <.001). Fewer than 1 percent of older drivers (two individuals) reported that they had driven after drinking at least five drinks, compared to 12 percent of younger adults (p <.001).

Older drivers were significantly less likely to have been stopped by the police while driving in the month before the survey (13 percent versus 25 percent; p <.001) and significantly less likely to report that they had been drinking before they were so stopped (1 percent versus 4 percent; p <.001). They also reported that they received significantly fewer traffic tickets than their younger counterparts: 5 percent had received any tickets, versus 11 percent of younger drivers (p <.001).

There is a possibility that older drivers are at lower risk of driving after drinking, not beause they are more cautious or law- abiding, but rather because they drive less. However, analysis of variance shows there is an independent and significant relationship (p <.001) between age and driving after drinking, even controlling for respondents' estimates of their mileage over the past year.

Further analysis of the data shows that not all older drivers are equally likely to report that they drove after drinking. Divorced people drove after drinking significantly more than others (33 percent versus 17 percent, p <.001). Otherwise, marital status is not significantly related to driving after drinking, nor is age nor employment status, all of which are closely correlated with alcohol use by older adults.[22] (Employment status was measured in terms of both retirement versus economic activity and the nature of the occupations of those who were employed.) The most striking differences are associated with gender and social class: males were significantly more likely to report that they drove after drinking during the month preceding the survey than were females (26 percent versus 7 percent p <.001), as were those with annual incomes in excess of $15,000 (28 percent versus 9 percent, p <.001) and those with college degrees (28 percent versus 15 percent, p <.001). Those with postgraduate college educations resembled those with less education more than they resembled college graduates: 18 percent reported driving after drinking alcohol.

Divorced people are also more likely to report that they frequently drive after drinking (seven times or more during the month before the interview). This datum must be treated with caution, however, since the number of divorced people in the sample was small ($N = 18$). Otherwise, males (8 percent) and college graduates (11 percent) distinguished themselves by their tendency toward frequent driving after drinking. There is also an income gradient in frequent driving after drinking: 2 percent of those with annual incomes in the range of $15,000–$20,000 reportedly did so, compared to 8 percent in the $20,000–$25,000 range, 10 percent in the $25,000–$30,000 range, and 12 percent of those with annual incomes of $30,000 or more.

Like national crime statistics, survey data are subject to important biases: above all, they assume that respondents candidly and accurately describe their practices related to drinking and driving, an assumption that may be unsound. The possibility of bias notwithstanding, however, they too have implications for the problem of crime committed by older adults.

They suggest that older adults are less likely to drive after drinking than younger ones, and that insofar as they do so, they rarely drink five or more drinks before they drive. This does not necessarily mean that they pose any less of a threat to personal or public safety, because older people may have a lower sensitivity to the effects of alcohol, because of the effects of normal aging, age-related diseases, medication, or some combination of the three.[23] It suggests, however, that the older persons who drink and drive are unlikely to be alcoholics or heavy drinkers.

The data also show that the risk of drinking and driving is concentrated, particularly among relatively affluent older males and, perhaps, those who are divorced. Preventive efforts should be addressed at the same groups, rather than at the older population-at-large.

CONCLUSIONS

The most obvious conclusion about alcohol-related crime committed by older people is that there is a clear need for more research of better quality on alcohol and crime in old age. There must be more careful cross-sectional studies, to determine the prevalence of alcohol-related crime and the relationships between alcohol use and criminal behavior generally, including such offenses as assault, robbery, and white-collar crime, in which the role of alcohol is not self-evident, as it is, for example, in OUI. There should also be longitudinal studies to determine whether alcohol use and alcoholism in fact cause crime, or whether crime causes problem drinking, or whether there are other confounding or intervening variables—for example, social class, culture, or psychological traits—that affect both criminal behavior and alcohol use.

Insofar as possible, these studies should take place in the general population rather than among such special populations as hospital in-patients or nursing home residents or convicted offenders, if we are to understand the social and demographic contexts of alcohol-related crimes committed by older offenders and the risk factors associated with drinking and crime. Since both crime and alcohol use are relatively rare phenomena among older people (see page 55), study samples will necessarily be large and the studies themselves quite costly. It may, therefore, be more reasonable to do one or two intensive local pilot studies before undertaking larger-scale research.

There should also be studies of police behavior to determine whether there are reporting biases that distort UCR data and other similar reports. Police officers may, in fact, underreport alcohol-related crimes committed by older people. Or they may arrest the elderly on other charges. Or, they may divert them to detoxification centers, hospital emergency rooms, or treatment programs in the best interests of the offenders. Or, they may simply leave them in the streets. In any case, police officers play important parts in the lives of older offenders, regardless of the offenses for which they are arrested. It behooves us to understand this role better.

In the absence of these studies, existing data suggest several conclusions for social policy. Above all, they suggest a cautious approach to the problems of crime and drinking by older people. There are certainly older criminals and there is certainly a relationship between older adults' drinking and their criminal behavior. But there is no evidence that these problems are now more pressing than they have been—and some evidence that they are less so—and no evidence that there is any single effective intervention to prevent older adults from committing alcohol-related crimes.

There may be efforts that can address the special needs and circumstances of older drinkers and drivers. For example, there may be a need for special labels on bottled alcohol warning that older adults may be more sensitive to its effects. Graphs and charts that correlate alcohol consumption and blood alcohol content—which are often posted in bars and restaurants—may have to be modified to demonstrate the effects of aging, or of chronic illness associated with aging, or of prescription drug use. Perhaps educational materials should automatically be included with driving license renewals of every driver aged 55 or older or, in states that require reexaminations, distributed at the examination or included among examination questions themselves.

Police officers commonly speak to groups of older people about personal safety or crime prevention. Perhaps they should expand these programs to include messages about drinking and driving, as they often do with groups of teenagers and younger adults. Finally, older adults have more frequent contact with physicians and other health care providers than do their younger counterparts,[24] and physicians, nurses, and social workers have in turn expressed a growing interest in health promotion and disease prevention among older adults. Perhaps their encounters should also include discussions of the risk of alcohol use, both normal and pathological, stressing the fact that even normal moderate drinking may become dangerous as persons age, suffer the effects of chronic illness, or use more drugs.

If these efforts reduce the incidence of OUI by older people, they will most likely affect the light to moderate "social" drinker who rarely breaks laws and is generally concerned not to do so. They are unlikely to help older chronic alcoholics or problem drinkers who have had long histories of criminal behavior and who appear to account for most late-life crime. They, too, need help, although their problems appear to be much more resistant and the theoretical bases for intervention are much less clear. Although several sources report success in dealing with older adult alcoholics,[25] there have been no controlled experiments that indicate the superiority of any particular treatment mode. So, in this case, too, there is a need for a broad eclectic approach.

Alcohol-related crime and problem drinking take heavy tolls in human life, happiness, and public resources; they affect not only the offenders and problem drinkers, but also their victims, their own and the victims' families, health care providers, police officers, corrections officials, and the courts.[26] However, they represent only a very small component of the substantial problems that affect our society, in terms of both criminal justice and corrections and old age. There is a responsibility to address those problems—by means of prevention, rehabilitation, and correction—but an equal responsibility not to exaggerate them. This is important not only to avoid stereotyping the older population or falsely attributing to them disease and disability, but also to ensure that the commitment of resources corresponds to levels of need.

NOTES

1. David Shichor and Solomon D. Kobrin, "Note: Criminal Behavior among the Elderly," *The Gerontologist* 18, (1978): 213–218.
2. L. J. Epstein, C. Mills and A. Simon, "Antisocial Behavior in the Elderly," *Comprehensive Psychiatry* 11 (1970): 42.
3. Donald Cahalan, I. Cissin, and H. Crossley, *American Drinking Practices: A National Study of Drinking Behavior Attitudes* (New Brunswick, N.J.: Rutgers Center of Alcohol Studies, Monograph #7, 1969). Donald Cahalan, *Problem Drinkers* (San Francisco: Jossey-Bass, 1970). See also Cahalan et al., *American Drinking Practices*, passim.
4. Marc Schuckit and P. Miller, "Alcoholism in Elderly Men: A Survey of a General Medical Ward," *Annals of the New York Academy of Sciences* 273 (1976): 558–571.
5. Eloise Rathbone-McCuan, Harald Lohn, Julia Levenson, et al., *Community Survey of Aged Alcoholics and Problem Drinkers* (Baltimore: Levindale Geriatric Research Center, 1976).
6. Elizabeth Wells-Parker and Barbara Spencer, *Drinking Patterns, Problem Drinking, and Stress in a Sample of Aged Drinking Drivers* (Social Science Research Center, Report #53, Mississippi State University, Mississippi State, Mississippi, 1980).
7. J.H. Atkinson, Jr., "Alcoholism and Geriatric Problems, I and II," *Advances in Alcoholism* 11, 8–9 (1981): 1–2, 1–3. See also works cited in notes 8 through 14, passim.
8. Edith Gomberg, *Drinking and Problem Drinking Among the Elderly* (Ann Arbor, Mich.: Institute of Gerontology, University of Michigan, 1980).
9. Allan R. Meyers et al., "The Social Epidemiology of Alcohol Use by Urban Older Adults," *International Journal of Aging and Human Development*, in press.
10. Allan R. Meyers, Ralph Hingson, Marc Mucatel, et al., "Life Stress and Life Satisfaction in an Urban Environment and Problem Drinking in Old Age," *Journal of the American Geriatrics Society* 30 (1982): 452–456.
11. Shichor and Kobrin, "Criminal Behavior among the Elderly." (1982).
12. Michael J. Hindelang, Christopher S. Dunn, Alison L. Aumick, et al. (eds.), *Sourcebook of Criminal Justice Statistics—1974*, U.S. Dept. of Justice, Bureau of Justice Statistics (Washington, D.C.: U.S. Government Printing Office, 1975). See also Hindelang et al., *Sourcebook—1976* and *Sourcebook—1977;* Michael Gottfredson et al., *Sourcebook—1978;* Nicolette Parisi et al., *Sourcebook—1979;* Timothy Flanagan et al., *Sourcebook—1980;* and Hindelang et al., *Sourcebook—1981.*
13. Shichor and Kobrin, "Criminal Behavior among the Elderly."
14. U.S. Bureau of the Census, *Current Population Reports*, Series P-20, No. 336, "Population Profile of the United States: 1978" (Washington, D.C.: U.S. Government Printing Office, 1979).
15. See annual *Sourcebook of Criminal Justice Statistics.*
16. Norman Kurtz and M. Regier, "The Uniform Alcoholism and Intoxification Treatment Act: The Compromising Process of Social Policy Formulation," *Journal of Studies on Alcohol* 36 (1975): 1421–1441. Loren R. Daggett and Edward J. Rolde, "Decriminalization of Drunkenness: Effects on the Work of Suburban Police," *Journal of Studies on Alcohol* 41, (1980): 819–828.
17. See annual *Sourcebook of Criminal Justice Statistics.*
18. Shichor and Kobrin, "Criminal Behavior among the Elderly."

19. Epstein et al., "Antisocial Behavior in the Elderly."
20. Shichor and Kobrin, "Criminal Behavior among the Elderly."
21. One drink equals approximately 0.5 oz. (15 cc) of ethanol, 4.5 oz. (135 cc) of wine, 12 oz. (360 cc) of beer, or 1.5 oz. (45 cc) of spirits.
22. Grace Barnes, "Alcohol Use among Older Persons: Findings from a Western New York State General Population Survey," *Journal of the American Geriatrics Society* 27 (1979): 244–250. And see also Ralph Hingson et al., "Life Satisfaction and Drinking Practices in the Boston Metropolitan Area," *Journal of Studies in Alcohol* 42 (1981): 24, and Allan R. Meyers et al., "Evidence for Cohort or Generational Differences in the Drinking Behavior of Older Adults," *International Journal of Aging and Human Development* 14 (1981–1982): 31–44, as well as David Guttman, *A Survey of Drug-Taking Behavior of the Elderly* (Washington, D.C.: Alcohol, Drug Abuse, and Mental Health Administration, 1977).
23. Richard W. Shropshire, "The Hidden Faces of Alcoholism," *Geriatrics* 30 (1975): 99–102.
24. U.S. Department of Health and Human Services, *Health, United States, 1980* (Washington, D.C.: U.S. Government Printing Office, 1981), pp. 43–46.
25. Eloise Rathbone-McCuan and J. Bland, "A Treatment Typology for the Elderly Alcohol Abuser," *Journal of the American Geriatric Society* 23 (1975): 553–557. See also K. Gunnar Gotestam, "Behavioral and Dynamic Psychotherapy with the Elderly," in James Birren and R. Bruce Sloane (eds.), *Handbook of Mental Health and Aging* (Englewood Cliffs, N.J.: Prentice-Hall, 1980), pp. 775–805.
26. National Institute on Alcoholism and Alcohol Abuse, *Third Special Report to Congress on Alcoholism and Health* (Washington, D.C., 1978).

Chapter 5

Psychiatric Aspects of Crime in Old Age

Stephen J. Hucker

The criminal statistics of most Western countries show that crime is a phenomenon associated overwhelmingly with youth and rapidly declines with advancing age. It is therefore not surprising that elderly offenders have been little studied.

By far the most common reason for arrest among the elderly is drunkenness; more serious crimes such as sexual and violent offenses are rare.[1] Nevertheless, these crimes have received disproportionate attention from writers on crime in the aged and, indeed, have sometimes been regarded as typical of this age group.[2] This fallacy is almost certainly due to the fact that, until recently, most of the contributions to the literature were written by psychiatrists, who based their views on the highly selected cases with which they came into contact.[3]

While the relative rarity of the more serious offenses occurring in old age needs to be clearly acknowledged, the fact that previous studies of sexual and violent offenses by the elderly are few in number and sometimes contradictory shows that this area justifies further exploration. It is widely believed, for example, that sexual offenses involving child victims are the most common crime in old age.[4] Most of these are said to be committed by first-time offenders, who are often described as being of "blameless character."[5] Many authors have held that such offenders are suffering from dementia, but others do not confirm this.[6] Some have held that the commission of the offense is the "first sign of senile change,"[7] as typical features of established dementia may be lacking.[8] Other explanations that have been put forward to explain the behavior of the elderly sex offender have included "changes in the prostate," "regression" due to emotional factors, "intoxication," and "seduction by a child."[9] Children are most frequently selected as victims, according to East, because elderly men are unattractive to adult females and fear rejection by them.[10] Whiskin suggested that the crime is an attempt to restore a lost sense of masculinity.[11] Others, less charitably, have noted that a "grandfather" image tends to be trusted and that child victims are less able to defend themselves, easier to bribe, more amenable to threats and less likely to report the incident.[12] Hirschmann considered most elderly sex offenders to have been sexually well adjusted, but others have noted that many are unmarried, divorced, or have had sexual difficulties.[13] The combination of social problems—such as loneliness, social isolation, and poverty—which accompany old age has been noted frequently and may contribute to the offense.[14]

Violent offenses among the elderly have been even less frequently studied than sex crimes. It has recently been shown, however, that assaultive behavior is a common reason for elderly persons to be admitted to public psychiatric hospitals.[15] Furthermore, a study of offender-patients detained in British Special Hospitals also showed that the peak age for personal violence was in the over-60 group.[16] These studies and also a recent one based on violent patients from a geriatric psychiatric unit suggest that organic and functional mental disorders are strongly associated with violence in the elderly.[17] Similarly, both Lanzkron and Mowat indicated that paranoid syndromes, especially delusional jealousy, are important in this group.[18] Roth believes that homicide in the elderly rarely occurs in the absence of suicidal tendencies and is prone to occur in mental states characterized by fluctations in conscious awareness.[19] He states that dementia is unusual in these cases but that emotional blunting and diminished control over emotional expression are often seen.

Finding so few studies based on sizable samples of elderly offenders, M.H. Ben-Aron and I, both forensic psychiatrists, examined the records of all individuals aged 60 years or older who had been referred to the Forensic Service at the Clarke Institute between 1966 and 1979. We found only 70 such individuals—comprising 43 sex offenders, 16 violent offenders, and a group of 11 miscellaneous cases. We did not investigate the miscellaneous cases in great detail because their numbers were too small to allow comparative investigations. The other two groups, however, were large enough to match with comparison groups and were examined in greater detail. These are reported elsewhere;[20] following is a summary of the more important findings.

THE ELDERLY SEX OFFENDER

The 43 elderly sex offenders were compared with a group of 43 sex offenders aged 30 or younger, randomly selected from a list of sex offenders of all ages examined over the same period. We made no attempt to match the two groups with respect to legal charges, as the literature had suggested that certain types of sex offenses might be more common in the elderly group. The files of all 86 cases were reviewed, and relevant information was noted. We examined the files independently to document inter-rater reliability on certain items, for example, the presence or absence of seven broad diagnostic categories (organic brain syndrome, functional psychosis, neurosis, antisocial personality disorder, other personality disorder, alcoholism, and drug addiction) based on accepted criteria.[21] Multiple diagnoses were therefore possible. In analyzing the data, my diagnoses and ratings were used, as I was senior author.

The mean age of the elderly sex offenders was 66.1 years (range, 60 to 84 years). There were no striking differences between the two groups with respect to former occupation or intelligence. The older offenders were less well educated, probably reflecting the poorer educational opportunities available when they were young. Also, the elderly sex offenders were more likely to be or to have been married, although this was likely a function of the way the groups were pre-selected on the basis of age. Interestingly, of those who were or had been married at the time of the offense, about 70 percent of the elderly offenders and 50 percent of the young sex offenders were rated as having a "below-average" marital relationship ($\bar{\chi}^2 = 10.247$; 2 d.f.; $p < .01$).[9] Although the rating was crude, the two authors agreed in 90 percent of the cases. The elderly sex offenders had significantly fewer social contacts than their younger counterparts ($\bar{\chi}^2 = 19.711$; 3 d.f.; $p < .001$), although it proved difficult to obtain high inter-rater reliability (only about 65 percent agreement) on this item.

The most frequent psychiatric diagnoses in the elderly group were organic brain syndrome (14 percent), neurosis (19 percent), personality disorders other than the antisocial type (21 percent), and alcoholism (21 percent). In the younger group, the diagnoses were most frequently of personality disorders of the antisocial (19 percent) and other types (63 percent), alcoholism (26 percent), and drug abuse

(14 percent). Inter-rater agreement was never lower than 90 percent. Only six of the elderly offenders and eleven of the younger group were drinking at the time of the offense, none of the elderly and three of the younger offenders were intoxicated with drugs, and one younger offender was using both drugs and alcohol. Taking intoxication with drugs and/or alcohol as a whole, we found that the younger offenders were significantly more likely to be intoxicated than the older group ($\chi^2 = 5.103$; 1 d.f.; $p < .05$). While twelve of the elderly sex offenders and eight of the younger offenders had previous psychiatric histories, the difference is not statistically significant. The victim was at least known to the elderly sex offender in nearly 70 percent of the cases, whereas the younger sex offenders more often chose strangers as victims. This latter finding, however, is chiefly a reflection of the large number of exhibitionists in the younger group, who typically expose themselves to women who are unknown to them. Similarly, 70 percent of the older group chose child victims compared with 26 percent of the younger group.

Comparison of legal charges for the two groups showed that no members of the elderly group were arrested for rape or attempted rape, whereas 17 percent of the younger group were. When the nature of the sexual contact was examined more closely, it was found that elderly sex offenders usually engaged in rather passive sexual activity (79 percent), whereas nearly half the younger group attempted or achieved penetration of the victim. Similarly, the elderly group never used threats or force, whereas 17 percent of the younger men threatened or were aggressive toward the victim. Most commonly, the elderly sex offender committed the offense not on the street or local park but at his or his victim's home. A greater number of incidents by young sex offenders consisted of indecent exposure in a public place or from a private vehicle. Young sex offenders tended to have committed more previous offenses than their elderly counterparts, even though the latter had more time in which to have accumulated such a record. Nearly half of the elderly sex offenders had previous records, however, and nearly a quarter of them had sex offense records. The infrequency of subsequent convictions with the elderly group (7 percent) is no doubt attributable to the increasing likelihood of death or disability, which would prevent further antisocial behavior. The number of offenders whose case was adjourned indefinitely or whose charges were dropped was greater with the elderly than with the younger group. Where the court found sufficient evidence to render a guilty verdict, more elderly than youthful offenders denied the offense at the time of the assessment ($\chi^2 = 1.042$; 1 d.f. $p < .01$). Perhaps these elderly men have greater difficulty acknowledging the offense because of fear of further social ostracism, or perhaps they hope that their credibility will survive the accusation. The majority of both groups of offenders were punished by fines, cautions, or suspended sentences with or without probation. A significant finding was that only 1 percent of the elderly group was sent to prison, compared with 26 percent of the younger group. This may have been because the younger offenders more often committed rape and aggressive indecent assaults.

Treatment was recommended by the assessing psychiatrist for 35 percent of the elderly sex offenders; only 33 percent of those subsequently received it in the form of psychotherapy or counseling. Of the young sex offenders, 27 percent were recommended for treatment and 50 percent received it, almost half again more than were recommended. The cause of this discrepancy might be that the elderly were seen as needing social support rather than psychiatric treatment, or that the younger group were seen as more disturbed or more prone to recidivate.

Our study found that most elderly sex offenders referred for forensic psychiatric examination have molested children. The choice of a victim who was at least known to the offender, sometimes a relative or close friend, was also noteworthy, as was the typically nonaggressive nature of the sexual contact. These data agree with those collected by Zeegers, who found that many of the elderly sex offenders in his sample were either unmarried or, if they had been married, that their sexual relationships had been poor.[22] The fact that a quarter of our group and a similar number of Zeegers's cases had previous convictions for sexual offenses further supports the idea that these men have had sexual problems throughout their lives.

The differences in psychiatric diagnosis between the elderly and young sex offenders are worthy of special mention. As noted earlier, it has been widely believed that elderly men commit sexual offenses as a result of organic brain disease. While only 14 percent of our group of elderly sex offenders were suffering from dementia, Zeegers found 49 percent and Whiskin found 60 percent suffering from this condition.[23] As community surveys of the prevalence of organic mental disorders in the elderly population tend to give rather similar or higher figures, our data do not suggest that elderly sex offenders suffer from organic brain syndromes to any greater extent than the elderly population in general. Probably Whiskin and Zeegers found such high percentages of demented patients in their series because of differences in diagnostic practice. Whiskin, for example, admits that his criteria were vague and proposes a "pseudo-organic syndrome." Similarly, Zeegers uses rather puzzling existential terminology to define his demented patients. In studying cases of pedophilia in all age groups, Revitch and Weiss and Mohr et al. failed to find dementia in most of their elderly cases and saw greater importance in the observation that these offenders are often lonely and socially isolated.[24] Although we confirmed this finding, many elderly people have these difficulties, and our study was not able to clarify whether the sex offender group is any more handicapped in this way than nonoffenders of the same age. Perhaps social problems affect the judgment of the elderly sex offender to the extent that they act on deviant impulses that they have kept under control for most of their lives. Along with the fact that these men tend to be nonaggressive in their sexual behavior and to suffer notable social and mental problems, the low recidivism rate among elderly sex offenders justifies continued sympathetic treatment by the courts.

VIOLENT ELDERLY OFFENDERS

We compared the sixteen violent elderly offenders with two comparison groups. The elderly group itself consisted of ten cases of murder, three attempted murder, one wounding, two assault causing bodily harm, and one common assault. For comparison purposes, a list was drawn up of all the individuals who were 30 or younger at the time of their offenses and who had been examined during the same period. We grouped these men according to their charges, and from these lists randomly matched the cases with elderly violent patients charged with the same offense. To make comparisons between elderly violent offenders and elderly persons who had not been violent, we randomly selected a further contrast group of sixteen subjects from the forty-three elderly sex offenders described earlier. All the individuals selected in this latter group were charged with the sexual fondling of children, and aggression was not involved.

We reviewed all forty-eight clinical files and recorded relevant information. With respect to psychiatric diagnoses, we reviewed the files independently so that we could check inter-rater reliability. The procedure was similar to that used with the sex offender study, in that the presence or absence of each of a number of diagnostic categories (based on the 9th edition of International Classification of Diseases) was required. Multiple diagnoses were again possible.

SUMMARY

We found that younger violent offenders were much more likely to hold unskilled occupations than the more skilled men in the older two groups ($\bar{\chi}^2 = 16.474$; 4 d.f., p <.01). This perhaps indicates a greater lifetime stability among the older men. The two older groups were more likely to be or to have been married ($\bar{\chi}^2 = 26.875$; 4 d.f., p <.001), a difference no doubt relating simply to the age differences. Five (31 percent) of the elderly violent group had past histories of psychiatric hospital admissions, compared with ten (63 percent) of the younger group, although the difference is statistically insignificant ($\bar{\chi}^2 = 5.131$; 2 d.f., p = N.S.). In the case of the younger offenders, the psychiatric admissions were generally the result of drug- or alcohol-related problems or suicide attempts.

Among the young violent offenders, antisocial personality disorder was the most common psychiatric diagnosis (63 percent), compared with 13 percent in the older violent patients and none in the nonviolent elderly group. Alcoholism was slightly more frequent among the elderly violent offenders (50 percent) and nonviolent offenders (44 percent) than among the younger men (31 percent), but the differences are not significant. More striking was the large number of elderly violent patients suffering from a functional mental disorder (50 percent) such as schizophrenia or manic depressive or paranoid psychosis. The differences between this and the other two groups was highly significant statistically ($\bar{\chi}^2 = 15.590$; 2 d.f., p <.001). Organic brain syndromes, such as dementia or delirium, are more common among the elderly than the young, so that comparison between the groups would be misleading. Nevertheless, among the violent elderly group, organic and fucntional mental disabilities combined accounted for 75 percent of the group. Also of interest was the high frequency (44 percent) of paranoid symptoms (irrespective of basic diagnosis) among the elderly violent compared with the other two groups ($\bar{\chi}^2 = 10.667$; 2 d.f., p <.01). Inter-rater agreement for psychiatric diagnosis was always better than 90 percent. Close to 50 percent of both violent and nonviolent elderly groups had no previous criminal record, whereas 75 percent of the young violent offenders had previous convictions.

A number of victim characteristics were noteworthy. The victims of both old and young violent individuals were divided equally between the sexes. No statistically significant differences emerged between the two violent groups with respect to the relationship between the offender and the victim, although slightly more (69 percent) family or close friend victims were found with the violent elderly group than with the young violent subjects (44 percent). Clearly related to this was the observation that most of the elderly violent offenders (88 percent) committed their offense in their own or their victim's home, compared with only 12 percent of the younger group, statistically a highly significant result ($\chi^2 = 18.00$; 1 d.f., $p < .001$). Slightly more young violent subjects used knives in their attacks (56 percent versus 31 percent), whereas similar numbers in both groups used firearms or other weapons. Domestic quarrels accounted for 44 percent of the elderly offenders' attacks compared with 6 percent of the young men's. In the latter, the motive appeared to be jealousy in 31 percent of cases. Nondomestic quarrels constituted 13 percent and 25 percent of the elderly and young violent groups, respectively. Delusional motives predominated in the elderly group (38 percent versus 6 percent). Apparently motiveless murders were more common in the younger group (38 percent versus 6 percent). Fifty-six percent of the elderly group and 31 percent of the young group had harbored hostile feelings toward the victim before the crime, but the difference was not statistically significant. Only small numbers of both violent groups were suicidal after the crime. One elderly subject, the only female in all three groups, actually succeeded in killing herself before she came to trial. Although 63 percent of the young violent offenders and 38 percent of the elderly group were drinking at the time of the offense, the difference was not significant. Similar numbers of the elderly and young offenders were found guilty of the offenses with which they were charged. More (44 percent) of the elderly group rather than the young (19 percent) were found guilty of lesser offenses, but fewer of the elderly were found "not guilty by reason of insanity"—19 percent compared with 31 percent in the young group. Thus, in many important respects the elderly violent offenders resembled their youthful counterparts. They were as likely to be a relative or friend of the victim, as likely to have harbored hostile feelings toward the victim, and as likely to be under the influence of alcohol or drugs at the time of the offense. Similarly, they were not more prone to suicidal behavior following the crime. Young aggressors are, however, more likely to receive a diagnosis of antisocial personality disorder. The elderly violent group received a diagnosis of either organic or functional mental disorder in nearly three-quarters of the cases.

The group of elderly violent patients in our study shows close similarities with those in a recent study by Petrie et al.[25] Of the 222 patients admitted to a geriatric psychiatric unit, 18 had used guns or knives in acts of violence. Organic brain disease was found in only 17 percent, whereas the rest suffered from serious mental disorders such as paraphrenia, manic depressive illness, schizophrenia, or atypical paranoid disorder.

CONCLUSIONS

As this book itself demonstrates, there seems to be a renewed interest in antisocial behavior by elderly people. However, the focus has tended to be on sociological or legal rather than clinical issues. The two studies summarized in this chapter show that because they are relatively rare it is difficult to obtain large numbers of elderly offenders for study. In addition, the findings from these studies have to be viewed cautiously, as offenders were referred for psychiatric examination. Studies of incarcerated elderly offenders would also be expected to be biased, although perhaps in different ways: those with serious mental illnesses, for example, are usually filtered out of the prison population.

Although by our use of comparison groups we hoped to minimize this selection problem, it is clear that it is desirable to carry out prospective examinations and follow-up of a group of all elderly offenders coming before the courts in a specific jurisdiction over a specific period. Even this approach, however, would not capture offenders who are not apprehended (there seems no easy way around this problem) or those who are apprehended but not taken to court.

For the present, our studies provide the only controlled clinical investigations in this area. Despite the methodological problems already acknowledged, they help provide a clearer picture of the characteristics of cases likely to be seen at forensic psychiatric facilities and emphasize the need for very thorough psychiatric, neurological, and social work evaluation of elderly offenders.

NOTES

1. Leon J. Epstein, C. Mills, and A. Simon, "Antisocial Behavior in the Elderly," *Comprehensive Psychiatry* 11, 1, (1971): 42–46. See also, O. J. Keller and C. B. Vedder, "The Crimes That Old People Commit," *The Gerontologist* 8, 1 (1968): 43–50.
2. David Abrahamsen, *Crime and the Human Mind* (New York: Columbia University Press, 1944); J. Devon, "Age and Crime," *Police Journal* 3 (1930): 124; and Vernon Fox, "Intelligence, Race, and Age as Selective Factors in Crime," *Journal of Criminal Law, Criminology and Police Science* 37 (1946): 141, 152. See also

David Moberg, "Old Age and Crime," *Journal of Criminal Law, Criminology and Police Science* 43 (1953): 764–776, and Paul L. Schroeder, "Criminal Behavior in the Later Period of Life," *American Journal of Psychiatry* 92 (1936): 915–924.

3. Otto Pollock, "The Criminality of Old Age," *Journal of Criminal Psychopathology* 3 (1941): 213–235.

4. S. Bergman and M. Amir, "Crime and Delinquency Among the Aged in Israel," *Geriatrics* 28, 1 (1973): 149–157; Havelock Ellis, *Psychology of Sex* (London: W. Heinemann Ltd., 1933); Frederick E. Whiskin, "Delinquency in the Aged," *Journal of Geriatric Psychiatry* 1, 2 (1968): 242–262; and Michael Zeegers, "Dementie in Verbana met het Delict Ontucht," *Tijdschrift Voor Strafecht* 75 (1966): 265. See also Michael Zeegers, "Sexual Delinquency in Men over 60 Years Old" (abstract), personal communication with the author, 1978. See also Abrahamsen, *Crime and the Human Mind*; Devon, "Age and Crime"; Fox, "Intelligence, Race, and Age"; and Schroeder, "Criminal Behavior."

5. See Martin Roth, "Cerebral Disease and Mental Disorders of Old Age as Causes of Antisocial Behavior," in Ciba Foundation Symposium on *The Mentally Abnormal Offender*, A. V. S. de Reuck and Ruth Porter, eds. (London: J and A Churchill, Publishers, 1968), pp. 35–51. See also Moberg, "Old Age and Crime," and Zeegers, 1978. Eliot Slater and Martin Roth, *Clinical Psychiatry*, 3rd ed. (London: Bailliere, Tindall and Cassell, 1969); and Pollock, "The Criminality of Old Age."

6. For views that elderly offenders suffer from dementia, see W. Norwood East, "Crime, Senescence and Senility," *Journal of Mental Science* 90 (1944): 836–849; Ellis, *Psychology of Sex*; J. M. Henninger, "The Senile Sex Offender," *Mental Hygiene* 23 (1939): 436–444; Richard von Krafft-Ebing, *Psychopathia Sexualis*, English trans. by H. E. Weddeck (New York: Putnam and Sons, 1965); H. Rollin, "Deviant Behavior in Relation to Mental Disorder," *Procedures of the Royal Society of Medicine* 66, 1 (1973): 99–103; Clifford F. Rose, "Criminal Responsibility and Competency as Influenced by Organic Disease," *Missouri Law Review* 35 (1970): 326–348; D. Rothchild, "Senile Psychosis and Cerebral Arteriorsclerosis," in Oscar Kaplan (ed.), *Mental Disorders of Later Life* (Palo Alto, Calif.: Stanford University Press, 1945); S. H. Ruskin, "Analysis of Sex Offenses Among Male Psychiatric Patients," *American Journal of Psychiatry* 97 (1941): 955–968; Anthony Storr, *Sexual Deviation* (Hammondsworth, Middlesex, England: Penguin Books, (1964); Edwin H. Sutherland and Donald Cressey, *Principles of Criminlogy*, 9th ed. (Philadelphia: J. B. Lippincott, 1978); Whiskin, "Delinquency in the Aged"; Zeegers, "Dementie in Verbana"; and Zeegers, "Sexual Delinquency in Men."

For opposing views, see, for example, J. Allersma, "Ouderdom en Criminaliteit," *Nederlands Tijdschrift Voor Gerontologse* 2 (1971): 285–293; Ralph Brancale, D. MacNeil, and A. Vuocolo, "Profile of the New Jersey Sex Offender: A Statistical Study of 1206 Male Sex Offenders," *Welfare Reporter* 16 (1965): 3–9; A. Nicholas Groth, Ann Wolpert Burgess, H. J. Birnbaum, and P. S. Gary, "A Study of the Child Molester: Myths and Realities," *Journal of the American Criminal Justice Association* 41, 1 (1978): 17–20; J. Hirschmann, "Zur Kriminologie der Sexualdelikte des alternden Mannes," *Gerontologica Clinica Additamentum* 4 (1962): 115–119; S. K. Law, "Child Molestation: A Comparison of Hong Kong and Western Findings," *Medicine, Science and the Law* 19, 1 (1979): 55–60; Johannes Mohr, R. Edward Turner, and M. B. Jerry, *Pedophilia and Exhibitionism* (Toronto: University of Toronto Press, 1964); Eugene Revitch and Rosalie Weiss, "The Pedophiliac Offender," *Diseases of the Nervous System* 23, 2 (1962): 1–6.

7. See Henninger, "The Senile Sex Offender."

8. See Ellis, *Psychology of Sex*, and Roth, "Cerebral Disease."

9. See, respectively, Sutherland and Cressey, *Principles of Criminology;* Revitch and Weiss, "The Pedophiliac Offender"; Pollock, "The Criminality of Old Age"; and D. J. Meyers, "Psychiatric Examination of the Sexual Psychopath," *Journal of Criminal Law and Criminology* 56, 31 (1965); Matti Virkkunen, "Victim Precipitated Pedophilia Offenses," *British Journal of Criminology* 15, 2 (1975): 175–180. See also Allersma, "Ouderdom en Criminaliteit;" Henninger, "The Senile Sex Offender;" Slater and Roth, *Clinical Psychiatry;* Zeegers, "Dementie in Verbana"; and Zeegers, "Sexual Delinquency in Men."

10 See East, "Crime Senescence and Senility."

11 See Whiskin, "Delinquency in the Aged."

12 For the former view, see Roth, "Cerebral Disease." For the latter view, see Henninger, "The Senile Sex Offender."

13. For the former view, see the articles listed in the second paragraph of note 6. For the latter view, see Roth, "Cerebral Disease"; Zeegers, "Dementie in Verbana"; and Zeegers, "Sexual Delinquency in Men."

14 See Allersma, "Ouderdom en Criminaliteit"; Roth et al., "Cerebral Disease"; Meyers, "Psychiatric Examination"; Mohr et al., *Pedophilia and Exhibitionism;* and Revitch and Weiss, "The Pedophiliac Offender."

15. See Kenneth Tardiff and A. Sweillam, "The Relationship of Age to Assaultive Behavior in Mental Patients," *Hospital Community Psychiatry* 30, 10 (1979): 709–711.

16. Nigel Walker and S. MacCabe, *Crime and Insanity in England,* vol. 2 (Edinburgh: Edinburgh University Press, 1973).

17. W. M. Petrie, E. C. Lawson, and M. H. Hollender, "Violence in Geriatric Patients," *Journal of the American Medical Association* 248, (1982): 443–444.

18. John Lanzkron, "Murder and Insanity: A Survey," *American Journal of Psychiatry* 119 (1963): 754–758; J. Lanzkron, "Murder as a Reaction to Paranoid Delusions in Involutional Psychosis and Its Prevention," *American Journal of Psychiatry* 118 (1961): 426–427; R. R. Mowat, *Morbid Jealousy and Murder* (London: Tavistock Publications, 1966).

19. See Roth, "Cerebral Disease."

20. Stephen J. Hucker and M. H. Ben-Aron, "The Elderly Sex Offender," in R. Langerin (ed.), *Erotic Preference Gender Identity and Aggression* (Hillsdale, N.J.: Erlbaum Associates, 1983); and S. J. Hucker and M. H. Ben- Aron, "Violent Offenses in Old Age," in William Wilbanks and Paul Kim (eds.), *The Elderly Offender,* (forthcoming).

21. See World Health Organization, *Mental Disorders: Glossary and Guide to their Classification,* in accordance with the 9th revision of the *International Classification of Diseases* (Geneva: WHO, 1978).

22. See Zeegers, "Dementie in Verbana," and "Sexual Delinquency in Men."

23. Ibid., and Whiskin, "Delinquency in the Aged."

24. Revitch and Weiss, "The Pedophiliac Offender"; Mohr et al., *Pedophilia and Exhibitionism.*

25. Petrie et al., "Violence in Geriatric Patients."

Chapter 6

The Elderly Homicide Offender

William Wilbanks and Dennis D. Murphy

NATIONAL DATA ON ELDERLY HOMICIDES

Despite all the attention given to elderly victims, little or no research attention has been given to elderly offenders. A review of the literature failed to find even one article dealing with elderly homicide offenders, although some data on such offenders does appear in more general works on homicide.[1] This study will attempt to fill this gap by describing the rate and pattern of all 1980 criminal homicides in the United States committed by elderly versus nonelderly offenders.

The Federal Bureau of Investigation collects several items of information on every homicide reported to the agency via its *Supplemental Homicide Reports* (SHRs). For each homicide incident, the local police complete and send to the FBI data on the month of the incident; the number of victims and offenders in each incident; the age, sex, race, and ethnicity of victim(s) and offender(s); the weapon used; the victim/offender relationship; circumstance/motive; and the state, region, population group, county, Standard Metropolitan Statistical Area (SMSA), and city of occurrence.

We secured a data tape from the FBI of all homicide incidents reported to the FBI for the United States for 1980 (N = 21,911). Since some incidents involve multiple victims and/or multiple offenders, the actual number of victims and offenders was greater..

DATA LIMITATIONS

It should be recognized that there are several sources of error in this data base. First, some homicides may not be reported to the FBI. However, this number is likely to be quite small and insignificant given the procedures utilized by both the FBI and state data collection agencies. Furthermore, prior research has found that the figures from the FBI correlated highly with death certificate data (collected and reported by the National Center for Health Statistics in the *Vital Statistics of the United States*).[2]

Second, the data tape includes only "murder" and "non-negligent manslaughter" and thus excludes some types of manslaughter (those which are not "willful"). Also, only those deaths that are traditionally and legally defined as homicides are included. Deaths that many authors suggest should also be classified as "murder" (deaths due to defective automobiles, unnecessary surgery, etc.) are also ignored.[3]

Third, offender data on the SHRs may be faulty since data are submitted monthly and many offenders are not arrested until days or months after the crime. In theory, police departments are supposed to update the SHR with each arrest, but it is questionable whether this is always or even often done. No research has been published to test the accuracy of SHR offender data. Thus any data on homicide offenders from the SHRs must not be understood as "offender" data, but rather only as arrest (and perhaps only *early* arrest) data.

SAMPLE SIZE

We reduced the sample of 1980 U.S. homicide events to 21,002 by eliminating 452 incidents of justifiable homicide involving felons killed by private citizens and 457 incidents of felons killed by police. Because this is a study of a *criminal* homicide rate, we had two reasons for eliminating justifiable homicides. First, there is considerable evidence that the numbers of justifiable homicides on the tape represent a serious undercount since the police are not generally concerned with noncriminal homicides. Also, others have demonstrated that there are far more justifiable homicides by police officers than are reported in official data bases.[4]

The final sample of offenders was 14,608. This figure is smaller than the number of homicide events, because in many cases the offender is unknown or uncaught. On the other hand, the figure does not mean that 14,608 cases were solved, since some incidents resulted in the arrest of several offenders. Although the SHR tape allowed for up to ten victims and offenders for each incident, multiple offenders greatly complicated the analysis and, because the number of fourth through ninth offenders was minimal, only the first three offenders for each incident were included. The total sample of 14,608 eliminated 105 offenders who were recorded on the original SHR tape. This reduction did not seriously affect the analysis of elderly homicides, however, since elderly offenders accounted for only 2.8 percent of all offenders on the tape. Because elderly offenders were not generally involved in multiple-offender cases, it would appear that consideration of only the first three offenders resulted in a loss of no more than one or two elderly violators.

Data on age of offender were recorded for each of the 14,608 cases. The age of offenders ranged from 1 to 93. Obviously the single case listing the age of offender as 1 was an error on the tape. There was, however, another offender listed as being 5 years old, two as 6, three as being 9, and seven as being 10. Some of these are also likely to be errors, although 9- and 10-year-olds can be charged with homicide in some states. The oldest offender was 93, while three others were listed as being 90. Given this broad range of ages, we subcategorized the age of offender as follows: (1) under 18, (2) 18–19, (3) 20–24, (4) 25–34, (5) 35–44, (6) 45–54, (7) 55–59, (8) 60–64, (9) 65–74, and (10) 75 and over. Age of offender was also dichotomized as elderly (60 and over) and nonelderly (under 60). We chose these age categories because they coincide with categories established by the Census Bureau and thus enabled us to obtain population figures for each age category so that we could calculate rates. Population figures were taken from early reports of the 1980 Census.

POPULATION DATA IN RESEARCH SITES

Since data for homicides in Alaska were not available but data for the District of Columbia were, we studied fifty jurisdictions. Measures of various demographic and economic indicators were also taken for the fifty states from the *Statistical Abstract of the United States*.[5] Those measures included: (1) the percent of the population below the poverty level, (2) the percent of the population that is urban, (3) the percent of the population that is black, (4) the per capita income of residents, (5) the rate of active physicians for each state, and (6) the unemployment rate for each state. Most of these variables that were used to determine possible correlates of elderly and/or nonelderly homicide offender rates across the states have been found in prior research to correlate with various crime indices. The one variable that may not have an obvious relationship to crime is the rate of active physicians. Doerner, however, found that the number of physicians is important in explaining the differing homicide rates in the South versus the rest of the United States because where medical resources are in short supply victims who are shot are more likely to die.[6]

Pearson product-moment correlation coefficients were calculated for the elderly and nonelderly homicide rates for the fifty states with the rates for other age groups and for the demographic and economic indicators. Also, we used step-wise regression programs to determine the best predictors of the elderly and nonelderly homicide rates across the states and to determine the percentage of variance that could be accounted for in the elderly and nonelderly rates by combinations of predictors. (See Table 6.1.)

Table 6.1. Elderly Versus Nonelderly Offender Rates Correlated with Age, Demographic, Sex, and Race Rates for Fifty States, 1980

	Elderly Rate	*Nonelderly Rate*
Demographics		
% Below Poverty	.456 (.000)*	.427 (.001)
% Urban	.269 (.030)	.404 (.002)
% Black	.706 (.000)	.721 (.000)
Per Capita Income	−.066 (.324)	.199 (.083)
Physician Rate	.320 (.012)	.348 (.007)
Unemployment Rate	.285 (.022)	.316 (.013)
Age Rates		
20–24	.610 (.000)	.906 (.000)
25–34	.802 (.000)	.961 (.000)
35–54	.851 (.000)	.942 (.000)
55–59	.543 (.000)	.577 (.000)
60–64	.893 (.000)	.762 (.000)
65 and up	.936 (.000)	.689 (.000)
Elderly	—	.792 (.000)
Nonelderly	.792 (.000)	— (.000)
Age 20 and up	.335 (.000)	.983 (.000)
Total	.815 (.000)	.998 (.000)
Sex Rates		
Male	.311 (.000)	.991 (.000)
Female	.731 (.000)	.875 (.000)
White	.570 (.000)	.772 (.000)
Black	−.031 (.417)	.121 (.202)
Total	.815 (.000)	.993 (.000)

*Numbers in parentheses indicate level of significance.

HYPOTHESES ABOUT ELDERLY HOMICIDE OFFENDERS

Numerous studies of the "patterns" of criminal homicide have been conducted since the publication in 1958 of Marvin Wolfgang's *Patterns of Criminal Homicide,*[7] a prototype that stimulated similar research in a number of other jurisdictions. Wolfgang argued that the epidemiology, or patterns of "facts" of homicide, must be determined before explanations are set forth to account for this crime. The SHR data tape described earlier allowed us to examine the facts of homicides involving elderly offenders compared to those involving younger violators, so that we can make some tentative statements about how and why these patterns differ. While it may be true that facts should precede theory, nonetheless it is important to construct and present hypotheses so that the facts can be systematically ordered to answer significant questions. The major hypotheses, and the results of this study, were as follows:

1. *The homicide offender rate for the elderly will be relatively stable across jurisdictions (states), whereas the overall homicide offender rate will fluctuate sharply.* Verkko, who formulated certain "laws" of sex and homicide, states that female (victimization and offender) homicide rates were stable across jurisdictions and over time in a single jurisdiction. He reasoned that females were less subject to the broad sociological and economic forces that influence homicide rates and thus that their rate would remain stable while the male and overall rate would fluctuate in response to broader social conditions.[8] Research has failed to confirm Verkko's "laws,"[9] and thus we believe it to be likely that elderly homicide offenders will not be "carriers" of a subculture of violence or be influenced as greatly by broader sociological conditions as people in younger age categories.

Table 6.1 presents correlation coefficients for the elderly rate versus the nonelderly rate for three types of variables: (1) the demographic/economic factors, (2) the homicide offender rates for the other age groups and the total rate, and (3) the homicide offender rates for males, females, blacks, and whites. Contrary to expectations, it is shown that the elderly offender rate is *not* stable across jurisdictions as it varies greatly from state to state. In fact, the elderly rate is strongly and positively related to the nonelderly rate ($r = .792$) and with the rates for the other age categories (e.g., $r = .610$ with the rate for offenders from 20 to 24 years of age).

We found evidence to contradict the first hypothesis by examining the elderly versus the nonelderly rates across the fifty states. The elderly rate varied from 0.00 in five states (Delaware, South Dakota, North Dakota, Vermont, and New Hampshire—states with small populations) to 5.09 in Alabama, to 5.79 in the District of Columbia. The states with the highest elderly homicide offender rates were D.C., 5.79; Alabama, 5.09; South Carolina, 4.33; Arkansas, 3.79; Hawaii, 3.51; and Tennessee, 3.49. The *nonelderly* homicide rate ranged from 0.88 in South Dakota to 14.24 for Texas and 18.91 for the District of Columbia. The *total* homicide offender rate *for all ages* (for the United States for 1980) was 6.44. The rate for the nonelderly was 7.35, and the elderly rate was 1.61. Thus the nonelderly to elderly ratio was 4.6 to 1.

Table 6.1 also indicates that the elderly offender rate is closely associated with the poverty level of a state ($r = .456$), with the percent of the state that is urban ($r = .269$), and with the percent of the state population that is black ($r = .706$). It also appears that the nonelderly rate is more closely associated with each of the six demographic/economic indicators than is the elderly rate. Thus it appears that the elderly offender rate is not as closely tied to selected demographic/economic indicators as is the nonelderly offender rate.[10]

2. *Homicides by the elderly will be disproportionately "domestic" in terms of the victim/offender relationship.* Prior research has demonstrated that female homicide offenders tend to have a domestic relationship with their victim rather than being acquaintances or strangers.[11] This hypothesis states that, similar to female murderers, conflicts involving the elderly are more likely to be domestic and less likely to be outcomes of committing other felonies and that elderly offenders will be disproportionately involved in domestic homicides.

Table 6.2 presents a breakdown of elderly versus nonelderly homicide offenders by victim/offender relationship. Elderly homicide

Table 6.2. Elderly Versus Nonelderly Homicide Offenders, Classified by Victim/Offender Relationship

	Acquaintances Friends, or Employer of Offender	Family Member or Lover	Stranger	Unknown	Total
Nonelderly (under 60)	6,092 (43.4%)	3,828 (27.3%)	2,311 (16.5%)	1,805 (12.9%)	14,036 (100%)
Elderly (60 and over)	244 (42.7%)	253 (44.2%)	44 (7.7%)	31 (5.4%)	572 (100%)

$\chi^2 = 111.302$, significant at .001 level
Cramer's V = .086
lambda = .001 (predicting victim offender relationship from age of offender)
tau = .002

offenders tend to be disproportionately (44.2 percent versus 27.3 percent) involved in domestic (family, lovers) homicides. Thus the second hypothesis appears to be confirmed. It is also noteworthy that the elderly are far less likely (7.7 percent versus 16.5 percent) to be involved in homicides against strangers than are the nonelderly.

3. *Homicides by the elderly will be disproportionately intraracial.* Most interracial homicides are incidental to robberies and burglaries, and since it is unlikely that elderly persons will be involved in these types of crimes, it is hypothesized that their homicides are likely to be disproportionately intraracial.[12]

Table 6.3 presents data on the extent to which elderly versus nonelderly homicide offenders are involved in intraracial versus interracial homicide events. The third hypothesis is confirmed, in that elderly

Table 6.3. Race of Offender by Race of Victim for U.S. Criminal Homicides, 1980, by Elderly Versus Nonelderly Offenders

Race of Offender	Black Victim	White Victim	Asian Victim	American Indian Victim	Total
Nonelderly					
Black	5,952	856	17	8	6,833
	(87.1%)	(12.5%)	(0.2%)	(0.1%)	(100%)
White	295	6,243	24	32	6,594
	(4.5%)	(94.7%)	(0.4%)	(0.5%)	(100%)
Asian	1	22	57	1	81
	(1.2%)	(27.29%)	(70.49%)	(1.2%)	(100%)
American Indian	6	37	2	61	106
	(5.7%)	(34.9%)	(1.9%)	(57.5%)	(100%)
Elderly					
Black	271	10	0	0	281
	(96.4%)	(3.6%)	(0.0%)	(0.0%)	(100%)
White	12	269	0	0	281
	(4.3%)	(95.7%)	(0.0%)	(0.0%)	(100%)
Asian	0	0	3	0	3
	(0.0%)	(0.0%)	(100%)	(0.0%)	(100%)
American Indian	1	0	0	1	2
	(50%)	(0.0%)	(0.0%)	(50%)	(100%)

Note: The 13,614 nonelderly offenders and 567 elderly offender cases (for a total of 14,181 cases) represent the victim/offender relationship for all the offenders/victims who were listed as the first offender and victim in each incident. Thus this figure differs from the 14,608 cases reported in other tables (those tables combined data on the first, second, and third offender of each homicide event). We have a different total (14,481) in this table because we used only the first offender and victim, but also because in a few cases the victim/offender relationship data were missing.

black offenders are more likely than nonelderly black offenders (96.4 percent versus 87.1 percent) to be involved in intraracial homicides. On the other hand, elderly white offenders are just as apt as nonelderly white offenders (95.7 percent versus 94.7 percent) to be involved in intraracial homicides.

4. *Circumstance/motive of homicides differ sharply by sex and race, and differences by sex and race found for other age groups will also be found for the elderly.* It is hypothesized that elderly offenders are not a homogeneous group and that sex and race subgroups of elderly homicide offenders are likely to differ sharply by "circumstance," the SHR term for the motive or type of homicide event. It expected that sex and race differences found for other age categories will also apply to the elderly since sex and race, both such dominant correlative influences, will not change when one becomes elderly.

Data on the circumstance/motive of elderly versus nonelderly offenders for various subgroups of the population indicate that the fourth hypothesis is *not* confirmed, in that we found no sharp differences for elderly offenders in circumstance or motive by sex and race of offender. The data suggest that the circumstance patterns for the black elderly varied little from the white elderly, although there were some differences in patterns between male elderly and female elderly. For example, although the percent of felony or suspect felony (0.0 −0.0) for females differed sharply from the figures (2.0−1.6) for the male elderly, overall there were few differences in circumstance or motive patterns for various subgroups of the elderly. This suggests that the elderly offender category is more homogeneous with respect to victim/offender relationship than was hypothesized. However, the offender rate among various categories of the elderly (and nonelderly) did vary significantly. For example, the offender rate ranged from 0.11 for elderly white females to 19.25 for elderly black males.

Although the data indicate no sharp differences in the circumstance or motive categories for various subgroups (sex and race) of the elderly versus nonelderly offenders, there is strong evidence that the relative frequency of homicides by these subgroups does vary sharply. The offender rate for the nonelderly varies from the 0.99 for nonelderly white females to the 50.05 for the nonelderly black males. Thus it would appear that while the *patterns* of elderly versus nonelderly homicides do not vary with respect to victim/offender relationships, when subgroups (by sex and race) are considered, the *relative frequency/rates* of the elderly versus the nonelderly offenders by subgroups do vary sharply. In short, the elderly and nonelderly offenders are homogeneous (with respect to sex and race subgroups) with respect to patterns of offenses but heterogeneous with respect to relative frequency/rates. Thus, although sex and race do not appear to affect patterns of homicides, they do affect relative frequency.

5. *Homicides by the elderly will be predominantly incidents involving one victim and a single offender.* Most multiple-offender homicides involve some type of felony-related activity, such as drug deals, robberies, burglaries, and other crimes. Because the elderly are not as likely to be engaged in these types of activities, it is hypothesized that elderly offenders will seldom be involved in multiple-offender slayings.

Table 6.4 presents data on the number of victims and offenders in the homicide event by elderly versus nonelderly offenders. The fifth hypothesis was confirmed, in that the elderly offenders were more likely to be involved in homicide events with only one victim and offender than the nonelderly (96.9 percent versus 86.2 percent). The figures suggest that multiple offenders were involved in only 0.4 percent (0.2 + 0.2) of the elderly offender cases versus 11.5 percent (10.9 + 0.6) of the nonelderly cases. Although the chi-square was significant, the elderly versus nonelderly differences are not very great.

6. *Elderly offenders will be more likely to kill those of their own age than offenders in other age categories.* Many homicides by the young involve victims who are older and who are killed during the course of robberies and other felony-related activities. Once more, because the elderly are not likely to be involved in these felony-type activities, their homicides are likely to involve victims with whom they live or closely associate. Since the elderly in the United States

Table 6.4. Type of Homicide Event (Number of Victims/Offenders) for U.S. Criminal Homicides, 1980, by Elderly Versus Nonelderly Offenders

	One Victim, One Offender	One Victim, Multiple Offenders	Multiple Victims, One Offender	Multiple Victims, Multiple Offenders	Total
Nonelderly (under 60)	12,094 (86.2%)	1,527 (10.9%)	327 (2.3%)	88 (0.6%)	14,036 (100%)
Elderly (60 and over)	554 (96.9%)	1 (0.2%)	16 (2.8%)	1 (0.2%)	572 (100%)

$\chi^2 = 121.827$, significant at .0001 level
Cramer's V = .069
lambda = .000 (predicting type of homicide event by age of offender)
tau = .004

do not generally live in extended families, it is hypothesized that the conflicts that resulted in homicides are more likely to involve other elderly people with whom the offender is in close association.

The data on the categorized age of the offender by the categorized age of the victim (reflecting only the first offender and victim in a homicide event) indicate that, contrary to the sixth hypothesis, it appears that elderly are *not* more likely to kill those of their own group. In fact, the opposite appears to be true. It appears that the middle-aged (those 25 to 34 and 35 to 44) are more likely to kill those of their own age than the old. By contrast, those 60 to 64 and 65 to 74 were less likely to kill someone of their own age (12.0 percent and 14.6 percent). However, the *very* elderly (those 74 and over) do not fit the pattern for the *younger* elderly, in that 33.8 percent of those over 74 kill someone of their own age category.

7. *Elderly offenders will be more likely to use firearms than offenders in other age groups.* Since the elderly are not as strong as younger persons, it is hypothesized that they will be more likely to use a gun to kill another. It is unlikely that an older and presumably weaker person would approach a younger person with a knife, stick, or a blunt instrument that could be seized and used by the intended victim. Guns are "equalizers," and thus the elderly are more likely to use this weapon to compensate for lack of physical strength.

Table 6.5 presents data on weapon choice by the elderly versus the nonelderly. The seventh hypothesis was confirmed, in that the elderly do appear to be more likely to use firearms than the nonelderly (78.1 percent versus 63.3 percent). The measures of association at the bottom of the table, however, suggest that the relationship between weapon choice and elderly versus nonelderly is not strong.

8. *Monthly patterns of homicides by the elderly will be similar*

Table 6.5. Weapon Choice for U.S. Criminal Homicides, 1980, by Elderly Versus Nonelderly Offenders

	Firearm	Knife	Other	Total
Nonelderly (under 60)	8,888 (63.3%)	2,936 (20.9%)	2,212 (15.8%)	14,036 (100%)
Elderly (60 and over)	477 (78.1%)	71 (12.4%)	54 (9.4%)	572 (100%)

$\chi^2 = 56.474$, significant at .001 level
Cramer's V = .060
lambda = .000 (predicting weapon choice by age of offender)
tau = .002

to those of other age groups. There appears to be no reason why the elderly homicide offender would be more active in particular months of the year. Thus it was hypothesized that the monthly pattern of the elderly would be no different from that of the nonelderly offender. Data on month of the homicide event by elderly versus nonelderly offenders confirm the eighth hypothesis: little or no differences were found for the elderly versus the nonelderly. Measures of association indicate a lack of relationship between month of the event and elderly versus nonelderly. It might be noted that the peak months for the elderly were July and August, and the same was true for the nonelderly. However, the fewest elderly homicides were in November and May, while the fewest nonelderly homicides were in February and March.

CONCLUSIONS

The facts do not lead to an obvious theory of why the elderly commit fewer or different kinds of homicides than do the nonelderly. The types of facts that we would need to draw such conclusions or to build a theory are currently not available from the FBI data tape. For example, it would be useful to know the types of conflicts that erupted in homicides for elderly versus nonelderly. Likewise, it would be useful to have data on the prior record of elderly offenders versus nonelderly offenders; on the relative availability of weapons; on the relative adherence to values that reflect a subculture of violence; on the relative level of frustration; and so on. The facts presented here would appear to support the following conclusions in the absence of a general theory:

1. The elderly offender is affected, but to a lesser extent, by the same sociological forces that appear to create different rates of murder from state to state. Although the elderly offender rate in several states is greater than the nonelderly rate in other states (e.g., the elderly rate in D.C. was 5.79 while the nonelderly rate in South Dakota was 0.88), the ratio of elderly to nonelderly rates was similar across all the states (the state with the lowest elderly to nonelderly ratio was Hawaii, with a ratio of 1.2).

2. The incidence of homicide also varies by sex and race. Elderly homicide offender rates vary significantly, from 0.11 for elderly white females to 19.25 for elderly black males. The male and female and black and white rates also varied from state to state but in proportion to the overall homicide rate. Thus there ap-

pears to be a certain level or degree of the homicide incidents in each state and in each sex and race subgroup for the individual states. The extent of each state's homicide rate varies sharply, although the relative frequency *within a state* for various subgroups (whether elderly or nonelderly, blacks or whites, males or females, etc.) does not appear to vary greatly.

The major research issue would appear to be what constitutes the sociological forces/homicide subculture of the various states and the sex and race subgroups within the states. Overall, the most significant question about elderly versus nonelderly homicide offenders does not appear to be why they commit significantly different kinds of homicides (they do not), but why they commit fewer homicides of the same kind.

NOTES

1. Marvin Wolfgang, *Patterns of Criminal Homicide* (Philadelphia: University of Pennsylvania Press, 1958).
2. Michael Hindelang, "The Uniform Crime Reports Revisited," *Journal of Criminal Justice* 2 (1974): 1–17.
3. Jeffrey H. Reiman, *The Rich Get Richer and The Poor Get Prison* (New York: John Wiley & Sons, 1979). See also Joel Swartz, "Silent Killers at Work," *Crime and Social Justice* (Spring–Summer, 1975): 15–20.
4. Lawrence Sherman and Robert Langworthy, "Measuring Homicide by Police Officers," *Journal of Criminal Law and Criminology* 70, 4 (1979): 546–560.
5. *Statistical Abstract of the United States, 1982–1983:* National Data Bank and Guide to Sources, 103rd. edition. (Washington, D.C.: U.S. Department of Commerce, Bureau of Census, Dec., 1982).
6. W. E. Doerner, "Why Does Johnny Reb Die When Shot?—The Impact of Medical Resources upon Lethability" (unpublished paper, School of Criminology, Florida State University, Tallahassee, 1981).
7. See Wolfgang, *Patterns of Criminal Homicide.*
8. Veli Verkko, "Static and Dynamic 'Laws' of Sex and Homicide," in Marvin Wolfgang (ed.), *Studies in Homicide* (New York: Harper & Row, 1967), pp. 36–44.
9. William Wilbanks, "A Test of Verkko's Static and Dynamic 'Laws' of Sex and Homicide," *International Journal of Women's Studies* 6, 7 (1981): 173–180.
10. A regression analysis not reported in Table 6.1 provided the best predictor of the elderly offender rate across the states: the nonelderly homicide offender rate in the fifty states. The R^2 with the nonelderly rate as the first variable entering the equation was .627. Four of the six demographic/economic variables listed in Table 6.1 also entered the equation, but the R^2 with their inclusion was only .749, and thus only 12.2 percent of the variance unaccounted for by the nonelderly rate was accounted for by the demographic/economic variables. The R^2 with the elderly rate as the dependent variable and the demographic/economic variables as the independent variables (thus removing the nonelderly rate as an independent variable) was .560 (with percent black entering the equation first and producing an R^2 of .498). When the demographic/economic variables were entered

first and the nonelderly rate allowed to enter the equation last, an R^2 of .741 resulted (thus an increase of .189 over the .560 figure). When we used the nonelderly offender rate as the dependent variable, the elderly rate entered the equation first (R^2 = .627) with five of the demographic/economic variables also entering and producing a final R^2 = .855. Thus it appears that the best predictor (of those utilized) of the elderly rate was the nonelderly rate and the best predictor of the nonelderly rate was the elderly rate.

11 See Alan Blum and Gary Fisher, "Women Who Kill," in I. L. Kutash, S. B. Kutash, L. B. Schlesinger, and Associates (eds.), *Violence: Perspectives on Murder and Aggression* (San Francisco: Jossey-Bass, 1979), pp. 187–197, and also Wolfgang, *Patterns of Criminal Homicide.*

12. The offender rates among the elderly by race and sex varied as follows: black male elderly, 19.25; white male elderly, 1.95; black female elderly, 2.61; white female elderly, .011; male elderly, 3.33; female elderly, 0.32; black elderly, 9.54; white elderly, 0.88; all elderly, 1.58.

PART III

The Elderly In The Criminal Justice System

This part addresses the problems encountered by elderly suspects caught up in our traditional criminal justice process as well as problems elderly offenders create for the agencies and personnel in the system itself. At present, the number of elderly people encountering the criminal justice system has not created any major strains, except perhaps in some Sun Belt communities, whether they are charged, convicted, and sentenced or diverted. However, as the number of older people increases, the fit between our customary methods of crime control and a population of elderly offenders will necessarily be tested. The chapters in this part deal with elderly law violators as they encounter the police, prosecutors, trial courts, jails, and prisons.

Most of our crime control practices, including those of the police, are designed to deal with young criminals, those roughly between 16 and 24 years old, who pose issues of danger and the necessity of restraint, neither of which is a major issue with elderly offenders. Young criminals, who are often strong, healthy, and active, have a potential for physical violence that older suspects do not. In addition, the young, more than the elderly, have a proclivity for flight and escape. Danger and flight have resulted in offender control that is cautious and repressive. Accoutrements of all criminal justice agencies reflect these concerns. Sidearms, handcuffs, and leg irons all are designed to control the young, the dangerous, and the mobile. Are these techniques really necessary with the aged?

Unlike most younger offenders, elderly violators may present special medical problems. They may be subject to hypertension or heart disease, for example. The trauma of arrest and public disclosure may cause problems the police and the courts have no desire to precipitate. In Chapter 7, James J. Fyfe discusses the police decision of whether to take elderly offenders into custody and, if so, the amount of force that is necessary and can be used. He presents alternative ways the police have developed for handling older violators.

Chapter 8 is devoted to the court stages of the process, including legal defenses to criminal liability that may be raised on the basis of age and accompanying conditions. Fred Cohen discusses not only age as a defense but also the possibility of developing a new set of court procedures to deal with elderly offenders. For at least half a century we have operated separate juvenile justice systems in all states, systems that are akin to, but distinct from, those used to process adult criminals. The juvenile justice system is designed to be beneficent, to determine "the best interests" of young people (not simply to prove them guilty), and has a mandate to use the least restrictive methods of control and treatment once delinquency has been determined. Would elderly offenders be better processed by such a separate and "benevolent" system than in the regular channels of adult crime control?

Although they are at opposite ends of the offender age spectrum, elderly criminals and juvenile delinquents have common traits and conditions that make law violation more likely, if not inevitable. Comparing lifestyles of the young and the old can be carried too far, however. Youngsters falling into the juvenile delinquent category trade some rights for protection from the harshness of adult law. It is unlikely that elderly persons view, or would want to view, the state as *parens patriae*, to be treated as children—not only in respect to criminal liability, but in other aspects of their lives as well. Juveniles are "incompetent" in a number of ways other than criminal responsibility. Licensing, contracting, managing resources—all would be risked if the elderly were to be treated as children. Cohen discusses these issues and others as well.

In Chapter 9, Delores Golden discusses from her own experience in a medium-sized jail the problems encountered when elderly suspects and offenders are placed in such facilities. She does this against the backdrop of jails in general. Again the point is made that because jails are designed for a much younger population unique problems are encountered not only by older inmates but by jail personnel as well.

The next chapters in this section deal with older inmates in prison. In Chapter 10, Dan Rubenstein provides a review of relevant research literature, which he says is both sparse and sporadic. He decries the apologies of the various authors for methodological shortcomings, maintaining that poor research perpetuates myths. He believes it important to do careful and comprehensive research in this area, for in the foreseeable future the number and perhaps the types of elderly prison inmates will increase.

In Chapter 11, Ann Goetting details the findings of her survey of the prisons in all fifty states and concludes that "program facilities and treatment based on age are rare and never comprehensive." Prison administrators face the same dilemma inside the walls that gerontologists confront in society as a whole: the advantages and disadvantages of age segregation for housing, medical care, and types of treatment and job placement.

Because elderly criminals ordinarily present less of a continuing threat to society than younger offenders, and because we have no desire to punish people excessively for late-life, first-time crimes, alternative criminal justice programs have been developed to keep older offenders in the community. One such program, the Broward Senior Intervention and Education Program, is described in Chapter 12 by Gary Feinberg, Sidney Glugover, and Irene Zwetchkenbaum. This program, in Broward County, Florida, is a voluntary alternative to prosecution and correction for first-time elderly shoplifters who have admitted their guilt. After successful participation in the program, which combines individual counseling, and participation in various cultural and social activities at a senior center, and after community volunteer work, any criminal record of the elderly shoplifter is expunged. To date the program has shown a remarkably low recidivism rate of only 1.5 percent.

Diversion involves alternative programs, not simply letting elderly offenders off. And a major component of most diversionary programs, pre- or post-conviction, is counseling. In Chapter 13 Mindy L. Gewirtz discusses social work counseling with elderly offenders, clearly a field of direct practice that will become even more important in the future.

Chapter 7

Police Dilemmas in Processing Elderly Offenders

James J. Fyfe

In America's largest and most heterogeneous cities, police officers are trained to deal with a great variety of population subgroups. The New York City Police Department's recruit training manual, for example, includes separate sections treating police interaction with such clientele as heroin addicts, the mentally ill, preschoolers, adolescents, crime victims, the blind, the retarded, epileptics, drunk drivers, violent and nonviolent demonstrators, juvenile offenders, crowds, family disputants, youthful offenders, potential suicides, families of the suddenly deceased, welfare recipients, diplomats, and persons of black, Native American, Italian, Jewish, Chinese, Japanese, and Puerto Rican descent.[1]

Like most other police training manuals and task-prescriptive texts, the New York City publication also includes lengthy sections on circumstances in which elderly citizens are likely to come to police attention. These, however, are generally limited to descriptions of the elderly as extremely vulnerable targets of crime, as parties to culture conflicts with more recently arrived immigrant groups, or as persons whose diminished physical and mental capacities may require officers to take part in locating their homes, relatives, or institutions to care for them. Nowhere does this text discuss police interaction with elderly offenders.

That omission is understandable given the historical comparative

Table 7.1. Total U.S. Arrests and Arrests of Persons Aged 65 and Older, 1971 and 1980[a]

Offense	Total, 1971[b]	Total, 1980[b]	Change, 1971–1980		Aged 65+		Change, 1971–80	
			n	%	1971	1980	n	%
Murder (non-negligent manslaughter)	14,549	18,745	+4,196	+28.8	217	248	+31	+14.3
Forcible rape	16,582	29,431	+12,849	+76.2	36	107	+71	+97.2
Robbery	101,728	134,476	+37,748	+37.1	75	151	+76	+101.3
Aggravated assault	140,350	258,721	+118,371	+84.3	1,429	2,424	+995	+69.6
Burglary	315,376	479,639	+164,263	+52.1	282	527	+245	+86.9
Larceny	674,997	1,123,823	+448,826	+66.5	5,274	12,857	+7,583	+143.8
Auto theft	130,954	129,783	−1,171	−0.9	126	164	+38	+30.2
Arson	11,154	18,459	+7,305	+65.4	61	84	+23	+37.7
Other assaults	307,107	456,887	+149,780	+48.8	2,511	3,014	+503	+20.0
Forgery	45,340	72,643	+27,303	+60.2	108	169	+61	+56.5
Fraud	95,610	261,787	+166,177	+173.4	580	1,447	+867	+149.4
Embezzlement	7,114	7,885	+771	+10.8	41	26	−15	−36.6
Stolen property	75,516	115,514	+39,998	+53.0	210	340	+130	+61.9

(Total: 155,446,000[b] | 209,194,225[b])

Vandalism	121,850	233,857	+112,007	+91.9	275	582	+307	+111.6
Weapons	114,569	157,157	+42,588	+37.2	1,271	1,510	+239	+18.0
Prostitution	52,916	85,815	+32,899	+62.2	205	331	+126	+61.5
Other sex offenses	50,695	63,453	+12,758	+25.2	796	917	+121	+15.2
Drugs	400,606	533,010	+132,404	+33.1	251	691	+440	+175.3
Gambling	86,698	46,697	−40,001	−46.1	4,521	2,287	−2,234	−49.4
Family offenses	56,456	49,991	−6,465	−11.5	283	185	−98	−34.6
Driving while intoxicated	489,545	1,303,933	+814,388	+166.4	9,858	19,761	+9,003	+100.5
Liquor law violations	231,192	427,829	+196,637	+85.0	1,741	2,157	+416	+23.9
Disorderly conduct	1,491,782	1,049,614	−442,168	−29.6	57,468	25,513	−31,955	−55.6
Vagrancy	80,180	29,348	−50,832	−63.4	1,651	320	−1,331	−80.6
All other offenses	869,270	1,658,738	+789,468	+90.8	7,407	11,538	+4,131	+55.8
Suspicion	54,374	16,241	−38,133	−70.1	287	63	−224	−78.0
Totals	5,165,785	8,443,266	+3,277,481	+63.4	48,644 (0.9%)c	68,472 (0.8%)c	+19,828	+40.8

Source: Federal Bureau of Investigation, Crime in the United States 1971, pp. 122–123; Crime in the United States, 1980, pp. 200–201.
aExcludes drunkenness, curfew, and runaway violations.
bPopulation of reporting police jurisdictions.
cPercentage of total arrests.

rarity of police encounters with elderly offenders. Table 7.1 shows that, as a percentage of all arrests, police apprehensions of persons aged 65 or older remain infrequent. In 1971, such arrests accounted for 0.9 percent of all arrests reported to the Federal Bureau of Investigation; by 1980, they accounted for 0.8 percent. The table also shows that, in absolute terms, arrests of the elderly increased dramatically (but not so greatly as arrests of younger persons) between 1971 and 1980. Reporting police arrested 48,644 elderly people in 1971, and 68,472 in 1980. Thus, it appears that, while the percentage of total police business involving arrests of the elderly remains small, individual officers are now more likely to make such arrests than has previously been the case.

Further, several trends indicate that there will be continuing increases in the frequency of police arrests of the elderly. First, as other sections of this volume point out, people are living longer and the representation of elderly citizens in our population is increasing daily. Even if the *rate* at which elderly offenders came to official police attention were to remain constant, therefore, we could anticipate continued increases in the *number* of such occasions.

A second trend exaggerates the effects of these changing demographics on the frequency of police arrests of the elderly. Many older people live on small, fixed incomes and have suffered great real-dollar losses during the unprecedented inflation of the last several years. Thus, one might reasonably expect more members of the growing elderly population to succumb to the temptation to engage in shoplifting and other forms of property crime simply as a means of making ends meet. Further, the probability of continuing increases in elderly property crime is especially great when, as is the case, so many of the elderly live in areas in which the cost of living is particularly high.[2]

A third consideration concerns not the actual frequency of offenses and apprehensions of the elderly, but the manner in which their offenses—when discovered—are resolved by victims and by the police. Over the last several years there have been dramatic changes in public perceptions and in official policies regarding at least three of the offenses committed at comparatively high rates by elderly people: shoplifting, drunken driving, and criminal family violence.

SHOPLIFTING

Table 7.1 shows that the number of persons 65 or older arrested for larceny jumped by 143.8 percent between 1971 and 1980, an increase that far outstripped the change in all arrests for larceny (up 66.5 percent). Further, while larceny arrests accounted for only 10.8 percent of all 1971 arrests of the elderly, in 1980 they constituted 18.8 percent of the total. Although the FBI presents no information regarding the percentage of these larceny arrests of elderly citizens that involved shoplifting, this percentage is probably high.[3]

During 1971, (my ninth, and last, year of police patrol) I worked in an area of New York City that included several major department stores, each of which maintained its own security force. Several times daily, those stores generated police radio reports that "store security is holding one," but I can recall only one incident of a report that store security officers had apprehended an elderly shoplifting suspect.[4] During those years, it is doubtful that calling the police and initiating prosecution against elderly shoplifters were deemed desirable by either store management or their security personnel. Since such calls typically resulted in processions of uniformed police officers, store detectives, and handcuffed senior citizens who walked past aisles of surprised—and usually appalled—shoppers, out onto crowded streets, and into police cars, such parades did little to enhance the images of department stores as friendly places to shop. Thus, this unscientific recollection suggests that department store security personnel during that period opted for good customer relations over arrests of elderly offenders by resolving apprehensions of such offenders without calling them to official police attention.[5]

Since that time, several things have changed. It is clear that merchants now perceive shoplifting as a much greater threat to their economic survival than they did in the halcyon days of 1971. Shoplifting is taken much more seriously today than it was in the days when the "ripoff" was viewed as a political act,[6] and it is unlikely that many offenders are presently treated leniently in the interests of good public relations. In addition, in recent years, it has become far easier to initiate shoplifting prosecution without exposing shoppers to the spectacle of parading police officers, store detectives, and handcuffed senior citizens. The increasingly widespread police use of summonses as alternatives to physical arrest, as well as the grant of "special officer" status and arrest powers to store detectives, has meant that petty larceny prosecutions can be started quietly within department store security offices, sometimes without the involvement of public police.[7] Thus, over the last several years, there has been both an increase in the pressures encouraging arrest and prosecution of shoplifters, and decreases in the pressures that formerly inhibited such arrests and prosecutions.

DRUNKEN DRIVING

In 1971, driving under the influence of alcohol accounted for 9,858 arrests of persons 65 or over, or one in five (20.3 percent) arrests of the elderly. In 1980, 19,761 elderly persons (28.9 percent of total arrestees 65 or older) were arrested for these offenses. While the rate at which these arrests increased is not as great as is true for people of all ages (65 or over increased by 100.5 percent; all ages increased by 166.4 percent), only 15.4 percent of arrests of all ages involved charges of driving under the influence.

Again, however, it is difficult to tell whether the great increase in these arrests—for all age groups—evidences increased actual apprehensions for these offenses or changes in police dispositions of such apprehensions. In the past, it was not unusual for police officers to resolve drunken driving cases informally without resort to arrest. Recent and justified concern over the great toll in lives and property taken by drunken drivers, however, has almost certainly led to great increases in the percentage of apprehended drunken drivers against whom police elect to intitiate prosecution.[8] Further, since the elderly have almost certainly been disproportionately the beneficiaries of past police discretion not to arrest,[9] it is likely that the present sentiment to rid the highways of drunken drivers has particularly reduced their chances of "getting a break" from officers who catch them driving while intoxicated.

FAMILY VIOLENCE

In former years, "family disputes" were regarded by officers on patrol as events best handled by such informal means as mediation, by "sending the old man out for a walk" to cool him off, or by maintaining the peace while one of the parties packed and left. It was, in fact, regarded as a failure by officers if they were unable to "resolve" such situations without resort to arrest.

There were many reasons for this view. First, officers were well aware that attempts to arrest spouses who had in fact assaulted their mates often turned *both* parties against officers, sometimes violently. Second, officers often found that, even among those spouses who did insist on or consent to arrest in the heat of the moment, very few remained willing to pursue assault prosecutions against his or her mate after passions had cooled. Finally, and perhaps most important, officers generally strongly adhered to the principle that a man's home is his castle, that family disagreements are best handled by the parties involved, and that official intervention by police almost certainly irrevocably destroys the relationships of those involved.[10]

Police training materials of that time are illustrative. In 1967, the International Association of Chiefs of Police wrote:

> Once inside the home [of family disputants], the officer's sole purpose is to preserve the peace and by his presence prevent the parties from committing a battery....
>
> *The power of arrest should be exercised as a last resort when dealing with family disputes.* The officer should never create a police problem when only a family problem exists. *There will be times, however, when it becomes necessary to arrest a member of the family. A crime may have been committed in the officer's presence, a warrant may have to be executed or one of the spouses will demand to sign a complaint.*
>
> In these arrest situations, the officer should be very cautious. A strong familial bond may exist between members of the family even though one of the parties may have been the victim of a battery or had obtained an arrest warrant several days previously. Because of this sense of solidarity, the members of the household may decide to assist one another, posing a great risk to the officer. It is not uncommon for a grieving wife who had just wanted her husband arrested to suddenly turn and attack or verbally abuse the arresting officer.[11]

By contrast, in discussing police reponse to street fights and brawls, the same text states:

> A call of a fight in progress occurring either on the street or in a bar must be given immediate attention. There is always a possibility that the disturbance may be a struggle between an attacker and his intended victim. Prompt service can prevent serious injuries, the commission of a homicide, or reduce the amount of property damage....
>
> If the fight has ended before the arrival of the police and there are no serious injuries, no property damage and *no one present who is willing to file a complaint, the officer should obtain the names and addresses of those involved and disperse the crowd....*
>
> *If none of the parties involved is willing to sign a complaint or make a citizen's arrest, the officer's efforts are limited to rendering aid and restoring order.*[12]

Since that time, much has happened to change the police's philosophy that intrafamily violence should be treated more leniently than other forms of violence. Women's groups have pointed out the inconsistency of police attempts to avoid arresting those who had committed acts that, if committed against nonfamily members, would surely have resulted in arrest and prosecution. It has also been suggested that police have failed to distinguish adequately between mere family disputes and family violence, and have wrongly attempted to apply crisis intervention techniques to situations in which arrest was appropriate. Finally, it has been argued that police reluctance to arrest in incidents of family violence serves to license and encourage future, and often more serious, acts of violence.[13]

Both the courts and police administrators have heard and acted on these arguments. As a result, police discretion to resolve incidents of family violence without arrest has been severely restricted.[14] Because it is likely that change in police handling of family violence has disproportionately affected the elderly,[15] it is also likely that the increases in arrests in 1971 to 1980 for aggravated assault and other assault (69.6 and 20.0 percent, respectively, as shown in Table 7.1) are largely a result of changes in police policy rather than the result of substantial increases in the actual frequency with which police become aware of such offenses.

IMPLICATIONS FOR THE POLICE

Regardless of whether the increases in these arrests of persons aged 65 and older are indicative of increased criminality among seniors or merely an artifact of change in policy and in reporting practices, their implications for those who run police agencies and for those who make arrests are substantial. It is far simpler for police at all levels when offenses never come to their attention, or when they may be readily disposed of informally, than it is when there exist pressures to arrest. The police chief need not be concerned about issues regarding custody of elderly drunken drivers when his officers routinely handle such apprehensions by parking offenders' autos, stealthily removing ignition keys, returning keyrings to offenders, and finding them taxi rides home. Such practices are also quite simple for officers, who usually find that the victims of such thefts are usually too embarrassed or too grateful for the "breaks" given them to lodge complaints against the officers involved.

Thus, while *Uniform Crime Report* figures are merely surrogate measures of the frequency with which offenses come to officers' attention, the increases in arrests they include pose real problems for police. To police executives, these figures signal a need for a review of existing policies and training regarding use of force, custody provisions, and the effects on community relations of increased arrests of the elderly. For the field officers who implement policy, increased exposure to elderly offenders and increased pressures to arrest demand that officers carefully balance the possible negative effects of their actions on the lives and health of elderly offenders against the risk of endangering themselves and other innocent persons by dealing too leniently with these offenders.

POLICE DILEMMAS IN PROCESSING ELDERLY OFFENDERS

Many observers have marveled at the frequent near absence of guidelines on the broad discretion of field police officers, and at the often dismal training received by police. In 1970, Bittner wrote of the former that

> No other aspects of police practice have received more scholarly attention in the recent past than the procedures and decisions connected with invoking the law. The principal result of these inquiries was the discovery that policemen have, in effect, a greater degree of discretionary freedom in proceeding against public offenders than any other public official.... The condition creates something of a legal paradox because, according to the discovered facts, the policeman who is in terms of the official hierarchy of power, competence, and dignity, on the lowest rung of the administration of justice, actually determines that "outer perimeter of law enforcement," and thus actually determines what the business of his betters will be.[16]

In 1973, the National Advisory Commission on Criminal Justice Standards and Goals commented about training: "A 1967 study of the International Association of Chiefs of Police showed that the average policeman received less than 200 hours of formal training...and barbers more than 4,000. No reasonable person could contend that a barber's responsibility is 20 times greater than a police officer's."[17]

Since those observations were made, legislators and police administrators have generally attempted to give more direction to officers by formulating less ambiguous statutory and policy guidelines for police discretion. As noted earlier, however, police training programs continue to omit references to elderly offenders. Further, given increased pressures to arrest for offenses in which police typically encounter elderly offenders, it is ironic that, when interpreted literally, the broad statutory provisions regarding arrest procedures to which Bittner alludes may be overly restrictive. Regardless of the breadth of the statutes, police have little discretion when victims of shoplifting insist on arrest. Similarly, when outraged citizens' groups demand that more forceful action be taken in instances of family violence or drunken driving, police discretion is greatly constrained. If the police are to handle elderly offenders humanely and in a way that minimizes police exposure to civil liability, such restrictiveness may be unwise. Police often encounter elderly offenders whose criminal acts and general manner suggest that they are mentally disordered—or senile—and who therefore are most appropriately diverted out of the justice system to the care of family or a social service institution as expeditiously as possible. They are often unable to do so, however, because of statutory restrictions.

A vignette in "The Police Tapes," a video documentary on policing in the South Bronx, is illustrative.[18] A limping, poorly dressed 69-year-old woman with a cane has been arrested for striking her adult daughter in the face with either an axe or a wrench (weapon not recovered). The daughter has been hospitalized with severe injuries, and the old woman is brought before a young desk sergeant who, after agonizing over the lack of alternatives, patiently and reluctantly explains to her that she must be arrested and held in jail overnight before appearing in criminal court. In the minutes that follow, she explains to the arresting officer that she had been continually bothered by her daughter, and that she had struck the daughter to get her to stop. In front of the officer, who is obviously a reluctant participant in this process, she sits hunched in a chair, rocking back and forth, and quietly begins to sing gospel hymns. The officer gets up and walks away. In a follow-up interview of the officer several months later, the viewer learns that the old woman had resumed living with her daughter, because "she had no place else to go." We learn also that she had been jailed overnight, and that her case had been referred to family court by the criminal court judge because it was most appropriately "a case for a social worker."

If that is true, there arise questions concerning whether such a determination should not have been made before the old woman had been in jail overnight. A night in jail is a stressful experience, even for the young and healthy. For one who, even to the most detached observer, is apparently in an advanced state of both physical and mental deterioration, such an experience can be positively devastating.[19] In such circumstances, questions of police usurpation of the prosecutorial or magisterial function of determining whether a person who has committed a felonious act should be held criminally liable for that act seem of secondary importance.

Even when empowered to make determinations that persons such as the old woman should be detained in jail until the next session of the criminal court,[20] the police would face other dilemmas. The old woman in "The Police Tapes" wound up back at home because "she had no place else to go." While such a disposition may have been more satisfactory for her than incarceration in a prison or mental institution, it is doubtful that it has helped her daughter to rest easy—especially given the mother's apparent success in hiding from the police the weapon with which she had assaulted her daughter.

A major issue confronting the police in such cases, therefore, is that the pressure to arrest and the inflexibility of the prescribed arrest process may subject elderly offenders to the trauma of detention prior to court appearances that accomplish nothing. The old woman has spent a night in jail, and her daughter—presumably reluctant or unable to seek her mother's commitment—remains vulnerable to her mother's assaults. What may be needed is relaxation of the rule that only prosecutors and judges may decline to handle cases involving obviously incompetent defendants. With or without such a change, there also exists a need for some alternative to jail detention.

There exist other ironic dilemmas for the police in processing elderly offenders. While the public is concerned about shoplifting, family violence, and drunken driving, most people retain great sympathy for the elderly. In the abstract, there is great public support for police attempts to deal forcefully with these offenses, but in specific cases there frequently exists the perception of harshness when police arrest individual elderly offenders. The elderly axe wielder is a case in point. *Everybody* deplores assaults with axes but, in her case, the concern and sympathy of the documentary producers, the viewers (who are never shown the victim), the police, and, eventually, the court lie with the axe wielder rather than with her victim. It is difficult to imagine that a younger axe wielder would be seen as a sympathetic figure, or to imagine that the police would have been reluctant to arrest a younger assailant. How, for example, would police, documentary makers, viewers, and the courts have responded had the old woman been her daughter's victim in an axe assault?

Further, it is certain that individual elderly offenders charged with less serious offenses engender a greater degree of public sympathy than do axe wielders. For the police agencies, public reaction to arrests of the elderly for less serious crimes is likely to involve both sympathy for arrestees and a perception that the police have acted unreasonably.[21] The arresting officer in such a case is likely to suffer a negative reaction not only from the public, but from his supervisors and colleagues as well. Negative press or public reaction to the arrest of an elderly offender is apt to make the arresting officer's co-workers resentful of the heat he has brought on them, and to lead them to share the sentiment that the offense could—and should—have been handled otherwise.

A final irony is that police actions may unintentionally contribute to the commission of offenses by elderly citizens who take strong and/or irrational actions out of apparent fear of becoming crime victims themselves. Recently, for example, police responded to an apartment in which gas company employees thought there was a gas leak. The occupant of the apartment, a 94-year-old man who had been frequently victimized, refused to admit the gas company employees. When police arrived,

> the first officer on the scene tried to talk to Jackson through the closed door. Jackson opened the door, which was held by a chain lock, and pointed a pistol out through the crack. . . .
>
> When (Officer) Fox pulled up in front of the building, he was met by one of the gas workers who told him that the man inside had a gun.
>
> "I ran up the steps with my revolver drawn, when inside the residence I met Police Officer Lopit and said 'What's going on?'" Fox said.
>
> He said, 'There's a guy inside pointed a gun at me. I said 'What do you mean there's a guy inside pointed a gun on you?'
>
> "Then I said, 'Where at?' He pointed to a side door—first floor front apartment—at which time, with my right foot, I kicked the door in."
>
> In the apartment, Fox was confronted by Jackson, who pointed the pistol at him and Fox fired his service revolver, fatally wounding Jackson.[22]

For many reasons, the actions of this officer (who was dismissed by his department) were unwise. One is grateful, for example, that the apartment had not been filled with leaking gas, which surely would have been detonated by gunfire. Regardless of their extreme imprudence, however, his actions were a well-intentioned effort to apprehend someone who had pointed a firearm at his colleague.

But by his actions he failed to take into account the possibility that this suspect was a "scared, old and harassed"[23] man whose experience had taught him to trust nobody and who apparently regarded his home as a fortress. Such old people are, unfortunately, not uncommon in American inner cities. Nor is the incident the only one in which old people have been shot and killed by police whom they apparently perceived as intruding thugs.[24]

Thus, while one may criticize in general terms the wisdom of this officer's actions, they give rise to concerns specific to police encounters with the elderly. Many of the elderly, especially in inner cities, are nearly paranoid about their vulnerability to criminal victimization. Further, age has diminished the accuracy of many old people's perceptions. Consequently, police must be trained to understand that their well-intentioned actions may be perceived inaccurately, and may provoke protective and seemingly criminal reactions.

At the beginning of this chapter, it was pointed out that police in most cities are well schooled in the lifestyles, folkways, and perceptions of minority groups within their jurisdictions. One purpose of such schooling is to help officers resolve encounters with members of these groups without resorting to the use of force or arrest. Just as police learn to avoid triggering violent responses from ethnic and sexual minorities by refraining from using provocative words ("You people," "boy," or "fag") and actions, they must be carefully trained to avoid using the words and actions that turn the innocent elderly—a growing minority group—into assailants.

CONCLUSIONS

There are varying opinions concerning whether the increased number of arrests of the elderly are indications of increased senior criminality or merely the result of diminished police power to resolve such offenses informally. Such a debate, however, obscures the central concern for police: that the elderly are being arrested and processed by police in greater numbers than ever before, and that the trend is likely to continue. Regardless of how informal and unsanctioned the former relationship between police and elderly offenders, it is clear that it has changed, and that police and other officials must respond to that change. They must do so by examining carefully the limits on police power to process elderly offenders in a way that is best for victims, the public, offenders, and the police. That may mean that, contrary to general trends, police discretion in elderly offender cases should be broadened. Perhaps police should have available formally as many alternatives to jailing the elderly pending court appearances as they do for juvenile offenders. If that is so, both legislation and alternative services must be provided. Certainly police should be better trained to deal with elderly people who have already committed crimes, and to assure that the police themselves do not interact with vulnerable old people in a manner likely to make necessary the use of arrest or force.

NOTES

1. New York City Police Department, *Police Students' Social Science Guide* (1974).
2. According to the U.S. Department of Health and Human Services, *Facts About Older Americans* (Washington, D.C.: U.S. Government Printing Office, 1982, p. 3), 45 percent of persons 65 and over lived in seven states. California and New York had over 2 million each, and Florida, Illinois, Ohio, Pennsylvania, and Texas had over 1 million each.
3. It is difficult to imagine, for example, that more than a small percentage of these cases involved arrests for pocketpicking, thefts from motor vehicles, buildings, or confidence games (all of which require considerable skill), or pursesnatching, thefts of motor vehicle accessories, or thefts of bicycles (all of which require considerable strength and/or agility).
4. That incident involved an elderly bank vice president accused by store security personnel of collaborating with his teenage son in the theft of a jacket. While shouting denials at store personnel and at me, the elderly suspect suffered a sudden heart attack and died instantly.
5. This was usually accomplished by releasing shoplifting suspects directly from store security offices after searching them and requiring them to be photographed and to sign confessions of their thefts. These confessions included acknowledgment by offenders that they were thereafter banned from the store involved. Thus they would be subject to arrest for trespass if observed in the store in the future.
6. See, e.g., Abbie Hoffman, *Steal This Book* (New York: Grove Press, 1971).
7. See, e.g., New York City Police Department, *Patrol Guide*, § 110-63 (Desk Appearance Ticket, Participating Department Store Program) (November 4, 1977), which describes the process by which shoplifting arrests may be handled by store personnel without requiring appearances at police stations.
8. See, e.g., Greg Mitchell, "Driving the Drunks off the Road," *Police Magazine* (September 1982): 49–56.
9. Donald Black, *The Manners and Customs of the Police* (New York: Academic Press, 1980, pp. 1–40), for example, discusses determinants of police decisions to arrest or issue tickets, and observes (p. 35) that "[m]any police also tend to be more aggressive and severe toward young people."
10. See, generally, Nancy Loving, *Responding to Spouse Abuse and Wife Beating: A Guide for Police* (Washington, D.C.: Police Executive Research Forum, 1980), pp. 29–51.
11. International Association of Chiefs of Police, *The Patrol Operation* (Washington, D.C.: International Association of Chiefs of Police, 1967), pp. 200–201, emphasis added.
12. Ibid., pp. 201–202, emphasis added.
13. Loving, *Responding to Spouse Abuse.*
14. See, e.g., *Bruno against McGuire*, New York Supreme Court Consent Decree Index 21946/76 (1978), in which the New York City Police Department agreed that its officers could no longer attempt to mediate cases in which husbands committed crimes against their wives, but would instead effect arrests in such cases.

15. William Wilbanks and Dennis D. Murphy, in "The Elderly Homicide Offender in the U.S., 1980," (paper presented at the World Congress of Sociology, Mexico City, August 1982, p. 8), report that 44.2 percent of 1980 U.S. criminal homicides committed by persons 60 or older were intrafamily events, versus 27.3 percent for offenders under 60. Conversely, only 7.7 percent of 60+ homicides involved strangers, compared to 16.5 percent for all other offenders. Since, as Marvin Wolfgang (*Patterns of Criminal Homicide*, Philadelphia: University of Pennsylvania Press, 1958) suggests, homicides frequently differ from aggravated assault only in degree of injury inflicted, it is reasonable to assume that similar percentages would be found among elderly arrests for aggravated assault.

16. Egon Bittner, *The Functions of the Police in Modern Society* (Washington, D.C.: U.S. Government Printing Office, 1970), p. 107. (Reprinted by Oelgeschlager, Gunn & Hain, Cambridge, Mass., 1980.)

17. National Advisory Commission on Criminal Justice Standards and Goals, *Police* (Washington, D.C.: U.S. Government Printing Office, 1973), p. 380.

18. "The Police Tapes" (Schiller Park, Ill.: MTI Teleprograms, Inc., 1979).

19. In the specific case presented in "The Police Tapes," however, the negative effects of jail detention on the elderly axe wielder apparently were minimal. In his follow-up interview, the arresting officer responds to the interviewer's query about whether the old woman had "survived" her night in jail that she had done "fine." He then surprises the interviewer and the viewer by explaining that she had a lengthy arrest record, had spent time in jail previously, was not intimidated by jail, and had in fact loudly protested when a matron took away her cane as required by regulations. These revelations invariably produce titters and sighs of relief among first-time viewers of the documentary.

20. State laws usually require that officers bring to court for disposition persons who have committed crimes, regardless of apparent degree of mental instability. Conversely, police may often take into custody apparently mentally ill people who have committed no crime and transport them directly to mental health facilities for observation. See, e.g., New York State Penal Law, § 140; New York State Mental Hygiene Law, § 15.17, 29.19, 31.21, 31.37d, 31.41, 31.43, 31.45.

21. See "Money Collected for 91 year-old Shoplifter, " *Denver Post*, August 27, 1979, p. 6.

22. Dick Cooper, "Officer to Be Fired in Slaying of Old Man," *Philadelphia Inquirer*, July 2, 1980, pp. 1A–2A.

23. Ibid., quoting Philadelphia Police Commissioner Morton Solomon.

24. See Transcript of Proceedings, Coroner's Inquest upon the Body of Charles James, California Coroner's Court (San Francisco), Reg. No. 1117-78, August 9, 1978. In that case, police responded to a false report (given by an apparently hallucinatory woman) that gun-wielding hoodlums were terrorizing people in an apartment building. At 2:10 A.M. police entered the 66-year-old Mr. James's apartment, awoke his sleeping grandson, knocked on Mr. James's bedroom door (which was padlocked from the inside), and confronted Mr. James, who had reportedly armed himself with a shotgun. In the instants that followed, Mr. James—who was clad only in a t-shirt; was grossly obese, arthritic, and "slow-moving"; suffered from poor eyesight, and poor hearing; and had "difficulty moving voluntarily"—reportedly refused to drop his shotgun, and was struck and killed by sixteen shotgun pellets fired through the walls and door of his bedroom. Interestingly, for killing this "shotgun wielding assailant," in his own bedroom, the officers involved were awarded "silver medals of valor" by their department.

Chapter 8

Old Age as a Criminal Defense

Fred Cohen

The Criminal law, with its extensive list of dos and don'ts, is our most awesome vehicle for the official statement of behavioral norms. An accusation of crime puts the alleged perpetrator on a path that may wind through police lockups, jail, and several courts. While on that path, he may be subjected to public humiliation, may have to pay significant fees and expenses, and ultimately, may be condemned and punished.

The substantive criminal law—the dos and don'ts—is surrounded by a body of procedural law, which specifies the means by which accusation may lead to conviction and punishment. This package of substantive and procedural law fits within a larger entity: the criminal justice system. This system—the many arms of which are often criticized for failing to behave as part of an integrated body—comprises various institutions, agencies, and practices. It is a system that is populated by lawyers, judges, psychologists, high school dropouts, Ph.D.'s, and researchers. It serves a client group that ranges from merely accused to finally condemned.

In surveying the scope of this system, or in focusing on one step in the process, it is easy to lose sight of its purpose: to link *responsibility* for voluntary and harm-producing conduct with *punishment.*[1] This is the concept that gives our criminal law its soul and its special legal character. In our legal tradition, punishment must be deserved and may be inflicted only on those who are judged to have had the opportunity and the capacity to make voluntary choices about their behavior.

Our criminal law rests on the posit of free will, on a belief that competent adults when confronted with choices are free to choose rightly or wrongly. It states official norms of conduct and reserves to government the right to punish for violations. It is a "choose rightly or else" system, a system that links the power to punish to the concepts of blameworthiness and responsibility.

It is into this body of law and into this system that the elderly offender must fit, and it is not an easy fit.[2] The image of a shuffling, broken, old woman facing a stern judge evokes a wide range of emotions ranging from pity to dark humor. Anywhere we turn in this criminal justice system—from law enforcement practices, prosecutorial discretion, and sentencing practices to jails and prisons—the elderly offender presents some problems that go to the heart of our existing legal philosophy and enforcement practices.

Nowhere are these problems more conceptually acute than within the world of criminal responsibility. Despite this, the question of the criminal responsibility of the elderly offender has been almost totally ignored in the legal literature. We have an increasingly older population and a corresponding increase in crime by older persons— even crimes of violence (see p. 122)—and yet the legal literature is nearly bare of references to the elderly, and appellate court decisions dealing directly with age and criminal responsibility defy discovery.

Anecdotal material, however, abounds. "AILING WOMAN, 82, SLAYS 1; HAS SHOOTOUT WITH POLICE"[3] "GRANDMOTHER WHO GREW POT TO TREAT ARTHRITIS FOUND GUILTY."[4] Following is the news account of "AGED WOMAN ACQUITTED IN KILLING OF TEEN":

A 72-year-old woman wept when a [Connecticut] Superior Court jury Wednesday found her innocent in the shotgun slaying of a teenager and the wounding of another youth.

The parents of the dead boy also wept.

A jury of three men and three women acquitted [the defendant], who allegedly killed the teenager after a group of taunting youths tossed rocks at her East Haven home.

[The defendant] claimed she had been the target of harassment for two years by neighborhood youths who called her a "witch." She insisted she had acted in self-defense after being terrorized on the night of the incident in 1980.

The defense claimed [she] was "a prisoner in her own home" and was forced to patrol her yard at night and put wire mesh over her windows.

[The] jury foreman . . . said "not guilty" when the charges of first-degree manslaughter and first-degree assault were read off by the clerk.

[The defendant] was escorted from the courthouse by her 46-year-old twin daughters. . . .

The dead boy's parents . . . also cried and later said in a statement they did not understand how the jury had seen fit to acquit the woman.

[The defendant] said she feared for her safety and was acting in self-defense when she fired a shotgun from her home October 21, 1980. . . .

The prosecution said the woman's actions were "excessive" and suggested the youths were shot as they were leaving and the woman was standing in the street rather than on her own property when she fired the shotgun.[5]

Discussions with prosecutors, who ask not to be identified, provide similar anecdotal material as well as a glimpse of prosecutorial discretion in action. Consider this example:

You have this married couple, married for over 50 years, living in a Jewish retirement home. The guy sends the wife out for bagels and while the wife can still get around she forgets and brings back onion rolls. Not a capital offense, right? Anyway, the guy goes beserk and he axes his wife; he kills the poor woman with a Boy Scout—type axe!

What do we do now? Set a high bail? Prosecute? Get a conviction and send the fellow to prison? You tell me! We did nothing. The media dropped it quickly and, I hope, that's it.

Is this an example of Solomonic wisdom? Is it more likely selective enforcement of the law in an invidious fashion? Would the elderly offender have a defense to a charge of murder given these facts, or might a legitimate defense based, perhaps, on some mental impairment have surfaced had formal action been taken? Would this elderly man be competent to stand trial and, if not, what would be done with him?

THE IMPAIRMENTS OF OLD AGE AND CRIMINAL RESPONSIBILITY

What is it about being older that is significant to an inquiry concerning criminal responsibility? Are there certain characteristics associated with aging that are relevant to the legal question of criminal responsibility?

According to some experts,

> It is well established that the brain undergoes considerable alterations during senescence. The structural changes include a loss of neurons and other tissue, and an increase in the number of senile plaques and in the amount of neurofibrillary degeneration.
>
> Functionally, there is a reduction in the metabolic activity of the brain tissue involved. Some of these changes are probably associated with chronological aging; others are due to pathological processes in the brain or elsewhere in the body.[6]

If aging is defined as a change in living *systems*, some of which is normal and some of which may be pathological due to the passage of time, then it is also likely that the alterations experienced during aging are not limited to the brain. Indeed, such changes can be divided into the separate categories of antatomical, biochemical physiological, and behavioral. Within the last category, researchers describe the changes as alterations in sensory motive capacities, in mental function and capacity, and in drives, personality, and social rules.[7] The last category may not be of the same conceptual level as the first three, in that these behavioral alterations may well be an outgrowth of either anatomical, biochemical or physiological dysfunction. However that may be, the behavioral category is of most immediate relevance to our inquiry into criminal responsibility.

Inherent in sketching this broad picture is the risk of negative stereotyping, which in turn may lead to destructive policies. There appears to be broad agreement that

> Individuals vary enormously at any given age in respect to almost all human characteristics. In the case of the characteristics studied here, the variation increases as the age of people studied increases. Indeed this has been the finding in most works on the aging, and makes any generalizations about "the aged" very unsound. Chronological age is thus a very poor guide to the state of a man's . . . mental alertness.[8]

This variability in the capacity and functioning of those who are of the same chronological age will prove to be a central point in the further development of the criminal responsibility question. Thus, functional variability, standing alone, presents a powerful case against the creation of legal presumptions based only on age. On the other hand, the older the person, the greater the possibility that he has some impairment relevant to law. For example, if we are dealing with a 75-year-old man accused of attempted armed robbery, it would be reasonable to inquire into the possibility of the defendant's behavioral infirmities and their source. Given the same facts, it is unlikely that we would find the need to similarly inquire about the behavioral infirmities of, say, a 30-year-old.

Indeed, the case can be made that the older the accused, the stronger the concern about functional impairment. From the perspective of defense counsel representing an elderly client, the client's advanced years should serve as a basis for further inquiry and research. It is neither necessary nor desirable to create any presumptions of incapacity or impairment. But it is also unwise to blink at reality and ignore the increased possibilities of legally relevant impairment.

With age may come wisdom but certainly not an improvement or strengthening of one's physical and mental faculties. The aging-deterioration process may be normal or pathological, slow or fast, early or delayed, but it is inevitable. Thus, the variable but inevitable deterioration of some functioning—and especially those losses that may effect cognitive and volitional capacity and control—is of vital importance to criminal responsibility.[9]

An increasing number of arrests of older persons and attention by the media to elderly offenders are probably the immediate stimuli for the present flurry of attention. However, there can be no argument that the characteristics of normal or pathological aging (and how they bear on cognitive and volitional activity) are associated in a major way with basic notions of criminal responsibility.

Legal Alternatives for the Elderly Offender

Having established, if only in a stipulative fashion, that the elderly offender may well suffer from functional impairments relevant to criminal responsibility, we may now ask—should the criminal law provide some special doctrinal or procedural treatment for the elderly offender? If so, what? To address these very fundamental questions, a number of alternatives will be presented in heuristic fashion and thereafter in argumentative fashion. Finally, a preferred position will be suggested.

Aggravated Culpability. The first alternative might be to view the older offender as *more* culpable than younger offenders. In support of this position is the rationale that with age and experience there should be a concomitant increase in responsibility.[10] Older persons have, or should have, a greater ability and, indeed, a heightened desire to avoid criminal conduct. According to this view, when older people are involved in criminal activities they should be subjected to even more severe sanctions than their more youthful counterparts, although clearly they should not be convicted where younger persons would not be.

This position speaks less to criminal responsibility than it does to penal policy at the sentencing and correction stage. There are implications for criminal responsibility, however, in that this alternative denies to the elderly offender any defense or amelioration based solely on chronological age and would work to enhance sentences relying on the principles of "you should have known better."

Diminished Responsibility. Another alternative, resting on a very different premise, would be an argument for leniency, rather than a total exemption from criminal responsibility. In more traditional legal terms, this would be an argument for either diminished or partial responsibility. [11]

This rationale rests on at least a partial or tentative acceptance of a subjective theory of criminal responsibility, a theory that is willing to accept cautiously evidence of some individual infirmities even though such evidence falls short of the total lack of responsibility offered by the insanity defense. Why, it might be asked, should the elderly defendant's functional impairments serve to ameliorate responsibility while others who are similarly impaired are not similarly treated? For example, claims on the behalf of the drug addict and the chronic alcoholic, who are functionally impaired, have met with little or no success.

Perhaps the best answer is that the elderly defendant, when compared to the narcotic addict or the drunk, has a stronger moral and factual claim to a reduction in culpability. [12] The defendant's elderly status the argument would go, was achieved by nothing more than the passage of time and some happy combination of nature and nurture. Thus, the elderly defendant's claim to partial responsibility is not clouded by chronic drinking or narcotics use. While it may be argued that some alcoholics or addicts are predisposed to their status, or even born to it, the proof is by no means clear. However, even if the predisposition theory explains some alcoholism and addiction, this does not weaken the case for the elderly defendant but simply may provide arguments for expansion of the defense.

This approach would provide a doctrinal basis for the reduced responsibility of an elderly defendant. More specifically, it would operate to reduce what might be first-degree murder to manslaughter.

The elderly defendant would be permitted to show that by virtue of his age and consequent changes in his physical and psychological makeup he lacked "the equipment to deal reasonably with life's stresses."[13] If the homicide involves killing in the heat of passion and a claim of provocation, then the special characteristics of the elderly defendant, especially as they may bear on his perception and reaction to threats, would be the measure of the reasonableness of his action rather than the objective standard of the hypothetical "reasonable man."[14]

In the case of the 72-year-old Connecticut woman who shot the teenagers, age would seem to be an important factor in explaining why the woman had such a violent reaction to the provocation of the teenagers, who apparently had taunted her unmercifully over a period of time. According to the approach discussed here, she would have been guilty of manslaughter. Her attorneys went further, however, and were successful with a traditional defense of self-defense.

To invoke self-defense as an excuse for a killing, the actor must reasonably believe that he is in immediate danger of serious bodily harm and that the force used is necessary to repel this danger. Given the facts in the Connecticut case, the key problem would be the extent to which the elderly woman's age and the prior harassment by the youths caused her to reasonably believe that she was in a life-threatening situation. A purely objective approach to this question would limit consideration of the defendant's age and ask only if a "reasonable man" would have perceived a life-threatening situation and then reacted with the use of deadly force.[15]

Incapacity: No Responsibility. A third alternative, one that may appear to be as dubious as the first, is to provide that above a certain age there should be a total exemption from criminal responsibility and, along with this, a rebuttable presumption of irresponsibility between certain advanced ages.

Those familiar with the law's earlier legal treatment of juvenile offenders will recognize the inversion. As early as the fourteenth century, infants under the age of 7 were deemed to be without criminal capacity. In modern parlance this means an irrebuttable presumption of a lack of criminal responsibility. Infants between the ages of 7 and 14 also were presumed to be without criminal capacity, but this presumption might be rebutted by proof that the youthful accused had a knowledge of good and evil.[16]

Professor Derk Bodde's study of Chinese law during the Ch'ing dynasty (1644–1911) reveals an adherence to a principle of legalized inequality according to age.[17] The Chinese law arranged age and youth into three levels, or grades, for the purposes of ameliorative legal treatment:

	Aged	Youth
1st degree	70–79	11–15
2nd degree	80–89	8–10
3rd degree	90+	7 and below

As the chart suggests, the higher the degree, the greater the amount of privilege or exemption. The three degrees for the young offender, of course, correspond closely to the early Anglo-American legal position.[18] Our formal law, however, has nothing remotely comparable to the Chinese law with regard to the aged offender.

Thus, the third alternative would rest on a principle of total exemption based on age with one age group (80+ ?) needing to prove nothing but age and another (65–79?) presumptively irresponsible, but subject to the prosecutor's proof of culpability.

Age Neutrality. A fourth possible option might be characterized as age neutrality. More fully stated, in this position the criminal responsibility of the older or elderly offender would be dealt with on the same basis as any other adult accused of crime. Thus, age per se would not be a defense to a criminal charge.

While ruling out age per se as an exculpatory or even a mitigating factor, this option need not foreclose the allowance of evidence of the functional impairments commonly associated with old age. For example, cerebral atherosclerosis and senile dementia, the two most common mental afflictions of the population over age 65, involve symptoms (although not invariably so) that are directly relevant to criminal responsibility.[19] The atherosclerotic may suffer memory disturbance; disorientation, at first in time and place and then as to person; and impaired intellectual functions, including comprehension, problem solving, learning, and judgment.[20]

The general symptoms of senile dementia—again with wide variations possible,—are impairment of orientation; memory; all intellectual functions such as comprehension, calculation, knowledge, and learning; judgment; and lability and shallowness of affect.[21] Given the right symptom, or combination of symptoms, an elderly defendant might be able to negate the particular mental element required for the offense charged, establish the arcane defense of automatism, or be eligible for an insanity defense.[22]

EOs and OPINS: Benevolence and Prediction. The final option to be mentioned is somewhat different from the others. Some may argue that the elderly offender should not be subjected to the same procedures and institutional arrangements as other offenders. Their needs are different, and the objectives of the law necessarily are different—thus, as a matter of benevolence and wise policy, we should create a special court for the elderly, a Geriatric Court.

Such a court would assure an elderly accused of due process prior to any adjudication as an Elderly Offender (EO) and have available a number of dispositional options designed especially for older people. Taking a further cue from the juvenile court system, it may be desirable to invent a noncriminal category for the elderly person who appears to need help not otherwise or as easily available or who may be diagnosed as a pre-Elderly Offender. This new category might be termed Older Persons in Need of Supervision (OPINS).

What kinds of behavior might be subject to an OPINS petition? Without attempting to be exhaustive, one possibility is the noncriminal category of "wandering about."[23] Other possibilities include the more general categories of placing oneself in situations dangerous to life and limb, failing to maintain minimal dietary and personal hygiene practices and thereby causing a danger to oneself, and attempting to engage in shoplifting.[24]

The manifest objectives of an OPINS category would be protective and preventive: to deal with the struggling older person in a way that is physically, psychologically, and socially protective while striving also to cut short either further harm to the person or to the rights of others. The creation of this special tribunal and the OPINS category could entirely displace guardianship proceedings, euphemistically called protective services, which often "[deprive] the elderly of their personal autonomy, and often of their dignity, integrity, and self-esteem as well."[25]

Guardianship proceedings are designed primarily to protect the person or property of an individual when that individual is unable to care for himself or is incapable of managing his affairs. While we may properly be critical of the lack of due process and the excessive paternalism, few will deny that some elderly people need help managing their affairs and/or their persons. The question remains, however, whether a special tribunal along with an obviously paternalistic and vague new category such as OPINS is the direction to take.

THE SEARCH FOR POLICY

In arraying policy alternatives and then eventually selecting from among them, the first task should be to clarify what it is that one seeks to accomplish. And, to do that, one must identify what problem or problems stimulate the inquiry. Thus, the articulation of underlying problems and the statement of objectives go hand-in-hand as part of the threshhold inquiry.

The initial problem is that while the number of elderly people arrested for Index offenses—generally, felony offenses—is relatively minor, it has increased steadily over time.[26] Arrests for Index crimes as a proportion of total arrests have risen steadily since 1964. Shichor and Kobrin report that during the eleven-year period from 1964 through 1974, there was an overall 43-percent increase for all age groups while arrests of the 55-and-over population increased by 224 percent.[27] What is especially surprising is that the older offender group shows a more prominent pattern of crimes of violence than either the total arrested group or the youth group. Aggravated assault constitutes 80 percent of the total arrests for crimes of violence among the 55-and-over group.

As we might expect in the offenses against property—that is, burglary, auto theft, and larceny (theft)—larceny is by far the most common offense, constituting over 91 percent of such arrests in 1974, a total of 17,760 such arrests.[28]

The point, of course, is that we now have a crime problem of increasing magnitude and, with an older population that is multiplying, a problem that promises to continue to grow.[29] True, it may be that the data are incomplete or misleading; older persons may not actually be engaged in more criminal activity but simply may be

Table 8.1. Arrests by Offense Charged and Age, United States, 1979

Offense	Age of Offender		
	55–59	60–64	65+
Murder/non-negligent manslaughter	379	225	304
Forcible rape	214	125	130
Robbery	359	137	157
Aggravated assault	4,231	2,307	2,389
Total violent crimes	5,183	2,794	2,980
Percent of total arrests	1.2%	0.6%	0.7%

Source: Timothy J. Flanagan, David J. van Alstyne, and Michael R. Gottfredson (eds.), *Sourcebook of Criminal Justice Statistics—1981,* U.S. Department of Justice, Bureau of Justice Statistics (Washington, D.C.: U.S. Government Printing Office, 1982), p. 342 (Table 4.4).

arrested more often, or we may be seeing the results of improved reporting.

Real or artifact need not be resolved here. We can show some very real arrest numbers—almost 9,000 for crimes of violence in 1979 (see Table 8.1)—and those numbers, combined with the almost total absence of any considered legal policy on point, strongly suggest that there is indeed an elderly crime problem. It is a problem that has not been addressed by those who shape the law; to do so in advance of possible crisis clearly makes very good sense.

Many elderly people do suffer from age-related infirmities and suffer in such a way that their functional impairment often is relevant to our basic notions of criminal responsibility, which in turn trigger deeply held feelings about the propriety of inflicting punishment. The functional impairments commonly associated with senile dementia and arteriosclerosis mentioned earlier are pertinent examples. That these impairments appear with sufficient regularity in a significant number of people in a single category—that is, the elderly— would itself be an adequate basis for launching an inquiry of the sort undertaken here.

Thus, in addition to an increase in the reported crimes by older people, there is a constellation of functional impairments frequently associated with these older offenders that legitimately gives rise to an inquiry and a search for policy concerning criminal responsibility. No particular answer is thereby dictated, only the need to inquire.

The very silence that envelops this area is itself an aspect of the underlying problems. A survey of the leading texts and casebooks in criminal law uncovered only a single reference to the elderly or aged offender.[30] Similarly, appellate decisions and penal codes are silent when it comes to the criminal responsibility of the elderly offender.

The legal periodical literature is similarly barren. Robinson recently published one of the most comprehensive and thoughtful articles on criminal law defenses, and nowhere in the ninety-two pages does he mention the elderly offender.[31] In *Crime and Gerontology*, Malinchak includes a chapter entitled "The Elderly as Criminals."[32] The chapter, though, is simply a review of competing criminological theories that attempt to explain the causes of crimes committed by the elderly. Malinchak makes no effort even to speculate about competing theories of criminal responsibility.

Age: Condition or Excuse?

In addressing the basic question of the criminal responsibility of the aged offender, a threshhold problem is whether to view the category of aged as a condition or to deal with it as an aspect of excuses. This is a fundamental conceptual and practical problem.[33]

As a condition, age would parallel the legal treatment afforded the very young. That is, at a certain age all people within that category would be exempt from criminal responsibility. As noted earlier under "Incapacity" (p. 119), the only proof necessary for such a defense would be proof of age.

Analyzing age, or the dysfunctional conditions associated with age, as an excuse is a bit more difficult, but doing so may open the way to a somewhat more satisfactory policy solution. Any excuse in the criminal law initially concedes that the act in question was unlawful but challenges whether the actor is accountable.[34] Insanity, involuntary intoxication, duress and necessity, and mistakes in perception and mistakes about the law are representative of widely, although not uniformly, recognized excuses in criminal law.

It is not easy to uncover and present a unified theory of excuses, a unifying thread for all excuses that would allow exploration of the elderly offender to follow a clearly marked path. To illustrate the dilemma, let us briefly contrast the insanity defense with duress and coercion and then add a note about self-defense, treated here as a justification.

The insanity defense focuses on the defendant's mental condition at the time of the harm-causing event. Depending on the precise language of the test used for the insanity defense, the focus may be on the defendant's cognitive, emotional, and volitional impairment and control. Today the most popular test for insanity[35] is the formulation by the American Law Institute in the Model Penal Code:

Section 4.01. Mental Disease or Defect Excluding Responsibility

(1) A person is not responsible for criminal conduct if at the time of such conduct as a result of mental disease or defect he lacks substantial capacity either to appreciate the criminality [wrongfulness] of his conduct or to conform his conduct to the requirements of law.

(2) As used [here] the terms "mental disease or defect" do not include an abnormality manifested only by repeated criminal or otherwise antisocial conduct.[36]

The insanity test operates as an excuse to a criminal charge when the mental disease or defect is found to have seriously impaired the defendant's ability to think properly or to control his behavior.[37] The underlying excusing condition—the mental disease or defect—resides within the actor.[38]

Duress and necessity are also defenses that generally are categorized as excuses. Where the insanity defense grows out of an *internal* impairment, duress and necessity are defenses that focus on the compulsion of an *external* force. The defense of duress exists when one person unlawfully threatens another with death or serious bodily injury unless the person threatened engages in conduct proscribed by the criminal law.[39]

A person may succumb to the pressure of natural physical forces and in that emergency engage in conduct in violation of the literal terms of the criminal law. Necessity is the "choice of evils" defense, in that a person may be forced to choose between serious harm to his person or causing damage to the property of another. In that situation, the law will allow an action to preserve life and limb over damage to property. The pressure in this example is external and from a nonhuman source, such as a storm or privation. With duress the pressure is external but the source is human.[40]

To round out the picture, let us take a brief glimpse at the defense of self-defense. When this defense is available, a person who is not initially an aggressor, and who is under physical attack from another, may resort to the defensive use of physical force that is proportionate to the actual, or reasonably perceived, force initiated by the aggressor.[41]

There is much debate and disagreement about the precise meaning as well as the scope and application of the defenses discussed above. In my view, the defenses of coercion, necessity, and self-defense—which are traditionally characterized as "justification" and not "excuse"[42]—represent the criminal law's effort to articulate principles of defense where the harm-producing conduct falls within the range of acceptable (normal, if you will) behavior. Another way to put this is that these are defenses that recognize the harmful behavior as a normal and thus tolerable response to an abnormal situation.

Indeed, implicit within these defenses seems to be the view that when confronted with similar pressure, many—perhaps most—other people in the position of the actor (indeed, the actor himself) would behave similarly. This being the case, none of the traditionally recognized objectives of the criminal law would be served by a conviction and the infliction of punishment.[43] Deterrence, either general or specific, would be particularly inappropriate since the criminal law expects, without necessarily inviting or welcoming, similar behavior from others in similar circumstances.

Criminal Defenses: Subjective Versus Objective

Let us now look a bit more closely at the defense of coercion (or duress) and begin with the (partial) text of the Model Penal Code:

(1) It is an affirmative defense that the actor engaged in the conduct charged to constitute an offense because he was coerced to do so by the use of, or a threat to use, unlawful force against his person or the person of another, which a person of reasonable firmness in his situation would have been unable to resist.[44]

The crucial part of this definition is the reference to "a person of reasonable firmness." Should the law include any special characteristics of the elderly person as they might bear on that person's perception of the threat and the choices available to deal with the perceived threat? This question, in turn, goes to the heart of a perennial problem in criminal law: whether to apply an objective or a subjective standard in determining culpability. Recognizing an older person's greater susceptibility to fear from physical threats, for example, pushes in the direction of a subjective approach. If the fear must be "reasonable," and if reasonableness is a category excluding any special attributes of being older, then the elderly person's defense is in jeopardy.

The subjective-versus-objective test debate was introduced earlier and has been well rehearsed in the area of provocation. Provocation arises as a defensive matter in homicide cases when the accused claims to have acted "in the heat of passion" under circumstances where a complete defense would not exist but where the loss of control is such that what might otherwise be murder may be reduced to manslaughter.[45]

Provocation alone is not sufficient. The provocation must be adequate. This norm, in turn, often is decided on the basis of the objective "reasonable man" standard.[46] The danger here, as Fletcher rightly points out, is "that abnormal personal characteristics of the defendant will not be taken into consideration in assessing whether, as to him, the provocation was inadequate."[47]

The problem at the other extreme is that if the test for the adequacy of provocation is entirely subjective, then any person who is in fact provoked, for any reason, fits the test. We need not fall into the trap of ignoring all special personal characteristics or recognizing any claim of provocation as legitimate. There is a difference between reactions traceable to a head injury and a quick temper, between executing a promiscuous relative and being enraged at the sight of one's spouse copulating with another person, between an older person driven to violence after repeated threats and a young person who shoots a child crossing her lawn for the first time. Legal doctrine need not become trapped in these specious all-or-nothing binds, and it need not be driven from its moral underpinnings in search of some abstract doctrinal symmetry.

Selecting Among Alternatives

By now, it should be clear that in the development of the legal responsibility of the elderly I am inclined toward some version of the fourth option set out earlier: age neutrality. Anything resembling total exemption or irresponsibility based on age alone fits snugly into what Kalish describes as the new Ageism: "It stereotypes the elderly in terms of the characteristics of the least capable, least healthy, and least alert of the elderly."[48] Legal doctrine built on a generalized picture of the over-65 age group as sick, dependent, needy, and not competent would not comport with the facts and would needlessly contribute to this negative stereotyping.

If this is true of an approach providing for exemptions due to age, it is *a fortiori* so for the final option discussed somewhat tongue-in-cheek earlier—the creation of a Geriatric Court and the categories of Elderly Offender and OPINS. Any such court and special legal category, either the EO or the OPINS, clearly would trace its ancestry to the unhappy experience with the juvenile court. After reciting the long list of failures in juvenile justice, the historian David Rothman inquires, "So lengthy and unrelieved a recitation of the inadequacies of the administration of juvenile justice, so unambiguous a failure on the part of the juvenile court and the juvenile institutions to approximate the designs outlined in their rhetoric or to protect their charges from injury, raises the two recurring and troubling questions: why did such dismal conditions come to exist, and why did they continue to exist?"[49]

In the infancy of our legal concern for the elderly offender, we can extrapolate from Rothman's questions about a system-in-being and ask "why" in advance of spawning a new bureaucracy, new institutions and procedures, and new experts. Institutions and experts, once in place, have a remarkable penchant for remaining in place and using the fact of existence as the strongest argument for their own survival.

A representative checklist of the possible reasons for the failure of the juvenile justice system would include the performance of legislatures that never provided budgets to match the high-blown rhetoric of the child-savers movement. A lack of knowledge concerning the causes and control of delinquent behavior is another important factor in the failure of the juvenile justice system. This factor suggests that larger budgets would have contributed to a more expensive failure. Where theory pointed to causes of delinquency as a part of the socioeconomic fabric, it was clear that ultimate solutions lay outside the jurisdiction of the juvenile system, a system that at best could apply only palliatives. The juvenile justice system was built on the flawed vision of superimposing a medical model over a model based on fault or individual blame, and it could never reconcile the incompatability between coerced custody and treatment or that between the role of keeper and that of helper.

Do we know more about the "elderly delinquent" than about the juvenile offender? Do we have a clear vision of how to treat or rehabilitate? Are legislatures going to open the purse strings for the elderly where they would not for the young? Can we reconcile keeper and kept roles for the older person where we could not for the younger? Would we not, in fact, face the prospect of yet another liberal reform gone awry, constructed on a flawed and destructive incompetence model; of increasing the stigma associated with age through the invention of such new terms as OPINS; and, ultimately, of enlarging the number of people under the control of the state?[50]

A less cynical approach would frame questions on the premise that we can learn from the disasters of the juvenile system and use the Geriatric Court as a second chance. For example, the benefits of the procedural informality model could be preserved within a due process model without insisting on procedural parity with the criminal court.

Punishment and blame would have to give way to rehabilitation, which would form the core of the Geriatric Court system. Rehabilitation for the elderly must have highly specific, attainable, and measurable objectives. The Geriatric Court system would not tolerate the rhetorical and programmatic hoaxes of the juvenile justice system.

Rehabilitation of a 65-year-old, first-time shoplifter need not be aimed at preparing him for a long life of further education and industry. Just as rehabilitative objectives for the elderly may vary from those for the younger person, so must our notions of time. In a punitive system, the question would be whether a one-year sentence for an 80-year-old offender is actually a death sentence. If it is, might it be in violation of the cruel and unusual punishment of the Eighth Amendment as wholly disproportionate to the underlying offense? Aside from cruel and unusual punishment, there might be a question of equal protection, in that 70-year-old and 60-year-old offenders would have to receive correspondingly longer terms than the 80-year-old in order to equate the likelihood of death in prison with the age of the offender.

As troublesome as these questions may be for a punitive system, they can be avoided in a rehabilitative system. Since rehabilitation necessarily relates to achieving some desired change in the individual, and since one cannot know in advance when such change will occur, the dispositional structure must remain open-ended. Release from custody or confinement would be based on the achievement of some rehabilitative objective and not on any relationship between the seriousness of the offense and the amount of deserved punishment.

The questions posed earlier, of course, remain. In order to help, one must have some understanding of causation; once identified, the cause must be one that a justice system can address. If the "problem" is the way in which our society generally values the elderly, or the manner in which scarce resources for survival are allocated, then the limits of the justice system are clear.

Earlier it was noted that the insanity defense is one of the criminal law's recognized, however controversial, excuses. Every test to determine insanity rests on the defendant's having a mental disease or defect that almost certainly must be one of the major psychoses. This is not because the law formally requires that an accused have been psychotic at the time of the conduct in question. Rather, it is a practical or tactical requirement in connecting the defendant's mental impairment with the impaired functioning argued to be the cause of the harm-producing conduct.[51]

There is no doubt that some elderly offenders might present a successful insanity defense. The post-verdict consequences, however, make this defense especially troublesome for the elderly person. Following an acquittal by reason of insanity, it is virtually certain that the defendant will be civilly committed to and lodged in a mental hospital.[52] Thus, with an insanity defense the post-verdict choice is rarely freedom versus confinement; rather, it is a matter of the place of confinement. Should the place be a mental hospital, the term is indefinite and for an older person the effects may be devastating.

In the case of other defenses, the successful defendant typically is free of any restraint or coercion. There is, of course, a certain anomaly to committing an acquitted defendant whose mental disorder continues to exist and not even inquiring about commitability where an acquitted defendant's physical condition is the underlying basis for a successful defense.

Hawaii, drawing primarily on some obscure British cases, has a unique statutory arrangement in this regard. The state includes "*physical* or mental disease, disorder, or defect" in its statutory definition of insanity, which otherwise tracks the Model Penal Code's version.[53] The Commentary to the Hawaii Penal Code leaves no doubt that one major objective in the inclusion of physical disease or defect was to provide a basis for equality in commitment.

> The rationale for providing for acquittal conditioned on commitment (or 'hospitalization') in cases involving 'mental' disease, disorder, or defect ('insanity') is that commitment is necessary to protect other members of society (and the acquitted defendant) from the consequences of repetition of the prohibited conduct. The rationale is no less applicable or persuasive in cases of 'physical' conditions resulting in involuntary movements which threaten harm to others. These people too may present a public health or safety problem, calling for therapy or even for custodial commitment.... While it is true that mandatory commitment bears harshly on a person whose physical condition (or symptom thereof) may be non-recurrent—although the frequency of the latter instance may be less than that of the former.
>
> The answer does not lie in the black-and-white distinction posed by present law: an excusing mental condition means commitment; an excusing physical condition means an unqualified acquittal. The answer lies, as the Code suggests in later sections, in tailoring the disposition of a defendant, acquitted on the basis of disease, disorder, or defect, to the condition of the defendant and to the needs of society. Commitment need not be mandatory because the defendant's disease, defect, or disorder is labelled 'mental,' nor should it be precluded because his excusing condition is labelled 'physical.'[54]

The Hawaii approach poses significant problems for the elderly offender who might seek to avoid the post-acquittal consequences of an insanity verdict but who also seeks a finding of a lack of responsibility. The British case of Regina v. Kemp[55] illustrates the problem.

The defendant struck his wife with a hammer and in defense pleaded the excuse of automatism arising out of his arteriosclerotic condition. The medical testimony was in conflict over whether this condition should be characterized as physical or mental. The court ultimately determined that the accused did indeed suffer from a disease of the mind within the intendment of the British rule of insanity.

The broad submission that was made to me on behalf of the accused was that this is a physical disease and not a mental disease; arteriosclerosis is a physical condition primarily and not a mental condition. But that argument does not go so far as to suggest that for the purpose of the law diseases that affect the mind can be divided into those that are physical in origin and those that are mental in origin. There is such a distinction medically. I think it is recognized by medical men that there are mental diseases which have an organic cause, there are disturbances of the mind which can be traced to some hardening of the arteries, to some degeneration of the brain cells or to some physical condition which accounts for mental derangement. It is also recognized that there are diseases functional in origin where it is not possible to point to any physical cause but simply to say that there has been a derangement of the functioning of the mind, such as melancholia, schizophrenia and many other of those diseases which are usually handled by psychiatrists. This medical distinction is not pressed as part of the argument for the accused in this case, and I think rightly. The distinction between the two categories is quite irrelevant for the purposes of the law, which is not concerned with the origin of the disease or the cause of it but simply with the mental condition which has brought about the act. It does not matter, for the purposes of the law, whether the defect of reason is due to a degeneration of the brain or to some other form of mental derangement. That may be a matter of importance medically, but it is of no importance to the law, which merely has to consider the state of mind in which the accused is, not how he got there.

Hardening of the arteries is a disease which is shown on the evidence to be capable of affecting the mind in such a way as to cause a defect, temporarily or permanently, of its reasoning, understanding and so on, and so is in my judgment a disease of the mind which comes within the meaning of the [M'Naghten] Rules. I shall therefore direct the jury that it matters not whether they accept the evidence of [certain testifying doctors], but that on the whole of the medical evidence they ought to find that there is a disease of the mind within the meaning of the [M'Naghten] Rule.[56]

It is especially interesting to note that although the defendant was seeking a full acquittal based on the defense of automatism, the court instructed a verdict of insanity.

As Fox puts it,

whether the early common law decisions provide a basis for granting an outright acquittal, rather than an acquittal by reason of insanity when consciousness is lacking (and I would add, or impaired), becomes a crucial question in the presence of practically universal authority to commit to an institution those acquitted on grounds of insanity. It has, in fact, been suggested that one of the major reasons for recent developments on this subject has been the desire of defendants both to rely on abnormal mental conditions for exculpation and, at the same time, to avoid the consequences of being adjudged insane.[57]

Although it is not a defense, note should be taken of incompetence to be tried as it may relate to the elderly offender. The first point to note is that incompetence to be tried is not a defense to a criminal charge. Rather, it is a delaying device resting on the due process notion that it violates fundamental notions of fairness to subject a person to trial[58] when that person is unable to assist counsel properly or to understand the charges brought against him.[59]

There evidently are no data that provide an age breakdown on the number of older defendants who are found to be incompetent to stand trial. On the one hand, the concept of incompetence seems ready made for some elderly offenders: those who are disoriented, uncommunicative, or amnesiac.[60] On the other hand, competence to be tried does not become an issue in a criminal case until after arraignment and a formal charge.

It is probable that the obviously disoriented, elderly offender is diverted out of the criminal justice system before competence need be formally considered and decided. This can be only a hunch, although it is shared by some experts familiar with both the criminal justice and the mental health systems and is one of the many unknowns in the processing of elderly offenders.

Prior to 1972, a defendant who was found to be incompetent to be tried was not faced with many happy prospects. Such a defendant typically would be committed to a state mental hospital until "restored to reason," "competent," or "sane," depending on the jurisdiction's statutory language.[61] The issue of competence, or triability, could be raised by defense counsel, the judge, or the prosecutor. Thus, it could, and often did, happen that a person merely accused of crime, on suggestion of the prosecutor, was found incompetent to be tried and then subjected to what might amount to a commitment for life.[62]

In 1972, the Supreme Court of the United States decided Jackson v. Indiana,[63] a landmark case in this area and one that has changed some of the more egregious practices of the past. Theon Jackson is described as a mentally defective deaf mute with the mental level of a preschool child. He could not read, write, or otherwise communicate except through limited use of sign language. The prognosis for the defendant's future was extremely poor. Accused of two separate purse-snatchings involving a total loss of nine dollars, Jackson was found to be incompetent and committed until sane. In the Supreme Court, Jackson's lawyers successfully argued that this was tantamount to a "life sentence" based only on the accusation of crime. Justice Harry A. Blackmun wrote,

> We hold, consequently, that a person charged by a State with a criminal offense who is committed solely on account of his incapacity to proceed to trial cannot be held more than the reasonable period of time necessary to determine whether there is a substantial probability that he will attain that capacity in the foreseeable future. If it is determined that this is not the case, then the State must either institute the customary civil commitment proceedings that would be required to commit any other citizen or release the defendant. Furthermore, even if it is determined that the defendant probably soon will be able to stand trial, his continued commitment must be justified by progress toward that goal.[64]

Jackson thus created a constitutionally mandated two-stage proceeding offering substantial safeguards against prolonged confinement based only on incompetence to be tried.

A review of patients in facilities operated by the New York State Department of Mental Hygiene from 1977 through October 1982 reveals that elderly offenders are *not* being subjected to incompetence proceedings. In the 65-and-over category, patients classified as within forensic services—and that would include "incompetent to be tried" and "not guilty by reason of insanity"—in 1977, totaled eight; in 1978, seven; in 1979, ten; in 1980, eight; in 1981, fourteen; and in 1982 (partial), thirty-seven.[65] Whether as a result of *Jackson* or not, it is clear that incompetence to be tried as a disposition for elderly offenders is of no consequence in New York state.

However, another hypothesis involving the use of the mental health system may account for some older offenders. In New York a person accused of crime is not categorized as a forensic services case unless the case proceeds beyond arraignment.[66] Thus, if a police officer or a prosecutor encountered a severely disoriented elderly person accused of crime, and if early diversion was thought desirable, then a straightforward civil commitment could be sought.[67] Existing records in New York do not reflect the referral source, so it is not possible to do more than speculate at this point.[68]

To reiterate a point implied earlier, issues relating to competence to be tried, civil commitment, and the use of law enforcement or prosecutorial discretion obviously are vital to an understanding of how the elderly offender is actually treated.[69] As vital as these legal and administrative matters are, they are not central to an exploration of the doctrinal basis in criminal law for possible defenses related directly to age or to the functional impairments associated with conditions common to older people. Independent of our doctrinal concerns is a basic need to know how the elderly offender is processed. This calls for empirically oriented studies that are both descriptive and analytic.

It is commonly believed—and absent the studies proposed here, that belief is all one can go on—that the system simply buries these offenders, often hiding them from formal processing in the belief that this is an act of charity or mercy. I am not certain that I entirely disagree with this posture. However, we have to ask how long our study-and-assessment-oriented society will allow the gatekeepers of a system to make and enforce policy without scrutiny. Not long, I believe. Thus, even at the risk of upsetting some delicate social arrangements rooted in feelings of forgiveness, the need for formal exposure probably will, and should, win out.

At the doctrinal level, the problems are very difficult but less dependent on data then the questions of administration. While our law presently recognizes nothing that is identical to a defense of old age per se, we do have the analogies of the incapacity of the very young and the excuses associated with loss of, or the impairment of, consciousness. As noted earlier, age per se as a defense is not, in my view, a very desirable option.

This is *not* to say that a decent argument could not be made for a conclusive presumption of a lack of capacity above a certain advanced age. Rather, it is to say that the price may be too great for elderly people who seek to retain autonomy and responsibility during their final years. Little, if anything, is lost by taking another route, a route that focuses on the specific functional impairment that may be associated with a physical or mental condition suffered by the elderly accused. Such an approach, where successful, does lead to full exculpation and avoids the virtually automatic commitment that follows an acquittal by reason of insanity. Where such an approach cannot be taken, the consequence is that criminal responsibility with age will possibly serve as a mitigating factor at sentencing.

Efforts to create a special offender category or special benevolent court for the elderly offender would appear to be particularly dangerous to the publicly held concept of older persons and to self-image, and dangerous because of the risks of creating another treatment-rehabilitation establishment.

Let me make clear that my criticism of treatment-rehabilitation is not directed at efforts to treat and comfort elderly offenders. The critique is aimed at a system whose architecture and structure might be based on deprivations of liberty to achieve benevolent objectives. The criminal law system is, and should remain, a system constructed on the free-will posit and one that distributes punishment based on competent individuals being found culpable for their harm-producing voluntary conduct.

The very concept of a welfare or medical model simply is incompatible with our criminal law. The more equitable distribution of capital and medical care, of course, is perfectly sound and highly desirable in a humane and democratic society. Just as the determination that a juvenile is delinquent is the wrong time to decide that what he really needs is to learn to read, so the commission of a crime—be it a homicide or a relatively innocuous act such as shoplifting—by an elderly person is the wrong occasion to wring our hands about our neglected elderly.

NOTES

1. See Fred Cohen, *The Law of Deprivation of Liberty: A Study in Social Control* (St. Paul, Minn.: West Publishing Company, 1980), pp. 64–69.
2. References to the elderly or aged offender are meant to encompass those persons aged 65 or over. The arrest data referred to later include people aged 55 or over.
3. *Albany Times-Union*, July 20, 1982, p. 32.
4. *Schenectady Gazette*, August 25, 1982, p. 3.
5. *Schenectady Gazette*, September 30, 1982, p. 3. An extended quotation is presented because this tragic event raises some basic doctrinal questions of criminal responsibility and will be referred to later in the chapter.
6. Ewald Busse and Eric Pfeiffer, *Behavior and Adaptation in Late Life* (Boston: Little, Brown, 1969), p. 268.
7. J. Brooke Acker, Arthur C. Walsh, and James R. Beam, *Mental Capacity: Medical and Legal Aspects of the Aging* (Colorado Springs, Colo.: Shepards/McGraw-Hill, Supplement, 1981).
8. Alastair Heron and Sheila M. Chown, *Age and Function* (Boston: Little, Brown, 1967), p. 67.
9. The older a person is, the more likely that person is to disintegrate in the face of change and the more vulnerable he is to disorientation. Interview with Sheldon Tobin, Ph.D., Director of the Ringel Institute, State University of New York at Albany, Nov. 5, 1982.
10. Talcott Parsons has written, "If a society is able to conserve its 'moral capital' (if not, through wise management, even to increase it) why should this not be possible for the individual? It is submitted that this is in fact so, and that many persons—though of course by no means all—actually grow in moral stature as they grow older." Talcott Parsons, "The Aging American Society," *Law and Contemporary Problems* 27 (1962): 22, 33.
11. Abraham S. Goldstein, *The Insanity Defense* (New Haven, Conn.: Yale University

Press, 1967), pp. 194–202.

12. Narcotic addicts and alcoholics have frequently argued for some form of total or partial exemption from criminal responsibility and have done so with virtually no success.

In *Robinson v. California*, 370 U.S. 660 (1962), the Supreme Court did decide that it was a cruel and unusual punishment, and thus a violation of the Eighth Amendment to the United States Constitution, to criminally punish an addict *for his addiction.*

Whatever residual seeds for natural expansion existed in *Robinson* were rather quickly stunted by the Court's subsequent decision in *Powell v. Texas*, 392 U.S. 514 (1967), holding that chronic alcoholism had not been established as a constitutionally mandated defense to a charge of public intoxication.

Powell can be viewed as a loss for Leroy Powell but a doctrinal victory for his side. It was a 4–1–4 decision with the four dissenters clearly ready to accept chronic alcoholism as a disease that impairs the sufferer's volition and prohibits criminal sanctions for public intoxication for the same reasons that *Robinson* constitutionally forbids punishing drug addicts for their status alone.

Justice Byron White was the "swing man"—the single vote—taking the position that a chronic alcoholic with an irresistible urge to drink should not be punishable for drinking or being drunk. Given the facts in the case, however, Justice White was not convinced that Mr. Powell had not only a compulsion to consume alcohol but also to be on the street and for economic reasons could not resist his public appearances.

For a complete review of the cases after *Robinson* and *Powell*, see Annotation, "Drug Addiction or Related Mental State as a Defense to Criminal Charge," *American Law Review 3d* 73 (1981): 16.

13. Goldstein, *The Insanity Defense*, p. 195.

14. The rationale offered is limited to cases of homicide primarily because that is where the doctrine of diminished or partial responsibility currently is used. As an abstract proposition one might argue that by the same token burglary should become trespass; aggravated assault, simple assault; and shoplifting (larceny), a form of "joyriding," that is, a type of unauthorized use and thus less serious.

15. A defendant's characteristics may account for the jury verdict and, according to one important study, more often than not operate to acquit a sympathetic person, as I assume this woman would be. See W. Lance Bennett and Martha S. Feldman *Reconstructing Reality in the Courtroom* (New Brunswick, N. J.: Rutgers University Press, 1981), p. 159.

16. Wayne R. LaFave and Austin W. Scott, Jr., *Criminal Law* (St. Paul, Minn.: West Publishing Company, 1972), pp. 351–353. See also A. W. G. Kean, "The History of the Criminal Liability of Children," *Law Quarterly Review* 53 (1937): 364.

17. Derk Bodde, "Age, Youth, and Infirmity in the Law of Ch'ing China," *University of Pennsylvania Law Review* 121 (1973): 437. The extent of privileges or exemption accorded an offender varied not only with age but with the nature of the offense. Indeed for rebellion or treason no clemency or privilege may have been allowed. (See Bodde, p. 439.)

18. Professor Bodde suggests, without being certain, that the special and ameliorative treatment accorded aged offenders is based on considerations of Confucian humanitarianism and the fact (or belief) that their powers have already declined so that they are not in a position to repeat their offenses. Ibid., p. 440.

It is interesting to contrast this view of the reduced likelihood of recidivism concerning the aged and the more modern, and certainly increasingly criticized, version of the need to train and educate—i.e., rehabilitate—the young offender.

19. J. Brooke Acker, Arthur C. Walsh, and James R. Beam (eds.), *Mental Capacity, Medical and Legal Aspects of the Aging* (Colorado Springs, Colo.: Shepard's/ McGraw-Hill, 1977), p. vii.

20. Ibid., p. 121.

21. Ibid., p. 134. The symptoms noted in the text are derived from the American Psychiatric Association's *Diagnostic and Statistical Manual of Mental Disorders*.

      Insofar as memory impairment suggests the use of amnesia as a defense, our courts have taken the general position that amnesia is not a defense nor, standing alone, is it grounds to delay a trial. See Annotation, *American Law Review* 3d 46 (1981): 544. Review of the sixty-five cases discussed in this annotation does not reveal any pattern of use by older defendants. In fifty-seven of the cases, age is not even mentioned.

22. This approach would fit within the traditional realm of *excuses*, which include insanity, necessity, duress, and voluntary intoxication. As an example, the crime of larceny requires, inter alia, an intent to deprive the owner of his property permanently. Consider the elderly person accused of shoplifting, which is larceny, who, because of confusion attributed either to senile dementia or atherosclerosis, genuinely thought he had paid for the item. Automatism is more easily conceptualized as speaking to the absence of a voluntary act—a basic requirement for criminal responsibility—than to the lack of mens rea. The actor's movements, we might say, are not "willed." This defense has experienced some popularity in England but not in the United States.

23. In *Lake v. Cameron*, 364 F.2d 657 (D.C. Cir. 1966), one of the earliest decisions concerned with a right to the "least drastic alternative" in the field of civil commitment of the mentally ill, an elderly patient, Mrs. Lake, was given to "wandering about" the streets of the District of Columbia late at night often dressed inappropriately. Rather than deal with Mrs. Lake as a mental hospital patient or as mentally ill but under supervision in the community, a Geriatric Court proceeding could be less traumatic and less formal, and could make a more helpful disposition due to the Geriatric Court judge's greater expertise and knowledge of community resources. If this has a familiar and hollow ring to those familiar with the juvenile justice system and its history of benevolence and expertise gone awry, I have achieved (part of) my purpose.

24. The analogue to status offenders—termed Persons in Need of Supervision (PINS) in New York—is, of course, clear. Since the elderly are not required to attend school then there is no analogue to truancy and absent a parent-child situation there is no analogue to the unruly child. See generally Lee E. Teitelbaum and Aidan R. Gough (eds.), *Beyond Control: Status Offenders in the Juvenile Court* (Cambridge, Mass.: Ballinger Publishing Company, 1977); I.J.A./A.B.A., Juvenile Justice Standards Project, *Noncriminal Misbehavior* (Cambridge, Mass.: Ballinger Publishing Company, 1977).

25. Peter M. Horstman, "Protective Services for the Elderly: The Limits of Parens Patriae," *Missouri Law Review* 40 (1975): 215, 217. The author notes that in California four out of every five persons found in need of a guardian were over the age of 60.

26. David Shichor and Solomon Kobrin, "Note: Criminal Behavior Among the Elderly," *The Gerontologist* 18 (1978): 213.

27. Ibid., p. 213. It may be said that the 224-percent increase is not as significant as first appears since it is based on original numbers that are quite small. I would not argue that point primarily because my objective is simply to prove

that either the reality or the current perception of an increase in crime by the elderly constitutes one of the problems to which a policy alternative must respond.

28. Ibid., p. 215. Shoplifting is larceny; in order to qualify as felony theft, the value of the items taken must reach a statutorily determined, and jurisdictionally variable, value. Fifty dollars is the most common dividing line between felony theft and misdemeanor theft. See LaFave and Scott, *Criminal Law*, p. 634.

29. As a parallel point, in discussing the distribution of mental illness one authority states, "The elderly will therefore receive increasing attention in the future because of their mere numbers alone." Dan Blazer, "The Epidemiology of Mental Illness in Late Life," in Ewald W. Busse and Dan G. Blazer (eds.), *Handbook of Geriatric Psychiatry* (Princeton, N.J.: Van Nostrand Reinhold, 1980).

30. For a reproduction of one case and excerpts from one article on old age and crime, see Joseph Goldstein, Alan M. Dershowitz, and Richard D. Schwartz, *Criminal Law: Theory and Process*, 2nd ed. (New York: Free Press, 1974), pp. 1146–1148. The other sources cited have nothing on point. See Jerome Hall, *General Principles of Criminal Law*, 2nd ed. (Charlottesville, Va.: Bobbs-Merrill, 1960); Herbert L. Packer, *The Limits of the Criminal Sanction* (Stanford, Calif.: Stanford University Press, 1968); LaFave and Scott, *Criminal Law*; Sanford H. Kadish and Monrad G. Paulson, *Criminal Law and Its Processes*, 3rd ed. (Boston: Little, Brown, 1975); and George Fletcher, *Rethinking Criminal Law* (Boston: Little, Brown, 1978).

31. Paul H. Robinson, "Criminal Law Defenses: A Systematic Analysis," *Columbia Law Review* 82 (1982): 199. Cf. Sanford J. Fox, "Physical Disorder, Consciousness, and Criminal Liability," *Columbia Law Review* 63 (1963): 645.

32. Alan A. Malinchak, *Crime and Gerontology* (Englewood Cliffs, N.J.: Prentice Hall, 1980), Chap. 5. There is literature on point in anthropology although the author makes no pretense at having exhaustively researched it. For example Leo W. Simmons discovered that among the early Aztecs drunkenness was a capital offense. Those over 70, however, were exempted from any punishment, drinking being a prerogative of age. See Leo W. Simmons, *The Role of the Aged in Primitive Societies* (New Haven, Conn.: Yale University Press, 1945).

33. I am indebted to Professor George Fletcher's analysis of the insanity defense for the approach taken here. See Fletcher, *Rethinking Criminal Law*, pp. 836–843.

34. The criminal law also recognizes claims of *justification* where the actor concedes that the definition of the offense is satisfied but does not concede—as with an excuse—the wrongfulness of the act. For example, a police officer entering a private dwelling with a valid warrant need not offer an excuse for the "breaking and entering." His act is as legally justified as that of the hangman who carries out a lawful order.

Consent, where lack of consent is a material element in the offense, is another example of justification. The surgeon who wields his knife after a proper consent is not guilty of aggravated assault and battery.

35. See Annotation,"Modern Status of Test and Criminal Responsibility—Federal Cases," *American Law Review Fed.* 46 (1982): 326. All the federal circuits—with the exception of the First Circuit, which has not had a recent opportunity to address the issue—follow the Model Penal Code. Annotation, "Modern Status of Test of Criminal Responsibility—State Cases," *American Law Review 4th* 9 (1981): 526, indicates that most states follow some version of the Model Penal Code tests, but there is more diversity than in the federal system.

A review of the cases cited in both annotations discloses no data to indicate that the elderly make any significant, successful use of the defense.

36. American Law Institute, *Model Penal Code*, Proposed Official Draft, 1962, Sec. 4.01. A number of jurisdictions use only paragraph (1) in identical or slightly altered form, dropping the controversial paragraph (2).

37. Thomas Szasz has been one of the most persistent and energetic critics of the insanity defense, arguing that the defense should be abolished and, in Kantian terms, insisting that by "treating offenders as responsible human beings, we offer them the only chance, as I see it, to remain human." Thomas Szasz, *Law, Liberty and Psychiatry* (New York: Macmillan, 1963), p. 137.

38. The statement in the text is made with full awareness that Thomas Szasz and his followers dispute the very concept of mental illness, at least when used to explain or excuse conduct. See Szasz, ibid.

39. See LaFave and Scott, *Criminal Law*, p. 374. The authors point out that duress is not a defense to the charge of killing an innocent third party. That is, this is a choice that may be perfectly understandable and one that many persons would make when "looking down the barrel of a gun," but it is not a choice that the law allows.

40. Ibid., p. 381.

41. Ibid., p. 391.

42. "Claims of justification concede that the definition of the offense is satisfied, but challenge whether the act is wrongful; claims of excuse concede that the act is wrongful, but seek to avoid the attribution of the act to the actor. A justification speaks to the rightness of the act; an excuse, to whether the actor is accountable for a concededly wrongful act." Fletcher, *Rethinking Criminal Law*, p. 759.

43. The traditional goals of criminal sanctions are deterrence, incapacitation, rehabilitation, and retribution. If restitution—the rehabilitation of the victim—is added to the list, and if we can somehow evade the hurdle of not imposing criminal sanctions in the absence of culpability, then a case can be made for pursuit of this objective.

    It would be more accurate to refer to the concept of compensation—a civil type of remedy—as a way for society to make amends, or to spread a loss resulting from noncupable but damaging behavior. See, generally, Stephen Schafer, *The Victim and His Criminal* (New York: Random House, 1968).

44. American Law Institute, *Model Penal Code*, Proposed Official Draft, 1962, Sec. 2.09(1).

45. Typical examples of provocation would include the sudden quarrel where self-defense does not exist and the witnessing of one's spouse in the act of adultery. Provocation occasionally is referred to as failed self-defense.

46. See Glanville L. Williams, "Provocation and the Reasonable Man, *Criminal Law Review* (1954): 740.

47. Fletcher, *Rethinking Criminal Law*, p. 247.

48. Richard A. Kalish, "The New Ageism and the Failure Models: A Polemic," *Gerontologist* 19 (1979): 398.

49. David R. Rothman, *Conscience and Convenience: The Asylum and Its Alternatives in Progressive America* (Boston: Little, Brown, 1980), p. 282.

50. Rothman has tellingly chronicled the failures of liberal reform in *Conscience and Convenience*, cited above, and *The Discovery of the Asylum: Social Order and Disorder in the New Republic* (Boston: Little, Brown, 1971).

51. See Herbert Fingarette and Anne F. Hasse, *Mental Disabilities and Criminal Responsibility* (Berkeley: University of California Press, 1979), p. 17.

52. See Robinson, "Criminal Law Defenses," pp. 199, 286; Goldstein, *The Insanity Defense*, p. 19. Where commitment formerly was automatic and based solely on

the insanity defense, it is increasingly recognized that the need for commitment is a separable issue, requiring different facts and conclusions than the insanity defense. Thus, a hearing on commitability seems constitutionally required. See David Wexler, *Mental Health Law: Major Issues* (New York: Plenum Publishers, 1981), p. 124.

A recent study of the insanity defense in New York State revealed that persons found not guilty by reason of insanity (NGRIs) represented an older population than prison admissions, with an age range of 19 to 67 years. For males, the mean age of NGRIs was 33, while the mean age for the male corrections group was 26. Although 49 percent of the male NGRI cases were over 30 years old and 28 percent over 40, only 26 percent of the incarcerated population were over 30 and 9 percent over 40. For the women NGRIs, the average age was 37; for female prisoners, the mean age was 27. *A Report to Governor Hugh L. Carey: The Insanity Defense in New York* (Albany, New York: Department of Mental Hygiene, Feb. 17, 1978), p. 41.

53. Hawaii Rev. Stat. Sec. 704-400(1) (1956). Emphasis added.
54. Ibid., Commentary at 2591. Citations omitted.
55. [1957] 1 Q.B. 399 (1956).
56. Ibid., p. 408.
57. Fox, "Physical Disorder," pp. 645, 654.
58. In *Pate* v. *Robinson*, 383 U.S. 375 (1966), the Supreme Court concluded that it would violate due process of law to convict an incompetent defendant and that state procedures must be adequate to safeguard this right. The Court prescribed no particular test for incompetence or set of procedures.
59. Thomas Szasz, unalterably opposed to the insanity defense and involuntary commitment, states, "Nevertheless, as an abstract concept, the notion of competence to stand trial makes sense." Thomas Szasz, *Psychiatric Justice* (Westport, Conn.: Greenwood, 1965), p. 26. Szasz is not happy with the role played by psychiatrists or with the then-possible indefinite commitment.
60. Bernard Goldfine, prominent for his supposed influence with the Eisenhower administration, was found to be incompetent to stand trial, based on his arteriosclerosis, which a physician testified was irreversible and caused impaired judgment, disorientation, bad memory, the lability of affect, and, in general, intellectual impairment. Mr. Goldfine was released from a mental hospital and allowed to live at home with his son and undertake private medical care. The great majority of those found incompetent are not so fortunate. Excerpts from the transcript are in Jay Katz, Joseph Goldstein, and Alan M. Dershowitz, *Psychoanalysis, Psychiatry and Law* (New York: Free Press, 1967), pp. 687–693.
61. See generally, Cohen, *The Law of Deprivation of Liberty*, pp. 377–410. Incompetence to be tried is sometimes referred to as present insanity, and thus there is a certain semantic consistency to the requirement that a defendant be found sane prior to trial.
62. In 1962, Dr. Szasz was able to identify 1,167 patients at Matteawan State Hospital in New York—54.5 percent of all patients there—as having been found to be incompetent. Szasz, *Psychiatric Justice*, p. 50. After studying past records, two other authors of that era estimated that over one-half of those so committed would spend the rest of their lives in confinement. John H. Hess and Herbert E. Thomas, "Incompetency to Stand Trial: Procedures, Results, and Problems," *American Journal of Psychiatry* 119 (1963): 713, 718–719.
63. 406 U.S. 715 (1972).
64. Ibid., p. 738. The Court also found a violation of equal protection where Indiana

made it easier to commit and more difficult to release a person in Jackson's position vis-à-vis all other persons subject to commitment.

65. This information was provided by Pat Snyder and Judy Cox of the New York State Department of Mental Hygiene, and I am grateful for their assistance. I wish also to thank Dr. Henry Steadman of the same agency for providing me with very helpful insights into the area of the elderly person and mental hygiene facilities.

    With total admissions to these facilities ranging from 26,660 in 1977 to 24,538 through most of 1982, the number of older people treated as forensic cases is minute.

66. See N.Y.S., Crim. Pro. Law, Sec. 180.10.

67. In 1977, 1,205 persons 65 or over (875 were over 75) were in regular adult service facilities in New York state. By 1982, there were 1,529 persons 65 or over (646 were over 75). The decrease in the over-75 group is at least partially explainable by New York's emphasis on deinstitutionalization.

68. Dr. Henry Steadman suggested that while my hypothesis might be accurate and worthy of research, it may be that more elderly offenders would be found in local mental health facilities or in private care, given a state policy (in existence since 1968) to divert elderly patients from state facilities.

    The New York State Commission on Correction recorded a total of 105,000 admissions to jails in New York state in 1981. In the 65-and-over category, there were 461 males and 36 females, totaling 497 admissions. These figures lead to a further suggestion that elderly arrestees tend to not even be jailed as an incident to their further formal or informal disposition.

69. Dade County, Florida, which has a large population of retirees, has an "Advocate Seniors Program" that deals with elderly offenders and serves primarily as a diversion and counseling service. See Alvin Malley, "The Advocate Program Sees the Elderly Through," *Florida Bar Journal* 55 (1981): 177.

Chapter 9

Elderly Offenders in Jail

Delores Golden

The Bureau of Justice Statistics defines a jail as a "local government facility authorized to detain for at least 48 hours any adult suspected or convicted of criminal offense."[1] There are approximately 3,500 county and regional jails in the United States, having an average daily population of approximately 160,000, of which 9,500 are female. At any given time about 3 percent of jail inmates are over the age of 55. It is much more difficult to get an accurate census of jails and jail inmates than it is to obtain data about prison and prison inmates. One reason is that the definition of what constitutes a jail is less clear than what constitutes a prison.

There are fifty-seven county jails in the state of New York, which, like most states, requires its counties to support local jail facilities for two purposes. The first is to provide a secure setting for persons who have been convicted of an offense. This is similar to the state prison system except that state facilities house long-term inmates, and jails usually house prisoners confined less than one year. These inmates usually make up between one-fourth and one-half of the residents of any local jail. The second purpose is to provide a secure setting for persons who have been accused but not convicted of offenses. Here they wait further processing—bail considerations, indictment, trial, or sentencing. These persons need not be misdemeanants; they may be persons arrested for felonies from burglary to multiple murder. Technically, they are known as "detainees" rather than inmates, but in most jails they are not separated in any way from offenders serving sentences. Theoretically, people in this category present too great a risk to the community to allow bail or release on recognizance. The length of incarceration for these people can vary from one day to several months.

In addition to misdemeanant inmates and felony detainees, jails hold probation and parole violators who are awaiting revocation hearings or are awaiting transportation to, or back to, a prison. The number of revoked felons, typically only a few, varies depending on the caseload size of probationers and parolees in a given jurisdiction and the vigor with which these persons are supervised.

In the past few years, another category of inmates has been added to many county jails, especially those in the Northeast, South, and Southwest. These are criminals convicted of felonies and sentenced to state prisons who, because prisons are overcrowded, are held in local jails until "vacancies" arise in the state prison system. At the present time *all* state prisons are filled to capacity; early in 1982, 6,000 felons in sixteen states were in this category.

Commenting on the characteristics of jail populations, Mullen et al. say:

> Jails frequently house persons who come in contact with the criminal or juvenile justice system simply because no suitable alternative exists. Functions performed by a social service agency in one jurisdiction may be provided by jails in another. Thus, depending upon local custom, jails may hold runaway juveniles, public inebriates, material witnesses, persons in safekeeping, federal prisoners, and any number of other "residual categories."[2]

Furthermore, jails are usually county facilities (there are only a few regional jails) in contrast to prisons, which are state-operated. Jails, therefore, have to rely on county coffers rather than the bigger state budgets which support prisons. As can be imagined, most jails receive low priority when it comes to apportioning local money. They must compete with schools, health services, and other welfare programs.

Therefore, since money is not readily available at the local level, most jails rely on other community agencies and volunteers for any program resources and staff that can be obtained in this way. Counseling and educational programs for the most part focus on younger inmates. Programs geared specifically for the needs of the elderly offender are rare or absent altogether.

PROBLEMS THE ELDERLY FACE IN JAIL

Older inmates include two distinct groups. The first includes individuals who have grown old in the system—those who have been involved in criminal activity as a lifestyle and indeed have been familiar with jails for a long time. The other group is made up of persons who have been living noncriminal lives but for various reasons find themselves in trouble with the law at a late age. These latter criminals are commonly found in local jails rather than in state prisons.

Admission of a new inmate to a jail is a complicated procedure and is difficult for both the older inmate and the staff of the admissions unit. An individual who is being incarcerated for the first time will likely find the experience traumatic. During the admission process it is important that the staff gather as much information as possible, but there are many factors that can interfere, such as the influence of alcohol, drugs, or medications, mental problems, anxiety, misunderstanding of questions, and fear. Furthermore, prisoners, including elderly ones, are sometimes admitted under emergency conditions.

Since county jails operate around the clock, new inmates are received at all hours of the day. It is not uncommon to confront these newcomers when auxilliary units such as medical, mental health, and inmate services are not staffed. There is a popular misconception that when a person is arrested, the entire record of his existence is known to "authorities." Such information is not generally available to jail personnel, and it takes time to gather the pertinent data.

One of the most important aspects of admission of older inmates is medical screening. Information received by the medical staff may be vague, or the inmate may not relate his medical concerns. The staff may learn that the individual takes medication for a heart disorder, but not the type of medication. When a person is admitted in the evening or late at night, attempts to reach his doctor may be difficult at best. After obtaining some basic information in accordance with standard medical procedure, the nurse has to decide whether the individual will be all right until morning. The facility doctor is asked to examine the prisoner and to advise the security staff whether it is medically necessary or desirable to transport him to a hospital. It must be remembered that the main function of a jail is security, and that an inmate may feign a medical problem in order to be taken out of the facility in order to escape. The possibility of escape attempts must be considered with every inmate, including those who are elderly.

The physical layout of a jail can also present problems for the older inmate. Most cells are approximately six feet by eight feet and equipped with a toilet, sink, table, seat, bunk, shelf, and wall light. Cells are usually lined up next to each other, with all cells facing in the same direction so that officers can readily view all areas of each cell without obstruction as they pass by. The front door of the cell is barred but otherwise open to view; only the sides and back have solid walls, which afford the inmate his only privacy. The lack of privacy sometimes frustrates the individual to the extent where medical or mental health help is necessary. Everything is secured in a fixed position for additional security, which can present problems for older inmates, who because of reduced physical flexibility may have difficulties with standard seating and raised sleeping heights. In addition, fixed lighting can present a reading problem for the sight-impaired.

The layout of the jail can create additional problems for older inmates if worship services, recreation, family visits, or other programs are located at some distance from the cell area. Special arrangements must be made for inmates who have difficulty walking or suffer from other handicaps.

Because of the age of most prisoners, jails are geared toward younger offenders (see Table 9.1). This presents a major problem for older inmates. Younger inmates are often noisy and assaultive. Programs are geared toward younger inmates, and even the physical layout of the jail is meant for people in good physical condition. Older inmates are subject to various abuses by their younger counterparts, from harassment to assault and robbery.

The older first-time inmate may find it difficult to adjust to the daily life of the jail. By the time an individual has reached age 55 his lifestyle has become set in many ways. Older people may not enjoy the variety of foods they once did and find annoying the noise and the loud talking so common among younger inmates. Being transplanted to a new environment and losing control over their movements can be especially frustrating to them. These changes are very difficult for elderly prisoners to accept and internalize.

Because of impairment and/or fear of younger inmates, most older inmates remain inside their cells, which further reduces their physical activity and may cause emotional problems. Most often they serve their entire sentences in idleness.

The older inmate can easily be misunderstood by the staff and by other inmates. For example, the staff may wrongly diagnose a state of depression as merely a desire to be left alone growing out of the elderly person's lack of interests in common with those of the younger inmates. If the signs are not correctly interpreted, severe consequences, even suicide, can result. The role of the cell house correction officer is thus of extreme importance with the older inmate. Officers have in many instances prevented crises by referring the inmate to auxiliary units such as medical, mental health, or inmates' services when they have noticed changes in an individual inmate's behavior. Timely referral in a jail setting is critical. This referral is usually not for extended treatment. Because jail inmates are usually transitory, it is commonly assumed by judges, administrators, and the general public that prisoners will receive whatever medical or psychiatric help they need once they move from the jail either back to the community on release or probation or into the prison system.

The Albany (New York) Jail

Albany County jail is large as jails go; in calendar year 1981, 3,516 prisoners were admitted. As can be seen in Table 9.1, inmates between the ages of 16 and 29 made up 71.8 percent of the population; consequently, as is typical, the greatest attention (and accommodation) is given to this group. To understand the elderly inmate, it is important to look at this group separately. (See Table 9.2)

Table 9.1. Calendar Year Jail Admissions, 1981, Albany County Jail

Total Number Admitted = 3,516

Sex:		*Classification:*	
Male	88.5%	Unsentenced	76.3%
Female	11.5%	Sentenced	23.7%
Race:		*Age:*	
White	65.1%	16–20	32.8%
Black	32.9%	21–29	39.0%
Other	2.0%	30–34	25.2%
		55 and older	3.0%
Education:		*Occupation:*	
8th to 12th grade	45.7%	None	45.2%
High school graduate	33.0%	Laborers	26.9%
Some college	12.3%	Students	17.3%
Elementary	7.9%	Craftsmen	6.0%
None/not stated	1.1%	Other	4.6%
Marital Status:		*Charges/Convictions:*	
Single	75.3%	Felonies	44.1%
Married	16.3%	Misdemeanors	42.0%
Divorced/separated	7.3%	Miscellaneous	13.9%
Length of Stay:			
1–15 days	56.6%		
16–60 days	25.1%		
60–180 days	9.0%		
6 months or more	9.3%		

Table 9.2. Inmates Aged 55 or Older, Admitted July–September 1981

Total Inmates Admitted During Period = 910 (100.0%)
Inmates Aged 55 or Older = 35 (3.9%)

Sex:		Classification:	
Male	88.6%	Unsentenced	74.3%
Female	11.4%	Sentenced	25.7%
Race:		Education:	
White	88.6%	Elementary	45.7%
Black	11.4%	8th to 12 grade	31.4%
		Some college	20.0%
		None/not stated	2.9%
Occupation:		Charges/Convictions:	
None	57.2%	Petty offenses	34.3%
Retired	20.0%	Misdemeanors	37.2%
Disability	11.4%	Felonies	28.5%
Employed	11.4%		

The older inmate in the Albany County Jail can be described as a white, unemployed male, who probably lacks a high school diploma. The majority of these inmates have been charged with violations (petty offenses) or misdemeanors less than a felony grade, which means they will stay within the local criminal justice system, including the jail, if convicted. Since 34 percent were charged with petty offenses, the longest they could stay in the jail would be fifteen days. Since 28 percent were charged with felonies, even if convicted they will not complete their sentences in the jail, but rather, in all probability, they will be transferred to some state prison. It is possible, therefore, that only 37 percent (the misdemeanants) will be in the facility for more than fifteen days (the longest one can be sentenced for a misdemeanor is one year).

CASES HISTORIES

The following case history synopses should give a more realistic idea of the problems of older inmates. Both the first and the last describe first-time offenders. The second describes an offender who has been held at the facility for several months before conviction of a felony and subsequent transfer to a state prison. The third and fourth present pictures of two differing individuals who have been jailed previously on minor charges.

Case 1
Mr. A: Elderly First Offender

Mr. A was a 60-year-old with no prior history of incarceration in this jail; he apparently had lived a noncriminal life. He retired from work early because of medical disability, and his wife died shortly thereafter. He began to rely on alcohol as a means of coping with his problems. Mr. A arrived at the facility late in the evening in an intoxicated state. According to the arresting agency, nonjail alternatives had been used on three previous occasions when Mr. A was arrested for petty offenses. On the evening of his arrest, Mr. A was walking on a busy highway and stopping traffic. Upon admission, and although almost incoherent because of drink, he mentioned in a vague manner that he had high blood pressure. At the time he was arrested, no medical information was available. The medical staff decided that Mr. A did not need to be transported to the hospital, but they did find it necessary to strap him to his bunk to prevent him from falling and hurting himself. The next morning Mr. A received a complete medical screening. He was shown the picture of himself that was taken by the admissions unit the night of his arrest; it was a shocking awakening for him. After several days his son was located, and the judge released Mr. A to his custody.

Case 2
Mr. B: An Elderly Felony Inmate

Mr. B was a 65-year-old with a long history of criminal activity. He was detained in the jail on a felony charge. He has a heart problem, arthritis of the spine, and disc-degeneration. Because of his age and his medical problems, Mr. B saw himself as having a limited life expectancy; to him, incarceration seemed like death itself. The mental health unit closely monitored Mr. B because of his view, which they believed made him a high risk for escape or suicide attempts. Mr. B stayed in the jail for several months before his conviction on the felony charge of assault and subsequent transfer to a state prison. The demands on staff time in Mr. B's case were particularly heavy.

Case 3
Mrs. C: An Elderly Shoplifter

Mrs. C, 67 years old, was arrested for shoplifting. She had been previously incarcerated in the jail for a few days on the same type of charge. Mrs. C was also a crime victim: she was abused by her daughters and their boyfriends. According to Mrs. C, the reason she shoplifted was fear that they would either physically abuse her or threaten to do so if she didn't shoplift. She seemed to want to break the relationship with her daughters but felt she could not maintain herself without them. It was difficult to be of any assistance to her during her sentence since the only visitors she had were her daughters. In addition to visiting her, they corresponded with her and put money in her account so she could purchase items from the facility commissary.

Attempts were made to arrange consultations with agencies that could help and support Mrs. C. She claimed she would cooperate with and visit the agencies after she left the facility. Accordingly, she was provided with the complete information about the agencies when she left. On her release, however, Mrs. C was picked up at the jail by one of her daughters and a boyfriend; when she embraced them both, it was apparent that even though she wanted to break the relationship she could not. Like an abused child, Mrs. C felt they loved her even if they abused her.

Case 4
Mr. D: An Elderly Alcoholic

Mr. D, a 68-year-old, was a chronic alcoholic who suffered many of the debilitating medical problems caused by long-term drinking. Jail for him was really a revolving door. At each admission, the medical department thoroughly screened him for injuries, medication, and potential for withdrawal.

Mr. D's memory seemed to have stopped when he was 50; he did not recall any events after that. Among other things, the memory lapse made it difficult to find any of his relatives. Mr. D's explanation for his latest arrest was that the judge had had his picture placed in the store where he (Mr. D) got his cigarettes so the police could arrest him. According to Mr. D, he didn't steal the cigarettes, the store owners just didn't ask him to pay for them. Mr. D said he was going to fool them by going to another branch of the market to get his cigarettes. He saw no particular problem with his drinking. Given his advanced age, referral to a long-term rehabilitation setting seemed unlikely and futile, especially given his reluctance to take part in any program. Jail was not the appropriate place for Mr. D, but there was no better alternative.

Case 5
Mr. E: An Elderly Man Jailed for Harassing His Wife

Mr. E was 67 years old, retired, and separated from his wife. He was arrested for harassing and threatening her. According to Mr. E, he felt he shouldn't have to pay money to her each week because she already had the house and the furniture. Mr. E said their marriage hadn't been the best, but it had survived until he retired. He said he couldn't stand being with her all the time, so he moved out and took his own apartment. He seemed too proud to talk to anyone about the problems he was having with his marriage and chose to express his resentment toward his wife by harassing her.

Summary

All these elderly people did violate the law, but with the possible exception of Mr. B, incarceration in a jail did not seem to be the best solution. One of the factors that gives rise to situations like these is the fact jails cannot refuse to accept custody of people committed to them by the courts. This is not to say the fault can be laid to the courts, either. Judges have a responsibility to the community for security and order, but, in general, incarceration for older offenders is not the best alternative.

With complicating factors such as the limitations of the physical plant, the high cost of programs, and the problems of interpersonal communications with various inmate groups and staff, it becomes obvious that serious thought to finding alternative ways to deal with the older offender is necessary. The proportionate statistics are not staggering yet, but the demographic projections indicate that the older population will become proportionately larger with each passing day.

To deal effectively with the high cost of programs and the need to involve more people in research, one must look beyond only county jails. Another large bureaucracy clearly is not the answer either; rather, it might be to establish a closer relationship among practitioners in the fields of corrections and aging, community agencies, the courts, the academic community, and the community at large.

NOTES

1. *Survey of American Jails* (Washington, D.C.: Office of Justice Statistics, 1980), p. 3.
2. Joan Mullen, Kenneth Carlson, and Bradford Smith, *American Prisons and Jails, Volume 1: Summary Findings and Policy Implications of a National Survey* (Washington, D.C.: U.S. Department of Justice, 1980), p. 21.

Chapter 10

The Elderly in Prison:
A Review of the Literature

Dan Rubenstein

> Old criminals offer an ugly
> picture and it seems as if
> even scientists do not like
> to look at it for any con-
> siderable amount of time.
>
> —(Pollak, 1941: 213)

The older inmates of our prisons[1] are not of major importance in the totality of the prison system; they constitute only a small proportion of the ever-growing total aged population. So unimportant are they considered that Ham (1976) was moved to call them "the forgotten minority." While they are not totally forgotten, the literature about them has been both sparse and sporadic. It could be that "the sad aspect of the old criminal" has certainly had something to do with this neglect (Pollak, 1941).

In all probability, since the numbers of older prisoners are so few and the problems of the correctional system so many, awareness and efforts would naturally gravitate to the general population. One could also venture the proposition that since the condition of the elderly is decremental and not socially productive, the attitude is one of "why bother?" However, growing interest in the aging process and condition is creating an awareness of more and more situations that affect the elderly.

While older prisoners constitute a small, select population, there are unique aspects, both interesting and unexplored, of that population that need to be examined and understood. When society removes people from its midst, it assumes the responsibility for their care and well-being. The older prisoner's care and well-being depends on society's degree of caring and capacity for understanding.

HOW OLD ARE OLDER PRISONERS, AND HOW MANY OF THEM ARE THERE?

Here we consider older prisoners as those elderly people who have committed criminal offenses, have been found guilty of those offenses, have been officially sentenced, and are serving time in penal institutions. It is less easy to define at what chronological age one becomes "older."[2] Our review finds inmates are considered older at the widely varying ages of 25 (Straus and Sherwin, 1975), 40 (Silfen, 1977), and 82 (Aday and Webster, 1979). The majority of the studies, however, use age 50 or 55. While there has been no acceptable resolution to how to determine when an inmate is old, the FBI's *Uniform Crime Reports* (1980) contain an indicator for age determination. The FBI generally finds that in arrests by age there is a significant difference between the 50–54 age category and the 55–59 category. This substantially lower incidence continues through the age categories of 60–64 and 65 and older. From this spurious obversation, one might say an older inmate is anyone 55 and over. (It must be borne in mind, however, that the UCRs report only arrests, not prison convictions.)

How many older prisoners are there? To our knowledge, the literature has not shown any specific data to answer this question. By analyzing UCRs and using age 40 as "old," Aday (1976) reports that the elderly represent 5 percent of the prison population. A further refinement is produced by Krajick (1979), who reports that two studies (a twenty-six state survey by Contract, Inc., and a twelve-state study by *Corrections Magazine*) show that 1 percent of the prison population are 60 and over and 0.5 percent (1,500 people) are 65 and over. More specifically, the two studies found 180 prisoners over 60 in New York state, 170 in North Carolina, and 90 in South Carolina. A recent survey by the New York State Department of Correction Services could account for, as of February 1981, fifty-seven inmates who were 65 and older (Grossman and Macdonald, 1981).[3]

WHAT CRIMES HAVE THE OLDER INMATES COMMITTED?[4]—WHAT BROUGHT THEM TO PRISON?

From a knowledge of the number of older prisoners, a corollary question arises: what brought them to prison? What crimes have the older inmates committed? Why were they incarcerated? The major source for data about crimes reported and arrests made are the FBI's *Uniform Crime Reports,* in which the varied crimes are tabulated in five-year age intervals (55–59, 60–64, and 65 and above). The data are not too exacting, however, because in the listing of crimes, the UCRs may well report more than one crime committed by the same person. It must also be remembered that, as explained previously, the UCRs generally report only arrests and do not provide information about convictions.

Since the UCRs deal only with the number of crimes for which the elderly are arrested, the problem of the type of offenses that bring the elderly to prison must be approached with caution (Barrett, 1972; Fox, 1946). While the rates and crimes vary with age, the interpretations of prisoner characteristics and causality may also vary with specific populations and social conditions.

There are two distinctive types of elderly offenders (Wiegand and Burger, 1979–80; Teller and Howell, 1979): (1) recidivists or multirecidivists, or chronic offenders who may spend many years in and out of prison (Bergman and Amir, 1973); and (2) older people who commit a first offense after a lifetime of being law-abiding citizens (Teller and Howell, 1979). From these studies it is generally found that the first offender has a higher social status and was once more effective at social participation (including marriage), has a positive attitude toward life, and has affirmative religious attitudes. Thus this older first offender may find it more difficult to adjust to the deculturalization process that is part of prison socialization.[5] It is suspected that this difficulty may explain why they are extremely successful at resisting dependence on the prison. It is perceived that from their set ways and rigidity they resist being socialized into the prison system; on the other hand, multiply incarcerated older inmates have been found to more closely resemble younger inmates, in that they are familiar with the criminal way of life and thus assimilate readily into the prison culture (Keller and Vedder, 1968).[6]

What crimes do the elderly commit? Pollak (1941) and Moberg (1952–53) examine the context of capability that borders on the sociological concept of opportunity. Do the elderly in their later years have the physical agility to burglarize or the libidinal capacity to sustain erection long enough to rape? If one accepts a deprecatory perspective on aging, one could rationalize varied crimes as not "opportune" for the elderly. Physical changes prevent them from becoming involved in activities that demand stamina and strenuous effort (Bergman and Amir, 1973).

But there is a consensus in the literature that the older first offender will be found to have more often engaged in crimes against persons (Schroeder, 1936; Teller and Howell, 1979), and that these crimes will be violent crimes of passion, such as the murder of wives, neighbors, or relatives (Krajick, 1979). Shichor and Kobrin (1978) explain this by pointing out that as the range of social interaction contracts with advancing age, interpersonal primary relationships become intense, with a resulting increase in opportunities for conflict. The crimes will be murder and manslaughter (Aday, 1976; Panton, 1974). This phenomenon is also explained by Schroeder (1936), who points out that older inmates include "many men coming from foreign countries whose ability to adapt themselves may be expressed in the violence of their behavior." Studies in Israel have also recognized the difficulty of adjustment by foreigners (Bergman and Amir, 1973; Amir and Bergman, 1976).

The literature often refers to the fact that the elderly participate in sex crimes (Pollak, 1941). While these crimes include statutory rape and offenses against chastity, common decency, morals, and the like, they are rarely detailed and quantified. Moberg (1952–53) offers some weak and unsubstantiated explanations for sex offenses in later life: (1) that the elderly have normal sex drives, but weakened moral inhibitions; (2) that they have a revival of desires; and, (3) that they have an instinctive desire to leave descendants. Adams and Vedder (1961) venture that sex crimes have a psychological basis, "partly secondary to conscious or subconscious realization of physiologic impotence."

It must also be recognized that very few, if any, studies are conducted on the elderly female inmate. This review found no information for females.[7] While the female population was included in some samples, the numbers were so small as to preclude analysis.

It has also been mentioned in the literature (Keller and Vedder, 1968) that as age increases the incidence of arrest decreases, and that criminal involvement declines gradually with the advance of age (Moberg, 1952–53; Pollak, 1941; Schroeder, 1936).

THE PROFILE OF AN ELDERLY PRISONER

One of the functions of the reviewers of specific literature is to seek evidence of repetitive findings that permits them to create a generalization that could represent a fair definition of a particular population. As usual, the findings are not consistent but contradictory. On one hand, Weigand and Burger (1979–80) claim that the elderly inmate is competent, responsive, quick, and shrewd. These qualities are necessary since survival in prison requires living by one's wits, and the older inmate has lasted a long time. On the other hand, Panton (1974) finds that the aged inmate (age 60 and above) functions at a lower level of intelligence than the nonaged inmates, and has a considerably lower I.Q. and educational achievement level. Furthermore, he says, the number of mentally defective older inmates is more than twice the number of mentally defective younger inmates. The older prisoners are more likely to have histories of poor general health, more likely to be divorced or widowed, and more frequently classified as having no gainful employment, with a less stable work record. The aged have a high incidence of involvement in alcohol and have served a greater percentage of two or more prior sentences (recidivism). Shinbaum (1977) also finds them to be poorly educated.

To add further to the sorry state of older inmates, their physical and mental condition has been found to deteriorate rapidly during their prison terms (Bergman and Amir, 1973). The aging prisoners, according to these researchers, are at the mercy of younger, more aggressive, and difficult prisoners who tend to frighten, ridicule, or even harm them. The aged prisoners become depressed, anxious, and consequently dependent on the warden and prison staff for protection. They are deprived of friends, employment, and decent accommodations.

But to conclude these perceptions on a more positive note, Reed and Glamser (1979) found fifteen of nineteen subjects reporting that they felt younger in prison. The authors believe this perception to be accurate, given the social class background of most prisoners. Older prisoners are not exposed to heavy industry, hard labor, or heavy drinking. They eat well, rest often, and have ready access to medical care. This is unlikely to be the case among lower- and working-class men outside prisons.

Since there is no consensus on the profile of the older inmate in prison, a more particularistic examination is in order. What happens psychologically to the inmate? How is he socially affected? Before study findings can be reported, there must be a realization that prison experiences are affected by the characteristics of people who enter the system as well as by the dynamics of the intrasystem circumstances. Jensen (1977) and Hendricks (1981) both express the need to explore the direct and indirect influence of both imported characteristics and situational variables on inmate behavior and culture. The effects of prisonization on the aged could be as much a product of vulnerable individuals as they are of institutional structures (Reed and Glamser, 1979) and thus vulnerability accounted for by selection.

PSYCHOLOGICAL EFFECTS

Through the use of psychological tests, Eysenck et al. (1977) found that younger prisoners (those under 30) had positive extroversion scores and did not show elevated neuroticism scores; older inmates had negative extroversion scores (i.e., they were introverted), and high neuroticism scores.

From a sample of thirty inmates (nineteen black and eleven white) over age 65 Ham (1976) found a higher degree of insecurity, more expressed fear of pain, a constant fear of illness, more fear of correctional officers and of authority in general, and a heightened fear of young black inmates. He also found them to have a fear of the future and fear of having no place to live on the outside. Hormuth et al. (1977) found that "higher age led to generally low activity and less expectations, which in some cases might be evidence of a phenomenon of helplessness or the feeling of giving up." This "sedation by age" affected the inmates expectation for freedom. While they had fewer incidents of untoward behavior, they expected fewer furloughs. It has also been found that the older inmate would be more likely to refrain from participation in a riot than a younger person (Straus and Sherwin, 1975). With the use of the Minnesota Multiphasic Personality Inventory tests, Panton (1976–77) found older inmates to be more neurotic and less psychotic in responses than the general population, with greater anxiety, despondency, apprehension, and concern with physical functioning. They appeared to be naive and self-centered, were likely to be demanding of attention and support, and appeared inclined to avoid responsibility. They expressed fears of inadequacy and insecurity and were likely to be intimidated and easily influenced by younger, more aggressive inmates. They did not show a profile of serious mental illness. Through the use of the MMPI, McCreary and Mensh (1977) also found increases in neuroticism and less psychoticism. They also found less impulsivity and acting-out tendencies. Teller and Howell (1979), using a Bi-Polar Psychological Inventory of fifteen scales and seventy-five traits, found less psychic pain among the older inmates: they were depressed, impulsive, and hostile, but less socially deviant. It has also been found that older men cope satisfactorily. They cause less trouble because they are more mature and less sexually involved (Wooden and Parker, 1980). They are less future-oriented and acquire institutional neurosis, manifested by lack of expression of desire for freedom, mechanical behavior, and lack of emotional expression (Hicks and Alpert, 1978). It is encouraging to know that older inmates with longer records tended to benefit considerably from their involvement in therapy programs. It was further discovered that the longer these types of inmates remained in a treatment relationship, the lower was their recidivism rate (Carney, 1971). McCreary and Mensh (1977) also found that older offenders are in greater need of "noncriminal treatment" and rehabilitation programs.

SOCIOLOGICAL FACTORS

A very definite factor in the understanding of the older inmate is the length of time spent in prison, and how this time away from open society influences the inmate's relationships and reference groups. Aday and Webster (1979) note that "for many inmates, the prison environment helps to destroy relationships with those who, at one time, might have been significant others. Severing ties with family and friends may force inmates to either withdraw into themselves or turn to the prison environment for emotional support." Adams and Vedder (1961) associate long time served with certain consequences for institutional dependency by saying, "A long sentence may persist despite good prison conduct and parole may be denied reasonably because the prisoner has no family to whom he could go . . . If society has little place for the older man in general, it has even less place for the elderly prisoner or ex-convict."

When linked with the concept of social roles, the length of imprisonment is another potential frame of reference that may have an impact on prison adjustment. Sociological concepts of role theory (role loss, ambiguity, and gain) come into play. Here we would find, in prison, a loss of certain accustomed roles and the socialization into new roles in the new environment. Aday and Webster (1979) explain this:

Initial imprisonment is a type of forced social disengagement from

their customary social milieu, and axiomatic exposure to a new socialization process. In this light, institutionalization can be perceived as
a positive, as well as a negative, process. Prisonization gives the prisoner a new subculture, new role, new identity and new social group—
which are vital for social and psychological well-being. The longer the
normal roles of the life-cycle are disrupted, the more likely the older
prisoner will establish new roles in the inmate social system.

The length of imprisonment has often raised the question that
Ham (1976) asks: "Do the elderly who have been incarcerated for an
extremely long period of time (25 years or more) develop a dependency
from a so-called man-made disease called institutional neurosis that
manifests itself in their lack of not wanting to leave or be released
from prison?" Other writers have also suggested that long-timers
indicated increased concern about reentry into the community and
less willingness to attempt it. But the data to support such conten-
tions are scarce.

The sociological concept of social control is interspersed throughout the literature. This concept attributed to the aging condition
assumes that the elderly perform a vital function of maintaining
order in the prison society and hence serve as crucial aid to custodial
and institutional control.

Wiltz (1978) puts it this way: "Because older inmates are better
adjusted to prison life, and recipients of special privileges, the aged
inmates attempt to control the violent tendencies of younger inmates
which may disrupt their highly valued status in the social system.
It is because of their stake in the stability of prison that the treatment
received by older inmates differs from the treatment received by
young inmates." It has also been found that older inmates are less
prone to violate rules and do not try to escape (Jensen, 1977). The
presence of many old people in an inmate population may serve as
a stabilizing or deflating force on an institutional environment where
tensions seem persistently high and a riot is an ever-present possibility (Straus and Sherwin, 1975).

Concerns with social participation at both the primary and secondary levels are addressed in the literature. There is evidence that
marital status, visits with family and kin, and contacts with outside
reference groups tend to diminish with the length of imprisonment,
and that as time goes by the aged prisoner becomes more dependent
on the institution (Aday, 1976). Hendricks and Burkhead (1981)
found that older black inmates actually had fewer problems adjusting
to prison life than did younger prisoners because they were successful in their efforts to maintain family ties and supportive networks

while incarcerated.[8] Wooden and Parker (1980) also found older inmates more able to cope satisfactorily because they had family and outside social support. Social participation was studied by Gillespie and Galliher (1972) through tests for anomie. They found that for some, prison retarded the aging process and that friendships tended to be age-graded. The tests of participation in leisure-time activities, association with other inmates, and the extent of boredom found that inmates who aged more rapidly had fewer leisure-time activities, had fewer contacts with family, kin, or other inmates, and did not see time pass quickly. While it has been said that time served does not affect attitude (Gillespie and Galliher, 1972), the opposite was found by Hicks and Alpert (1978), who discovered that over time the older inmates increased their positive appreciation of police and decreased their positive evaluations of their lawyers. With further explorations of institutional participations, Silfen et al. in Israel (1977) found two distinct groups of older inmates: (1) those who balance through internal sources and (2) those who balance from external sources. The internal balance requires an acceptance of the prison social structure and provides for disengagement, while the external balance requires making prison demands flexible, with special considerations for a protective environment.

Family life for the chronic elderly offender was found to be more unstable, with higher incidence of divorce than for the late offender. The chronic offenders were less likely to receive visits and support from family and friends when paroled (Aday, 1976). In this same study that tested social participation with institutional dependency, an inverse relationship was found between the influence of outside reference groups and institutional dependence. The length of imprisonment has a direct relationship to institutional dependence; age at time of first imprisonment is inversely related to institutional dependence, and institutional dependence is greater for the chronic offender than for the late offender. Both Panton (1974) and Reed and Glamser (1979) found that older inmates take a greater interest in religion and participate more in religious activities. It has also been found that older offenders, especially those who have been incarcerated for long periods were relatively uninterested in prison education because of their low literacy levels (Shinbaum, 1977). While some researchers have found the imprisoned elderly joining organizations and taking interest in politics (Reed and Glamser, 1979), others have found that higher age led to generally lower activity and fewer expectations which in some cases might be evidence of helplessness or giving up (Jensen, 1977). "The older inmates are not as easy to motivate as the younger guys. They need a lot of coaxing to get them to do anything at all. It would be good for them if we could do that, shake them out of their boredom, you know, but that takes a lot of people and we don't have that.... There isn't much we have here that's of interest to them" (Krajick, 1979).

The Parole Commission is always investigating educational attainment, social participatory activity, and work ability. It will also consider a place to live for community reentry. It is not likely that the elderly will score well in any of these categories (Krajick, 1979). Wiegand and Burger (1979–80) found that the educational and vocational training were of no value to the elderly and therefore did not alleviate parole problems. They also found that the elderly were poor parole candidates because they were not active in any organizations, had no support systems, had no place to live, had health problems, were unemployable. The reviewers have noted a surprising finding, in that parole boards have shown a bias in favor of the release of older black inmates in preference to other inmates (Carroll, 1976). It has been rationalized that these events take place because there is a leniency attributed to a benign paternalism, a form of bias not uncommon in relations between blacks and whites and subordinate blacks who are perceived as nonthreatening.

AGE INTEGRATION VERSUS AGE SEGREGATION

The issue of age-integrated versus age-segregated environments is as alive in the field of corrections as it is in the general field of gerontology. Krajick (1979) and Roberg and Webb (1981) describe the virtues of separate facilities, as do Wiegand and Burger (1979–80) when they explain that "there has emerged in recent years a shared consensus that special programs should be implemented to meet the needs of aged prisoners. Age specific groups in institutions can contribute to the mental health of members." Their research reports that participation in age-specific groups (1) increases self-respect, (2) diminishes feelings of loneliness and depression, (3) reactivates desire for social exchange, (4) reawakens intellectual interest, (5) creates a sense of identification among members and a shared feeling of shared historical legacy, and (6) increases capability to resume community life. Ham (1980), however, does not concur. From a report on an evaluation of a special unit for older persons, he found that this limited-duty unit isolated them from the larger part of the prison and the general inmate population. The expressed function of this unit was to provide institutional housing for aged inmates to "alleviate discrimination of aged inmates by virtue of the fact that present programming was not commensurate with their physiological, psychological and sociological needs." The same services were provided to younger inmates who were physically unable to function in the routine correctional setting. "In reality, however," Ham writes, "the unit was administered in the same fashion as the various cell blocks and other units of confinement. No special privileges, treatments or programs were provided."

He goes on to say that "In fact because of isolation, immobility, and physical infirmities the inmates are worse off than those housed in main sections of prison," and to confound the issue even further, Aday (1976) hypothesizes that the dependence of older prisoners in a conventional prison will be higher than the dependence of older prisoners in a therapeutic (separate) prison environment. A comparative analysis of his two groups, with the use of an institutional dependence index, revealed no significant difference. Thus, failing to confirm his hypothesis, Reed and Glamser (1979) and Fuller and Orsagh (1979) advocated an annex for older inmates to protect them from aggressive young prisoners. The prison authorities also felt that they were protecting the younger prisoners by preventing the older ones from sharing too much knowledge with less experienced prisoners. But Straus and Sherwin (1975) believed it unwise to continue the practice of age segregation of inmates because their presence among the general prison population served as a stabilizing effect. Silfen (1977) and his colleagues believed that older prisoners should be placed in special units because they fail to adapt in the general institution. Even though opportunity for recreation and work is limited in special units or protective custody, it is found to be quieter and less troublesome (Krajick, 1979). From these varied opinions and findings, Wiltz (1978) suggested three ways to accommodate aged prisoners: (1) incarcerating aged inmates with other adult inmates, with special accommodations for the aged that would include specific housing areas, special diets, and job assignments; (2) segregating the elderly inmates, that is, incarcerating them in special facilities that are better equipped to handle their problems; and (3) releasing the aged inmates from prison, but reinstitutionalizing them into homes for the aged in the general society. This last option would be for inmates with no family, or for those with families that are unwilling to assume responsibility for them.

METHODOLOGICAL LIMITATIONS

The literature is fraught with methodological limitations in the conduct of the research, as well as unusual limitations due to the nature of the prison's closed society and the conditions that maintain it. Almost all the studies reviewed contained serious sampling problems. While the intent of the studies was to draw inferences about the characteristics of the populations, the authors frequently asserted that the sample should be drawn at random from the population, acknowledged that the sample used in the study did not approach randomness, and included the caveat that inferences can be drawn only from the group sampled. Other studies used disclaimers such as the following:

1. "Given the sampling procedures used, generalizations must be made with extreme caution. The findings of this research can perhaps be generalized to those inmates having similar characteristics as the inmates in our sample. Generalizations beyond this point would be hazardous" (Aday, 1976).
2. "Because of the lack of control groups, unidentified intervening variables may have influenced the findings" (Aday, 1976).
3. "Having specified a long list of errors and limitations, let's look at the findings of our research" (Carney, 1971).
4. "This analysis was based on an atypical sample" (Jensen, 1977).
5. "Our comparisons go well beyond the data of this limited study, and yet the decidedly heuristic quality of the study invites such license" (Reed and Glamser, 1979).
6. "Certain backgrounds were not investigated—there was no time" (Montgomery, 1974).

Some of the limitations that researchers confronted due to the nature of the system they were investigating were: (1) lack of access to records, (2) bureaucratic interference, (3) self-selection and voluntarism bias, and (4) the realization that the people they were interviewing were expert con artists. Regarding the last limitation, Aday (1976) states, "many subjects probably responded to the interview in such a manner to insure that good relations with the staff would be continued. Other questions may have been negotiated in a cautious fashion to insure that parole would not be hindered. Thus, establishing communications in an environment where little trust is evident is certainly no easy task and has a variety of built in limitations."

CONCLUSIONS

Both the weaknesses in the research reviewed and the scarcity of items indicate a strong need for more research on the elderly prisoner. These pioneer efforts have taught us that: (1) reliance on invalid and nonrepresentative data should be abandoned, (2) there should be more rigor in compliance with acceptable standards of research, (3) there should be a greater caution in the perpetuation of unsubstantiated beliefs (i.e., the elderly are disabled, dirty old men; the elderly are conservative), (4) there should be a wariness in accepting studies that reflect either an ignorance or naiveté about the prison environment, and (5) since many studies are found with inherent limitations due to singular disciplinary approaches (psychological, sociolgocial, etc.), more thorough work in investigating the phenomena could be achieved if undertakings could be interdisciplinary (Silfen et al., 1976).

Age has been cited time and time again as a significant correlate of behavior, particularly in adjustment to prison (Wolfgang, 1964). Many studies have also reported that age is a significant factor in the reformative process. If the older person is to adjust to prison or reform to return to the community, our institutions and programs will need to be responsive to the needs and capabilities of those unique individuals.

> The purpose and justification of imprisonment or a similar measure of deprivation of liberty is ultimately to protect society against crime. This end can only be achieved if the period of imprisonment is used to assure, as far as possible, that upon his return to society the offender is not only willing, but able to lead a law abiding and self supporting life (United Nations standard minimum rules for treatment of prisoners, cited in Silfen, 1976).

NOTES

1. "Older offender" and "criminal behavior among the elderly" are often associated with the older prisoner. However, not all older offenders are incarcerated. (See Shichor and Kobrin, 1978). One also needs to be aware that many elderly offenders do not go to prison because there may be a general tendency not to prosecute elderly or because their families tend to hide the deviance.
2. Wolfgang (1964), in his study of age and adjustment in prison, recognized the significance of age. He found as did the Gluecks, that the "great divide" occurred between the ages of 35 and 36, thus defining the older prisoner as over 35.
3. The numbers of the elderly in prison will be found to be small, hardly representative

of the percentage of the elderly in the general population. C. Murchison posited a conjecture that "older men either die or learn better methods" (Schroeder, 1936).

4. This review deals only with designated felons that are incarcerated in federal and state prisons, not with misdemeanants sentenced to local or county jails. It is of interest to note, however, that misdemeanant crimes of alcohol abuse and shoplifting may well be on the rise with older persons.

5. This process is often referred to as prisonization (Wolfgang, 1964).

6. Adams and Vedder (1961) attempt to describe the older recidivists as those who have "a decrease in the efficiency of their operations and a lessening in their ability to avoid detection and apprehension as effects of aging on their physical and mental capacities."

7. Tangential to this finding is the article by Foster (1975), who explains that the pseudo-family is probably a common phenomenon within relatively large, long-term female correctional institutions. He notes that when they are family participants, older inmates have often assumed the roles of mother or father, both of whom command considerable respect and influence within the group.

8. Roberg and Webb (1981) are among the few who write about the elderly black in prison. However, their speculations contradict those of Hendricks and Burkhead. This is not surprising, since their writings are conjectural and not based on any study findings.

REFERENCES

Adams, M. E., and Vedder, Clyde B. "Age and Crime: Medical and Sociological Characteristics of Prisoners over 50." *Geriatrics* (April 1961): 177–181.

Aday, Ronald Howard. "Institutional Dependency: A Theory of Aging in Prison." Ph.D. dissertation, Oklahoma State University, 1976.

Aday, Ronald H., and Webster, Edgar L. "Aging in Prison: The Development of a Preliminary Model." *Offender Rehabilitation*, 3 (1979): 271–282.

Amir, M., and Bergman, S. "Patterns of Crime Among Aged in Israel (A Second Phase Report)." *Israel Annals of Psychiatry and Related Disciplines* 14 (1976): 280–288.

Barrett, James H. "Aging and Delinquency." *Gerontological Psychology.* Springfield, Ill.: Charles C. Thomas, 1972.

Bergman, S., and Amir, M. "Crime and Delinquency Among the Aged in Israel." *Geriatrics* (January 1973): 149–157.

Carney, F. J. "Evaluation of Psychotherapy in a Maximum Security Prison." *Seminars in Psychiatry* 3 (August 1971): 363–375.

Carroll, L. "Racial Bias in the Decision to Grant Parole." *Law and Society Review* 11 (Fall 1976): 93–107.

Eysenck, J. B. G.; Rust, J.; and Eysenck, H. J. "Personality and the Classification of Adult Offenders." *British Journal of Criminology* 17, 2 (April 1977): 169–179.

Federal Bureau of Investigation. *Uniform Crime Reports, 1980.* Washington, D.C.: U.S. Department of Justice.

Fontaine, Walter J. *Characteristics of Inmate Population at the Adult Correctional Institution, September 1, 1977.* Cranston, R.I.: Rhode Island Department of Corrections, 1977.

Fontaine, Walter J. *Recidivism at the Adult Correctional Institution, Final Report 1974–1975*. Cranston, R.I.: Rhode Island Department of Corrections, 1979.

Foster, Thomas W. "Make Believe Families: A Response of Women and Girls to the Deprivations of Imprisonment." *International Journal of Criminology and Penology* 3, 1 (1975): 71–78.

Fox, Vernon. "Intelligence, Race and Age as Selective Factors in Crime." *Journal of Criminal Law* 37, (1946): 150–151.

Fuller, Dan A., and Orsagh, Thomas. "Violent Behavior Within the North Carolina Prison System." *Popular Government* 4 (Spring 1979): 8–11.

Gillespie, Michael W., and Galliher, John F. "Age, Anomie, and the Inmates Definition of Aging in Prison: An Exploratory Study." In Kent, Kastenbaum, and Sherwood (eds.), *Research, Planning and Action for the Elderly*. New York: Behavioral Publications, 1972.

Glueck, Sheldon and Glueck, Elinor, *Later Criminal Careers*, New York: The Commonwealth Fund, 1957.

Grossman, Judy, and Macdonald, Donald. "Survey of Inmates 65 Years and Over—February, 1981." State of New York, Department of Correctional Services, The State Office Building Campus, Albany.

Ham, Joseph Neal. *The Forgotten Minority . . . An Exploration of Long-Term Institutionalized Aged and Aging Male Prison Inmates*. Washington, D.C.: National Institute of Law, U.S. Department of Justice, 1976.

Ham, Joseph N. "Aged and Infirm Male Prison Inmates." *Aging*. Washington, D.C.: U.S. Department of Health and Human Services Pub. No. (OHD) (AOA) 79-20949, July–August 1980.

Hendricks, Jon, and Burkhead, John. "Older Black Inmates." *Quarterly Contact: National Caucus and Center on Black Aging* 4, 5 (Spring 1981): 4.

Hicks, Donald A., and Alpert, Geoffrey P. "Patterns of Change and Adaptation in Prison." *Social Science Quarterly* 59 (June 1978): 37–59.

Hormuth, S.; Hood, R.; Wicklund, R. A.; Mabli, J.; Pribble, M.; and Dallas, M. "Freedom in a Correctional Institution—Relationships Between Personal Variables, Expectations, and Behavioral Freedoms." Paper presented at the Annual Meeting of Southwestern Psychological Association, Fort Worth, Texas, April 21–23, 1977.

Jensen, G. F. "Age and Rule-Breaking in Prison—A Test of Sociocultural Interpretations." *Criminology* 14 (February 1977): 555–568.

Keller, Oliver J., and Vedder, Clyde B. "The Crimes that Older Persons Commit." *Gerontologist* 8 (1968): 43.

Krajick, Kevin. "Growing Old in Prison." *Corrections Magazine* (March 1979): 34.

Last, Gunter. "Sleep Disorders in an Asylum: Lack of Sleep in Elderly Prisoners." *Zeitschrift für Gerontologie* 12, 3 (May–June 1979): 235–247.

McCreary, Charles P., and Mensh, Ivan P. "Personality Differences Associated with Age in Law Offenders." *Journal of Gerontology* 32, 2 (1977): 164–167.

Moberg, David O. "Old Age and Crime." *Journal of Criminal Law and Criminology* 43 (1952–53): 764–776.

Montgomery, Reid Hood. "A Measurement of Inmate Satisfaction/Dissatisfaction in Selected South Carolina Correctional Institutions." Ph.D. dissertation, University of South Carolina, 1974.

Panton, James. *Characteristics of Aged Inmates.* Raleigh, N.C.: North Carolina Department of Correction, 1974.

Panton, James H. "Personality Characteristics of Aged Inmates Within a State Prison Population." *Offender Rehabilitation* 2 (Winter 1976–77): 203–208.

Pollak, Otto. "The Criminality of Old Age." *Journal of Criminal Psychopathy* 3 (1941): 213–235.

Reed, Monika B., and Glamser, Francis D. "Aging in a Total Institution: The Case of Older Prisoners." *The Gerontologist* 19, (1979): 354–360.

Roberg, Roy, and Webb, Vincent J. *Critical Issues in Corrections.* St. Paul, Minn.: West Publishing Company, 1981, pp. 165–167.

Schroeder, Paul L. "Criminal Behavior in the Later Period of Life." *American Journal of Psychiatry* 92 (1936): 915–924.

Shichor, David, and Kobrin, Solomon. "Note: Criminal Behavior Among the Elderly." *The Gerontologist* 18, 2 (1978): 213–218.

Shinbaum, Marian. "Development of a Model for Prediction of Inmate Interest in Prison-Sponsored Academic and Vocational Education." Ph.D. dissertation, Auburn University, 1977.

Silfen, P. "Adaptation of the Older Prisoner in Israel." *International Journal of Offender Therapy and Comparative Criminology* 20, 1 (1977): 18–25.

Silfen, P., et al. "Clinical Criminology in Israel." *International Journal of Offender Therapy and Comparative Criminology* 20 (1976): 18–25.

Straus, Alan C., and Sherwin, Robert. "Inmate Rioters and Nonrioters—A Comparative Analysis." *American Journal of Correction* (July–August 1975): 34–35.

Teller, Fran E., and Howell, Robert J. *Criminal and Psychological Characteristics of the Older Prisoner.* Salt Lake City: Utah Division of Corrections, 1979.

Wiegand, Douglas N., and Burger, Jane C. "The Elderly Offender and Parole." *Prison Journal* 59 (Autumn–Winter 1979–80): 59–60.

Wiltz, Carroll Joseph. "The Influence of Age on Length of Incarceration." Ph.D. dissertation, University of Iowa, 1978.

Wolfgang, Marvin E. "Age, Adjustment, and the Treatment Process of Criminal Behavior." *Psychiatry Digest* (July 1964): 21–35.

Wooden, Wayne S., and Parker, Jay. "Aged Men in a Prison Environment: Life Satisfaction and Coping Strategies." Ph.D. dissertation, California State University—Long Beach, 1980.

Chapter 11

Prison Programs and Facilities For Elderly Inmates

Ann Goetting

While offenses *against* the elderly are highly publicized and seem commonplace, we are simply unaccustomed to thinking of the elderly as offenders. But some elderly people do in fact commit crimes, some are arrested, some are convicted, and some are sent to prison. On December 31, 1981, an estimated total of 8,853 persons aged 55 and older were incarcerated in state and federal prisons in the United States.[1] It can be expected that that figure has increased and will continue to do so as the prison population continues its upswing, with an increasingly higher proportion of arrests of senior citizens being for serious offenses.[2]

Several explanations have been offered for criminal behavior and the resultant incarceration of the elderly. From a physiological point of view, Rodstein suggests that organic brain syndrome in the aged may be associated with loss of inhibitions resulting in unlawful sexual behavior such as exhibitionism and in rigidity, quarrelsomeness, and aggression.[3] Shichor and Kobrin propose that the declining range of personal contacts experienced by the elderly is conducive to emotional intensity with a resulting increase in opportunity for personal conflict.[4] Wiegand and Burger suggest that the frustrations of old age in the United States, including poverty, loss of occupational status, and boredom, may combine with long-time animosity and sometimes liquor to create an emotionally volatile situation conducive to violence.[5] According to van Wormer, some aged persons commit crimes in order to get into places where they can find care and shelter. She recalls the film, "Going in Style," in which George Burns's character declares, "What have we got to lose?" as he and two elderly peers set out to rob a Manhattan bank.[6] Finally, McCall places ultimate blame for the incarceration of at least some elderly on the 1960's civil rights movement. He explains that by focusing attention on the rights of individuals, the movement, encouraged society to rethink its policies of involuntary commitment to mental hospitals, where some elderly citizens without alternative housing facilities resided.[7] As a result, explains McCall:

> . . . we are confronted with lonely, old, bag ladies released from mental hospitals with a handful of pills and an appointment at the local mental health center. They were confused and lost the pills, and they never found their way to the mental health center. The legal people said they weren't dangerous; the health people said no more could be done for them in the institution so they were free to go out into the street. Now in New York City there are many old men and old women living out of shopping bags and sleeping in parking garages on cold winter nights. Some . . . become bothersome to their community. Some commit minor crime. Some even commit serious crimes.[9]

The fact that elderly inmates represent such a small proportion of the total inmate population, coupled with their double minority status as old and criminal,[9] renders them low-priority status in society as a whole and within the prison structure. It is within this context that they have been referred to as "forgotten people" or "the forgotten minority."[10]

The purpose of this paper is to describe the existence or lack thereof of special policies, programs, and facilities for elderly inmates in the U.S. A survey was conducted during the first half of 1982 to solicit information from the fifty states, the District of Columbia, and the Federal Prison System. The results reported here are based on a 100-percent response from prison officials associated with each of these political units. In a telephone call and/or a letter, respondents were asked to describe what policies, programs, and facilities, if any, were in operation that were designed to accommodate the elderly inmate.

Forty-seven states and the Federal Prison System reported no formal special considerations for this category of prisoner. Typically, all inmates including the elderly are screened in the admission process; housing and work assignments are commensurate with health and agility. In this way, the elderly who are designated as being infirm are granted special treatment based on their inferior health status. In some states (including Alabama, California, Georgia, Idaho, Michigan, Missouri, North Carolina, South Carolina, and Virginia), these elderly infirm are referred to special units for the "medical/geriatric," "elderly and handicapped," "geriatric and handicapped," "aged and infirmed," or simply "geriatric." Such designations are misleading, however, in that they suggest that the facilities select the elderly for special consideration. In reality, the units are simply medical or light-duty units that house infirm inmates, many of whom are elderly. In these typical prison settings, healthy elderly inmates are distributed without special consideration throughout the prison system. It should be noted that six of the forty-seven states reporting no special accommodations for the elderly prisoner indicated that they had provisions to exclude them from heavy duty work such as highway labor and maintenance. Unlike Texas, however, inmates in Virginia are not residentially segregated based on their medical status. Also for the benefit of the elderly inmates, Virginia operates the Aged Offender Program at its state penitentiary. This program accommodates sixty-two men over age 50, which represents approximately 13 percent of the total Virginia inmate population in that age category. Essentially, the Aged Offender Program functions to sanction regularly scheduled monitored meetings of these older men at the state penitentiary for the purpose of discussing specific concerns of incarcerated senior citizens. The District of Columbia Department of Corrections houses inmates aged 55 and older (except those with medical problems requiring hospitalization) apart from the general inmate population in two special dormitories, which are described as quieter, cleaner, and better controlled than other residential facilities. Special recreational facilities for sedentary activities such as checkers, cards, and television are provided in these dormitories. Diets accommodate special medical needs. Also, the case worker assigned to these older residents consults with them on Social Security, Veterans Administration activities and benefits and community social services where applicable. Such consultation helps prepare the elderly inmate for reentry into society.

It becomes apparent from the information provided by this survey that prisons do not commonly recognize a chronological age status independent of health status. Programs, facilities, and treatment based on age are rare and never comprehensive, possibly reflecting a lack of recognition of, and responsiveness to, the special needs of institutionalized senior citizens. The vast majority of prisoners are in their twenties, and the prison structure is designed to accommodate that general age category. The mainstays of prison programming are education, vocational training, and recreation, and the programs offered are typically of little value to the elderly inmate. Most older prisoners have been out of the educational system for decades and have no desire to resume their studies. Those who do show an interest in educational programs are often discouraged by prison officials, who believe that the limited openings should be offered to younger men and women who would more likely benefit from them. Often the staff are unwilling to place older prisoners in education programs. The same situation holds true for vocational training programs; they are of little interest or value to the elderly because chances are slim that an older ex-convict will find work available in the community.

Competitive sports are an important part of prison recreation programs. Again, few, if any, are suited to the physical needs and limitations of the elderly, especially when participation requires them to compete with the younger, more robust, and often violent residents.[11] In addition, older prisoners are often unwilling to participate in institutional activities that are open to the general inmate population.[12] At least part of their resistance to association with younger prisoners can be attributed to their fear of becoming victims of violence.

The needs of the elderly in terms of health care, life-cycle roles, friendships, and security remain constant regardless of where they find themselves. Imprisonment causes many of these needs to be left inadequately fulfilled while simultaneously intensifying the need for their fulfillment.[13] In response to the perceived frustration associated with such unfulfilled needs, numerous recommendations for policy change have been posed on behalf of the incarcerated senior citizen.[14] One of the most commonly cited recommendations is that older prisoners be housed together and isolated from the general inmate population. Such isolation provides the older resident with optimal opportunity for forming peer networks, and also reduces vulnerability to violence.[15] Recommendations directed toward the elderly's unique physical needs are also common. By virtue of age alone, people require special diet, exercise, and recreation programs. Furthermore, due to the progressive deterioration of sight, hearing, memory, and reflexes and also to a general slowing of movement and sometimes of mental responsiveness, older inmates need to be served by staff members who are familiar with the physical components of the aging process and have the patience to deal with them.[16] A third type of recommendation for policy change stresses the value of an institutional setting geared to accommodate all needs—physical, psychological, and social. The emphasis here is on an integrated, comprehensive program designed to promote life satisfaction and successful reentry into the community.[17]

Opposing views have been offered to these arguments. Some observers, for instance, see no need for or responsibility to provide special consideration to older offenders.[18] Others address the issue of age segregation specifically, suggesting that the distribution of older inmates throughout the prison system has a stabilizing effect on the general inmate population.[19] Another point of opposition to the perceived need for the implementation of special formal consideration for older inmates is not found in the literature, but some prison officials expressed it. Some administrators advocate the "total person perspective," and believe that the humanistic concept of special consideration of the elderly can be turned into age discrimination. From this viewpoint, inmates should be given housing and work assignments based on, first, the type of custody status that they require. Next should be considered health, followed by family and community status. If a prisoner has relatives and friends who are willing to visit him, he should be placed in a correctional unit accessible to them. Work skills should also be considered. If a person is trained in a certain occupation and prefers that kind of work, he should be placed in an institution that can provide him with that kind of job activity. Some prisons conduct farming enterprises, while others specialize in road work or industry. Placing an inmate in a special unit for the elderly could be detrimental to his security, family relationships, and occupational interests and needs.

The question of appropriateness of special policies, programs, and facilities for elderly inmates poses a true dilemma, and deserves recognition of professionals interested in the well-being of the elderly as well as those interested in prison policy. One point prison administrators should consider is legal immunity. The law grants certain rights to U.S. citizens, which are maintained during incarceration. Numerous lawsuits have been filed against departments of correction by inmates and civil rights groups for claims involving a wide range of negligence. Among them are inadequate health care, failure to protect an inmate from assault, and unsanitary living conditions. It is in the best interest of corrections administrators to accommodate the needs of their elderly residents, if not for humanitarian purposes, then to avoid legitimate charges of civil rights violations.

NOTES

1. This figure was reached by summing the total number of inmates aged 55 and older in federal prisons (1,013) with the estimated total number of inmates in the same age category in state prisons (7,840). Information on the Federal Prison System was furnished by U.S. Department of Justice, Federal Bureau of Prisons, *Profile Data Report* (Report No. 80.51, unpublished), February 8, 1982. The estimate on state prisons (including the District of Columbia) was reached by determining (1) that in 1979 an estimated 2.3 percent of state inmates were 55 years of age and older, (2) assuming that the 2.3 percent held true on December 31, 1981, (3) determining that the total state inmate population on that date was 340,876, and (4) computing 2.3 percent of 340,876 (7,840). The 1979 percentage of state inmates aged 55 and older was furnished by U.S. Department of Justice, Bureau of Statistics, *Survey of Inmates of State Correctional Facilities, 1979* (machine-readable data file). The data were originally collected by the Bureau of the Census for the Principal Investigator, The Bureau of Justice Statistics, 2nd ICPSR ed. (Ann Arbor, Mich.: Inter-University Consortium for Political and Social Research, 1981). The total number of state prison inmates on December 31, 1981, was furnished by U.S. Department of Justice, Bureau of Justice Statistics, *Prisoners in 1981*, Bureau of Justice Statistics Bulletin (Washington, D.C.: U.S. Government Printing Office, January 1981), p. 2.
2. David Shichor, "Patterns of Elderly Lawbreaking in Urban, Suburban and Rural Areas," presented at Second Annual Elderly Offender Conference, Florida International University, North Miami, February 24, 1983.
3. Manuel Rodstein, "Crime and the Aged: The Criminals," *Journal of the American Medical Association* 234, no. 6 (November 10, 1975): 639.
4. David Shichor and Solomon Kobrin, "Note: Criminal Behavior Among the Elderly," *The Gerontologist* 18, no. 2 (1978): 215.
5. N. Douglas Wiegand and Jane C. Burger, "The Elderly Offender and Parole," *The Prison Journal* 59, no. 2 (1979): 49.
6. Katherine van Wormer, "To Be Old and in Prison," in Sloan Letman et al. (eds.), *Contemporary Issues in Corrections* (Jonesboro, Tenn.: Pilgrimage, Inc., 1981), p. 86.
7. Jack McCall, "Special Problem Patients—Psychotic, Geriatric, Retarded, Sex Offender," Workshop Number V of the conference "Mental Health for the Convicted Offender Patient and Prisoner," sponsored by the North Carolina Department of Correction and the North Carolina Medical Society, Raleigh, October 27–29, 1976, p. 175.
8. Ibid., p. 176.
9. Members of minority racial or ethnic groups have triple minority status.
10. Kevin Krajick, "Growing Old in Prison," *Corrections Magazine* (March 1979): 34; Joseph N. Ham, "The Forgotten Minority—An Exploration of Long Term Institutionalized Aged and Aging Male Prison Inmates," unpublished Ph.D. thesis, University of Michigan, 1976.
11. Wiegand and Burger, "The Elderly Offender and Parole," pp. 50–51.
12. Michael T. Bintz, "Recreation for the Older Population in Correctional Institutions," *Therapeutic Recreation Journal* 8, (1974): 88; Marian Goldstein Shinbaum, "Development of a Model for Prediction of Inmate Interest in Prison-Sponsored Academic and Vocational Education," unpublished Ph.D. thesis, Auburn University, 1977.
13. Ham, "The Forgotten Minority."

14. George F. Baier, "The Aged Inmate," *American Journal of Correction* (March–April 1961): 4–34: S. Bergman and M. Amir, "Crime and Delinquency among Aged in Israel: An Experience Survey," *The Israel Annals of Psychiatry and Related Disciplines* 11, no. 1 (March 1973): 33–48; Bintz, "Recreation for the Older Population;" Harry L. Freedman, "Rehabilitation of the Older Prisoner," *Journal of Clinical Psychopathology* 9, (April 1948): 226–232; Dan A. Fuller and Thomas Orsagh, "Violent Behavior Within the North Carolina Prison System," *Popular Government* 44, no. 4 (Spring 1979): 8–11; Maureen McCarthy, "An Assessment of the Unique Needs of the Elderly Offender," unpublished paper, Florida State University, 1980; Ernest O. Moore and Ruth Phillips, "Two Prison Environments: Their Effect on the Elderly," unpublished paper, University of Nebraska, 1979; Wiegand and Burger, "The Elderly Offender and Parole."

15. Bintz, ibid., pp. 88–89; Bergman and Amir, ibid.; Fuller and Orsagh, ibid., p. 11; McCarthy, ibid., p. 119; Moore and Phillips, ibid., p. 15.

16. Baier, "The Aged Inmate."

17. Ronald H. Aday, "Toward the Development of a Therapeutic Program for Older Prisoners," *Offender Rehabilitation* 1, no. 4 (Summer, 1977): 343–348; McCarthy, "An Assessment of the Unique Needs."

18. Dennis Jurczak, "Special Problem Patients—Psychotic, Geriatric, Retarded, Sex Offender," Workshop Number V of the conference, "Mental Health for the Convicted Offender Patient and Prisoner," sponsored by the North Carolina Department of Correction and the North Carolina Medical Society, Raleigh, October 27–29, 1976, p. 184; Peter Silfin, "The Adaptation of the Older Prisoner in Israel," *International Journal of Offender Therapy and Comparative Criminology* 21 (1977): 57–65; Wayne S. Wooden and Jay Parker, "Aged Men in a Prison Environment;" Life Satisfaction and Coping Strategies," presented at the 1980 annual meeting of the National Gerontological Society, San Diego.

19. Alan C. Straus and Robert Sherwin, "Inmate Rioters and Non-Rioters—A Comparative Analysis" (Part 2), *American Journal of Correction* 37, no. 4 (July–August 1975): 54; R. H. McCleery, "The Governmental Process and Informal Social Control," in Donald Cressey, (ed.), *The Prison: Studies in Institutional Organization and Change* (New York: Holt Rinehart and Winston, 1961), pp. 149–188; Marvin E. Wolfgang, "Age, Adjustment and the Treatment Process of Criminal Behavior," *Psychiatry Digest* (August 1964): 24.

Chapter 12

The Broward Senior Intervention and Education Program: A Pilot Program

Gary Feinberg, Sidney Glugover, and Irene Zwetchkenbaum

The Broward County Senior Intervention Program (BSIE) had its beginning in October 1978, when an elderly woman, 79 years of age, who attended activities at the Jewish Community Center of South Broward County, Hollywood, Florida, walked into the Outreach office to see the supervisor. She was in a state of agitation and highly traumatized. She related to Herb Weiss, the Outreach supervisor, that she had received a notice to appear at Criminal Court. This was a citation (a summons) for a shoplifting offense.

The woman was incoherent, but after being calmed down she was able to describe the shoplifting incident that had taken place a week earlier. Mr. Weiss decided it would be helpful to this woman if he appeared with her at the arraignment in Criminal Court. If nothing else, he could give her emotional and physical support.

This was Weiss's first experience with a continuing trail of elderly offenders appearing before the Criminal Court judge, and dispositions that neither served the best interest of the criminal justice system nor provided rehabilitation for elderly offenders. As a result of this experience, Weiss thought it would be mutually advantageous to meet with the presiding Judge (John J. King) of Broward County, to discuss an alternative program for handling elderly shoplifting offenders. Judge King, confronted daily with elderly offenders, was most receptive to this suggestion. He indicated that other Broward

County judges were also witness to similar cases and were seeking some diversionary programs rather than incarceration, high fines, and court costs to deal with elderly offenders. The present system of revolving-door justice did not seem to be working.

Discussions were begun between the staff of the Jewish Community Center and the county court judges of Broward County. In addition, research was undertaken to explore existing data and programs dealing with elderly offenders in Broward County.

A one-year study of Broward County's Pre-Trial Intervention Program disclosed that of 1,442 clients in the program sampled from April 1978 through April 1979, 332 (23 percent) cases of offenders were 60 years of age and over.[1] After exhaustive research, no other diversionary programs were found to be available for the elderly offender. As a result, the Broward County Senior Intervention Education Program (BSIE) was founded in April 1979. The program is a voluntary alternative created specifically for elderly offenders (60 years of age and older) who have been arrested and who have appeared before the courts for misdemeanant shoplifting, first offense. The program has two major objectives: (1) to prevent the recurrence of shoplifting by the elderly and (2) to provide the courts with humanitarian and socially constructive sanctions for elderly shoplifters. To achieve these objectives, the BSIE combines individual counseling, participation of offender-clients in various social and cultural activities in camaraderie with others their own age, and community involvement in the form of externships: "volunteer" work at local hospitals, libraries, elementary schools, and so on.

Although it has no official legal status, nevertheless the BSIE is accepted informally by the legal community and widely used. It recognizes that elderly shoplifters are a special type of law violators, their crimes carrying a unique set of circumstances and sociolegal reactions that distinguish them from other forms of criminal deviance. More specifically, as a diversionary rehabilitation program, the BSIE takes as its point of departure the following understanding of elderly shoplifters and their offense:

1. They are typically first-time law violators who have otherwise led exemplary and socially constructive lives.
2. They are criminologically immature. Their experiential knowledge of the criminal justice system tends to be nominal or nonexistent. Concomitantly, they are anxious, embarrassed, and contrite in their confrontation with law enforcement.
3. Unlike offenders of other age groups, they usually lack the opportunity to restore any loss of status stemming from the stigma of their law violation.

4. The passage of time that allows society, family, and friends to forget the errant folly of the young is not a boon afforded offenders in their senior years.

5. Entailed here is a special case of role reversal. In court the relatively younger and inexperienced sit in judgment of those who are older and have endured most of life's trials and tribulations—and paid their dues accordingly.

6. Even in terms of misdemeanors, the theft tends to involve merchandise of nominal value, often under $5. This is well below the estimated $66 average loss per shoplifting incident, all age groups included.

7. The entire legal system—police, courts, corrections—is in a quandary regarding the most appropriate response to elderly shoplifting. Some legalists argue that the law has been violated and retribution must be had, even against the old and infirm. Others call for developing a special elderly justice system analogous to the juvenile justice system, including a designation of "Elderly in Need of Supervision," "Elderly Delinquents," "Elderly Offenders," and the like.

8. The ultimate victims are often other elderly persons, who absorb the cost of shoplifting losses through higher prices.

Prior to the creation of the BSIE, the judiciary had only a limited number of otherwise inadequate and inappropriate sentencing alternatives for cases involving elderly shoplifters. Fines, for instance, are especially punitive for an offender who must live on a fixed income. They may depress already subsistence-level standards of living, a problem exacerbated by limited opportunities to defray such costs through loans or supplemental income.

Probation is of equally questionable value. It often burdens the offender in much the same way as a fine, since probationers (in Florida) must pay a monthly probation fee. In addition, probation services don't especially articulate the elderly's interests and needs but focus more on those of juveniles. Similarly, the personnel associated with probation work typically are neither by training nor inclination in possession of skills necessary for working with the elderly.

Incarceration, in turn, seems both inappropriate and unusually punitive. Elderly shoplifters pose no major threat to the security of the community, nor could they likely benefit from any treatment program offerred under confinement. Furthermore, the seriousness of the offense pales into insignificance when considered in the context of this particular community's high rates of homicide, robbery, aggravated assault, and other crimes against persons and property.

At the same time, the consequences for the accused elderly shop-lifter are by no means insignificant: (1) they may be fined up to $500 (Fines of $150 to $200 are most common, even where the theft involved articles valued under $5); (2) court costs of about $15 may be levied against them; (3) if they hire attorneys, the fee can be $500 or more; (4) a criminal record is made, which may force the loss of certain occupational and licensing privileges. In addition, of course, are loss of trust and status within reference groups, and emotions such as embarrassment and guilt.

ORGANIZATION OF THE BSIE

A nonsectarian program, the BSIE is organized as a special service component of Jewish Community Centers of South Broward. Space is provided at several locations, which include the six Focal Point Senior Centers of Broward County. These Senior Centers are multipurpose facilities, which for many years have been offering to the elderly lectures, cultural activities, primary health care, free meals, therapy for the handicapped, an adult day care center, and so forth. The BSIE uses these centers as the base for its program. These centers offer the BSIE, free of charge, the use of telephones, and photocopying equipment, and office furnishings.

The BSIE program also maintains ties with other community ser-vice agencies. Included among these are local hospitals, alcohol re-habilitation facilities, nursing homes, Cancer Care, SCORE, the Sal-vation Army, as well as various organizations offering psychiatric counseling. These contacts are maintained informally and used on an ad hoc basis.

BSIE PERSONNEL

All four of the county's courts filter clients into the program. The BSIE personnel, a part of the Southeast Focal Point staff, consist of two counselors and one supervisor, who serve a large and populous geopolitical area. The two counselors work directly with the elderly shoplifting client. They are responsible for helping the clients work through the trauma of arrest and related legal proceedings. They also help clients unravel the personal woes that may underlie the shoplifting episode, channel them into needed special services offered elsewhere in the community (e.g., alcohol rehabilitation centers), place them as volunteers in understaffed local community organizations (e.g., libraries, elementary schools, hospitals), and generally monitor their rehabilitative progress.

ELIGIBILITY

Eligibility for the BSIE program is strictly prescribed. The offender-client must be: (1) 60 years of age or more; (2) a first-time offender; (3) charged with only misdemeanant shoplifting; (4) convicted after entering a plea of guilty; and (5) willing to accept participation in the BSIE.

PROGRAM COMPONENTS

The BSIE program has three components: (1) individual counseling; (2) required participation in Senior Center social, cultural, and educational activities; and (3) externship with a community service organization (e.g., hospitals, the Salvation Army, SCORE.

Each client must participate in the first two components; some must also donate time to a community service organization directed and overseen by the BSIE counselor.

Acceptance into the program depends on the consent of the presiding judge, then a "memorandum of acceptance" and a "waiver of speedy trial" are filed with the court and state attorney. The client is informed that arraignment will be continued and sentence deferred until completion of the program. In addition, he is informed that he will have to meet general requirements:

1. To attend twelve weekly sessions consisting of social, cultural, and educational classes offered to the senior public-at-large at the various senior activity centers.
2. To participate in a selected community volunteer program.
3. To attend one-on-one confidential counseling sessions (usually bimonthly, but anywhere from weekly to once every three weeks depending on client need). Weekly telephone contact is also required for all who see a counselor less than once per week. This is especially necessary where the client is not participating in a senior center activity but is working as a community volunteer. Home visits are made by the counselor when necessary.

The client then decides whether to accept participation in the BSIE as outlined or to accept the sentence of the court. It is estimated that approximately 82 percent of those cases offered this choice opt for the BSIE.

FUNDING AND SERVICE

Funds for the low-budget program are secured from Title III, the Older Americans Act, through the Area Agency on Aging of Broward County, Florida, and the Jewish Federation of South Broward. Unlike many probationary programs, the BSIE charges no fee to the elderly offender-client. Approximately 400 clients are served annually, with each counselor maintaining an average monthly case load of about twenty clients. The program takes three months—twelve weekly sessions—to complete.

PROGRAM OPERATIONS

The initial contact with elderly shoplifters occurs in the courtroom immediately following their hearing. BSIE counselors spend a portion of each week, ranging from four mornings to two full days, in the courts making themselves available to judges hearing cases involving elderly shoplifters. In preparation, and with the assistance of court bailiffs and administrative personnel, counselors receive a copy of the court's daily docket along with information indicating which shoplifting cases involve persons 60 years of age or older. This list is critical to locating potential offender-clients and helps ensure the presence of counselors when and where most needed. A preliminary interview is held to ascertain whether this is a first offense and if the person intends to plead guilty or no contest to the charge.

At the hearing, if the presiding judge finds the eligibility criteria for the BSIE, he has the discretion to offer the following sentencing option: to pay a fine (usually ranging from $75 to $150, although it may go as high as $500) and court costs ($10 to $15, most of which is used to defray victim compensation operations) and have a criminal record, or to accept participation in the BSIE.

Prior to making the sentencing decision, and to ensure a more reasoned consideration, the judge orders the potential offender-client to meet privately with a BSIE counselor in the courthouse that same day. It is at this session that the potential client is informed about the program, its goals and methods, and contracted responsibilities.

The offender is advised of what participation with the BSIE Program Offers: (1) it will remove the offender from the criminal justice system into a social agency trained to deal with "senior problems"; (2) one-on-one confidential counseling is provided; (3) the agency offers the ability to plug into social services as needed, including in-depth psychiatric and psychological evaluation and counseling; and (4) successful completion of participation will result in dismissal of charges with no court costs and no criminal record.

Once an offender-client has agreed to participate, he goes through several stages of counseling:

Stage 1: Introduction and Orientation

The offender-client completes an intake questionnaire. This form includes standard biographic data (e.g., age, sex, marital status, length of residence in the community, occupation, education level, amount and sources of income), as well as questions regarding feelings of alienation, loneliness, health status, attitudes toward the victim and the criminal justice system, type of article(s) purloined, treatment by store personnel, self definition as a criminal law violator, and so on. Usually this form will continue to be completed with the help of the counselor over two or even three sessions. The resulting case profile serves several functions. It may be used: (1) in direct counseling; (2) for purposes of causal analysis, and (3) in program evaluation. (An exit interview to measure certain attitudinal changes is anticipated.)

Stage 2: Catharsis

Having submitted certain pertinent information, offender-clients are given an opportunity to explain the shoplifting incident and ensuing events in their own words. Offender-clients, in many instances, have not discussed the shoplifting incident with anyone during the four or five weeks of waiting that typically precede the arraignment or hearing. At the same time, they are often highly traumatized by the events and processes that mark their transit through the criminal justice system from the time of accusation by store security and subsequent police arrest to actual appearance before a judge. Consequently, providing an opportunity during the first and second session to reduce the trauma and enjoy the release of tension becomes a critical therapeutic dimension of the program. Many clients lose control over their emotions and confide the pervasive embarrassment they feel and the humiliation they've suffered after a lifetime of commitment to law and order.

Throughout this catharsis, counselors remain relatively passive and objective. They do not sit in judgment. Instead, they seek to enhance self-esteem, reassure, and provide needed emotional support and practical information, especially regarding future procedures and expections.

Stage 3: Selecting Center Activities for Required Participation

The Senior Centers offer a wide range of social, cultural, and educational activities to all seniors in the community, including lectures, dances, self-awareness sessions, hobbycrafts, music, plays, and games. The counselor selects the activities in which the elderly offender-client will participate over the next twelve weeks with input from the client regarding his interests, needs, preferences, and experiences. Several factors are used to make the final determination, including observation of what the client is telling the counselor.

For the client who lives alone, has few friends, has an ill spouse, or in similar ways presents a lifestyle that affords little communication with the outside world, an activity in a group setting maximizing personal, informal interaction with others would be most appropriate. The multipurpose Senior Centers already offer a number of such groups in an established, on-going basis, for example, self-awareness groups, discussion groups covering various health and health-related issues, art and ceramics classes, and current events groups. These are led by a professional staff and instructors from local community colleges.

For offender-clients who already have an established pattern of activity and sociability in their present environment, a more diversified outlet in the form of volunteer community service work may be contracted. One of the most popular and rewarding is at a local hospital, where they may assist in a variety of functions such as admitting and discharging patients, escorting patients to various therapies, visiting patients who receive little or no attention from family or friends, and so on. Other more creative externships include transporting seniors to clinics, delivering "meals-on-wheels" to shut-ins, serving as library aides, helping elementary schools provide special attention to students requiring it, doing in-service activity with SCORE, and teaching some well-honed skill such as music or cooking to others in the center. Under consideration is an effort at implementing a "Helping Hand" program, in which the elderly are trained to help other seniors deal with grief, psychosocial crises of terminal illness, and the like.

A major objective of such externships is to help offender-clients transcend personal woes and entertain a broader *weltanschauung*. The secrecy of the clients' offenses is maintained, but counselors monitor their participation regularly.

Stage 4: Continuing Personal Counseling

The development stages of continuous counseling sessions become more revealing as the counselor strives to unravel some of the underlying problems that may have precipitated the shoplifting. This is done through intensive probing, especially with regard to the shoplifter's relationships with friends and family—or lack thereof—their use of available time, community awareness, and involvement.

REASONS FOR SHOPLIFTING

Most clients say they "don't know why" they shoplifted. Others admit to an impulse of the moment, to temptation, or to observing others shoplifting and trying to get away with it, too. Still others say they put the item or items in their pocket until they arrived at the checkout, and "forgot to pay." Some walk by the checkout station without stopping to pay, carrying items very visibly in their hands. They state that they were thinking of other things, such as recent loss, illness in the family, or other problems, and didn't realize what they were doing, possibly due to medication. Others are too impatient to wait in long lines, and so put the item in their bags or pockets and attempt to walk out of the store—only to be stopped by the security officer or manager. A number of clients feel that they were entrapped.

Specifically, counselors find that the elderly may shoplift for any one or a combination of the following:

1. fears about future financial security
2. impulse; the temptation to try to get away with it
3. a need for attention; loneliness, no friends, lack of family contact and concern; "a cry for help"
4. boredom; looking for excitement through inappropriate behavior
5. too impatient to stand in lines
6. irritability; anger at society for the position retirement has placed them in
7. inability to cope with physical or emotional changes of aging
8. forgetfulness, possibly due to physiological changes and/or medication

Contrary to supposition, the BSIE group of shoplifters were not indigent. Based on income reported to the counselors, only eight clients were receiving food stamps at the time of the shoplfiting, and four clients were in need of procuring food stamps.

The counselors help offender-clients sort out their feelings about the offense, its ramifications, and consequences. They attempt to give the act de facto and de jure status as a criminal law violation, and they offer a view that the store and other customers—especially elderly customers—are the ultimate victims of the shoplifting. In essence, they seek to make client-offenders fully aware of what they have done, and provide a proper perspective on it. Some offender-clients—those who, torn by grief and remorse, exaggerate the seriousness of their crime—may require more palliative statements and reassurances. Those who minimize or even decriminalize the act of shoplifting may require a more firm approach.

During the process of aging, various problems may occur. These may be physical, mental, social, economic, psychological, or any combination thereof. Furthermore, aging is not limited to any one aspect of an individual's life. Adaptation to major changes in life is seldom easy. Lost roles, activities, or capacities are often irreplaceable, agents facilitating resocialization may be lacking, and coping mechanisms themselves may be attenuated (reduced incomes, physical debilitation, etc.).

Concomitantly, it is recognized that shoplifting by the elderly is not an isolated event with no consequences and no ramifications. It originates and terminates in a highly charged social, psychological, cultural, and biophysical field. Counselors are attuned to the special dilemmas of aging—role loss, role vacuity, role reversal, disengagement, status transition, and accompanying losses of power, income, prestige, and so on. Many of these more salient age-related problems will be addressed at such counseling sessions, again in the context of the shoplifting act.

During the study year (April 1978–April 1979), the BSIE made referrals to other appropriate social service agencies when needed, such as clinics for psychological evaluations, where approximately twenty-eight clients were provided service. Other networking was done with Home Health Services for homebound spouses, Home Companions or Respite Care, which would allow the clients to attend the BSIE Program and give them time to attend to their own errands such as shopping. Of the approximately 1,400 clients the counselors have seen to date (April 1979–April 1982), the recidivism rate is only 1.5 percent.

PROGRAM EVALUATION

Whether or not a program is evaluated as successful depends, in part, on its goal (or goals) and in part on one's definition of "successful." The BSIE's goal is to provide a more humanitarian and effective sentencing alternative for first-time elderly violators of misdemeanant shoplifting laws. This central goal has two objectives: (1) to reduce the likelihood of continued involvement of the elderly in shoplifting activity; and (2) to get them more involved with people and back into the mainstream of life, and thus to raise their self-esteem. In examining how the BSIE has fared, we can observe both several milestones of achievement and a number of pitfalls.

The traditional measure used to determine the success of programs designed to rehabilitate criminal offenders is the recidivism rate, that is, the numbers of those receiving the program who repeat their offense. Among the limitations of this measure are:

1. Recidivism is not simply a direct consequence of the rehabilitation program's effect on the actual behavior of the offender. It is also a function of police efficiency in clearing with an arrest offenses known or reported to them.[2] Concomitantly, relying on arrest statistics places the evaluator in the unenviable position of having to cope with the fact that an unknown proportion of larcenies are reported to the police; this is especially true for less serious instances such as misdemeanant shoplifting.[3]

2. By "recidivism" do we necessarily mean a repeat of the same offense that brought the offender to the rehabilitation program? What if the offender-client ceases all shoplifting activity after participation in the program but returns to the courts for a different, more serious offense? (Possibly a variant of iatrogenic disease?) What if the offender-client returns for a less serious violation? And, lastly, what if the offender-client returns to shoplifting, but the manner in which it is carried out suggests a more organized, better planned offense and a commitment to this way of life?

3. A time frame must be established, within which a violation will constitute an instance of recidivism or a program failure. Probably we would have little difficulty accepting a repeated act of shoplifting done five minutes after completing the program as an instance of the program's failure. But what if it occurs five months later, or five years later? The decision here is subjective and arbitrary. Moreover, the problem compounds when one considers plotting the number of reoccurrences on a time grid.

For example, compare three repeats within five weeks and no other instances over the next fifteen years, to three repeats, once every five years? Are these measures of equal failure? Which, if any, is the more successful? Again, subjective and arbitrary elements enter into the decision and evaluation processes.

There are, of course, other limitations and problems in using recidivism rates as a measure of a program's rehabilitative success.[4] Keeping these in mind to dampen any overly enthusiastic conclusion, one must still admit that the BSIE nevertheless has an impressive track record. Since its inception, as stated previously, approximately 1,400 cases have been treated, but the recidivism rate is only 1.5 percent.

In addition to recidivism, however, there are internal validating sources for establishing the BSIE's success with respect to its rehabilitative objective:

1. Of the approximately 1,400 individuals treated by the program, 98.5 percent completed it without incident. In only four cases was it necessary to inform the court that the offender-client was not attending the Senior Center meetings or otherwise living up to contracted program responsibilities. This figure compares favorably with standard probation violation rates, about 20 percent nationally.

2. Some clients, by personal request, have continued attending the Senior Centers, offering volunteer aid, and occasionally meeting with a counselor on an ad hoc basis even after their case has been officially—and successfully—terminated by the court.

Although its success rate appears extremely positive, some qualifications are in order. First, the number of clients who actually remain law-abiding is not known. In point of fact, we simply do not know, nor can we accurately estimate, the real volume of elderly shoplifting by examining cases known or reported to the police. Second, a control group needs to be established so that it can be determined what proportion of elderly shoplifters discontinue their shoplifting without benefit of participating in the BSIE. Third, an additional control group is needed to determine if it is the appearance in court and the surrounding trauma that serve as negative stimuli to extinguish the shoplifting behavior or participation in the BSIE. Comparing the recidivism rates of those cases going to court but rejecting participation in the BSIE and those accepting participation would be one way to make this determination. Fourth, the program is so young that not enough data are yet available for evaluating the durability of any cure effected. A zero-order or low recidivism rate within one year may be a measure of the program's achievement. Ensuring an abstention for three or five years or longer would be a still greater achievement. Best would be a longitudinal study over one generation. Lastly, it has not been determined whether any BSIE participants have been rearrested subsequent to completing the program, even for another type of criminal offense. The program is informed only about rearrests for shoplifting. (Even if clients were to engage in other crimes, it would not necessarily mean that the BSIE is not a valid program for remediating elderly shoplifting. Again, however, the iatrogenic potentiality might excite some interesting research.)

CONCLUSION

With high arrest rates in the United States and dramatic increases by both volume and rate, elderly involvement in criminal law violations has captured contemporary intellectual interest. Using the FBI's *Uniform Crime Reports* to trace the pattern of elderly arrest rates over almost one generation, 1966–1980, evidences escalations in forcible rape (+ 161 percent), robbery (+ 114 percent), and aggravated assaults (+ 56 percent) among other FBI Index crimes committed by the elderly. However, with a volume increase of 309 percent, and a rate increase of 265 percent, elderly larceny arrests are of especial concern, outstripping the growth of this offense for all age groups in toto. Most of these larceny-thefts by the elderly take the form of shoplifting.

Why people shoplift remains an open question. Some, in keeping with traditional psychosocial perspectives, contend that shoplifters suffer from low frustration tolerance levels, lack of insight into realistic problem-solving, poor self-images, feelings of inferiority, recent traumatic experiences, or deeper psychopathological reasons.[5] Others, pledging allegiance to more chic econometric models currently currying favor, in the quest to explain social behavior, assert that no pathological state underlies such acts. Instead, the reasoning goes, they are caused by the same economic forces that guide all shopping behavior: getting the most goods for the least cost.[6] Less analytical studies simply delineate the reasons typically given by shoplifters to account for their behavior, including, for example, desire for the item, lack of money, need for excitement, an unexplained urge, and so on.[7] The process of aging may exaggerate many of these potential causes, crystallize them into some unique pattern, or bring into focus other variables.[8]

While scholars theorize about and research into the cause(s) of elderly shoplifting, local communities must respond to an increasingly visible and voluminous population of these "elderly delinquents" and elderly law violators in general. Moreover, they must do so while recognizing that standard criminal justice policies and procedures, which work well with other adults, have dysfunctional sociolegal consequences when applied to seniors, often bastardizing their original mandate. The Broward Senior Intervention and Education program, with its combination of individual counseling, sociocultural participation, and externships at manpower-poor community agencies is shown to be a viable alternative for coping with the growing problem of elderly shoplifters. Its simple organizational structure operates with few administrative problems while enjoying an almost 99-percent success rate as measured by recidivism. Furthermore, it could be made self-supporting were offender-clients charged even nominal fees. Given a little imagination, the BSIE program might be elaborated into a strategy for assisting criminal justice systems in a meaningful, humanitarian, and socially constructive way with other types of elderly delinquents—and elderly offenders—while at the same time effectively dealing with undesirable, illegal behavior.

NOTES

1. Jacob Messina, *Evaluation Report: Broward County Pre-Trial Intervention Program* (July 1979), (Ft. Lauderdale, Florida: unpublished).
2. Donald Black, "Production of Crime Rates," in J. Susman (ed.), *Crime and Justice* (New York: AMS Press, 1972), pp. 336–346; Stanton Wheeler, "Criminal Statistics: A Reformulation of the Problem," in J. Teele (ed.), *Juvenile Delinquency* (Itasca, Ill.: Peacock, 1970), pp. 50–58; Nigel Walker, *Crime Courts, and Figures: An Introduction to Criminal Statistics* (Lexington, Mass.: Petersen-Smith, 1973).
3. Albert D. Biderman and Albert J. Reiss, "On Exploring the Dark Figure of Crime," *Annals of the American Academy of Political and Social Science* 374 (1967): 1–15; R. Chilton, "Persistent Problems of Crime Statistics," in Simon Dinitz and Walter Reckless (eds.), *Critical Issues in the Study of Crime* (Boston, Mass.: Little, Brown, 1968), pp. 89–95.
4. Robert Martinson, "What Works? Questions and Answers About Prison Reform," *The Public Interest* 35 (1974): 22–54.
5. Anthony C. Gaudio, *An Assessment and Evaluation of Shoplifters* (Richmond: Virginia Advisory Legislative Council, 1968), p. 17; Versele-Severin, Carlos, "Study of Female Shoplifters in Department Stores," *International Criminal Police Review* 24 (1969): 66–70.
6. Robert E. Kraut, "Deterrent and Definitional Influences on Shoplifting," *Social*

Problems 23 (1976): 358–368; Jean Sohier, "A Rather Ordinary Crime: Shoplifting," *International Criminal Police Review* 229 (1969): 161–166.

7. Jerry J. Tobia and Jay Reynolds, "Juvenile Shoplifting in an Affluent Suburban Community," *Law and Order* 18 (1970): 76–80.

8. Matilda White Riley and Ann Foner, et al., *Aging and Society: Volume 1, An Inventory of Research Findings* (New York: Russell Sage Foundation, 1968).

Chapter 13

Social Work Practice with Elderly Offenders

Mindy L. Gewirtz

This chapter presents a preliminary attempt at fusing theoretical knowledge with practice skills from two fields, social work and gerontology, in order to develop an intervention approach for working specifically with elderly offender populations. It presents a modified version of the Integrative Approach for gerontological practice based on the work of Edmund Sherman.[1] The relationship of the Integrative Approach to social work practice, as well as a description, application, and limitations of the approach in working with elderly offenders will be explored, and issues for additional research and clarification will be recommended. It is hoped that this discussion will stimulate interest into researching why elderly people turn to crime, and into developing the most effective intervention strategies for prevention, treatment, and rehabilitation.

The author wishes to express thanks to Professors Maureen Didier and Edmund Sherman, of the School of Social Welfare, SUNY/Albany, and special appreciation to Evelyn Newman, Associate Director of the Ringel Institute of Gerontology, for their helpful comments during preparation of this paper.

SOCIAL WORK GOALS, ATTITUDES, KNOWLEDGE BASE, AND PRACTICE SKILLS

Social work practice has evolved from a system of goals and objectives that has guided the development of a particular set of values and attitudes. These values and attitudes in turn have shaped the development of a knowledge base and ethical practice principles.[2] One of the most important goals of social work is to help people as individuals, in groups and as a community, to achieve their chosen objectives of sustaining or enhancing social competence. This goal applies to social workers working with elderly individuals, their families, and communities as well as with elderly offenders, both in and out of prison, who comprise small subpopulations of the elderly.

The attitudes and values in social work having been shaped by the above system of goals and objectives, are based on a humanistic view of man, "giving primacy to the values of human worth and dignity, of self realization, personal autonomy, secular rationality and historical continuity. As an ideology, social work is humanistic, positivistic and utopian, committed to the ideals of professionalism and social welfare."[3]

The knowledge base, guided by the goals and values of social work, has been developed through an understanding of various theoretical approaches to human behavior. Sherman's Integrative Approach to counseling the aging utilizes the knowledge base developed from the major theoretical approaches to human behavior (developmental, cognitive, and behavioral) and applies them to working with the elderly population. The application of the modified version of the approach specifically applies the knowledge base to elderly offenders.

Practice principles derived from a fusion of the goals, attitudes, and philosophical values of social work are merged with theoretical knowledge. Practice principles, in turn, have guided the development of methodologies and technical practice skills for implementing the interventive strategies based on theoretical knowledge.[4] Practice methodologies in working with the elderly—or in this case, elderly offenders—depend on one's theoretical orientation. In Sherman's Integrative Approach to counseling the elderly, workers borrow methods and techniques from various approaches to individualize the most effective treatment plan for clients.

In essence, the goals, attitudes, values, knowledge base, and practice skills of social work provide a framework for working with elderly offender populations. The proposed application of Sherman's Integrative Approach assumes the goals and knowledge base of counseling intervention in social work. However, I have conceptually modified and expanded the approach to include the possibilities for integration of case management services as alternative or complementary strategies to counseling.

For this purpose, the elderly offender is defined as anyone aged 55 or over who has been apprehended by a security guard or police officer for an alleged criminal offense. An inmate is defined as anyone incarcerated for any period in a local jail or state or federal prison system. The use of the age 55 is arbitrary in a sense, as it may be argued that it is too young. The literature, however, does not provide conclusively definitive guidelines, as the ages of 50, 55, 60, and 65 are often used in discussing arrest and incarceration figures.[5] Although there is no uniform chronological age system independent of health status recognized by prison policy, several states operate programs specifically based on age, which define elderly offenders as 55 and over.[6]

DESCRIPTION AND APPLICATION OF THE MODIFIED INTEGRATIVE APPROACH

Sherman's Integrative Treatment Approach is inspired by Kuypers and Bengtson's Social Breakdown–Social Reconstruction Theory,[7] but it goes one step further. Sherman explains the Social Breakdown Syndrome as involving a self-defeating, downward cycle. The triggering of vulnerability through a traumatic event common in the lives of the elderly—role loss, retirement, death, illness, and so on—begins the cycle. In the next step, the individual is labeled as incompetent, which leads to a self-fulfilling prophecy. The dependent role facilitates the atrophying of skills until the person believes he is sick, then labels himself as sick and begins the process again. The cycle becomes a downward spiral as the person functions at lower and lower levels.

As Sherman has further explained, the Social Reconstruction Syndrome involves a reversal of the downward cycle through social system inputs. The goal of the intervention is to increase self-confidence and reduce the susceptibility that leads to breakdown. When services are offered to help maintain and sustain these individuals, this leads them to self-label themselves as competent rather than dependent. Finally, workers help the client build adaptive coping mechanisms and an internal locus of control. This in turn, should reduce the susceptibility to psychological breakdown at times of crisis. The person labels himself as competent and reinforces his past success with future successes.[8]

There are four major inputs (A–D) in contrast to the three shown in the social reconstruction model. Each of the four inputs should lead to a set of objectives, each marking a different level of client functioning. That is, the first level achieved by the provision of maintenance conditions should be the relief of immediate stress and dependency. The second level achieved by the provision of emotional support and coping strategies is one that should be marked by the re-establishment of an equilibrium, in that morale and coping strategies are sustained. The third level to be achieved by encouragement of an internal locus of control should be a higher plateau of functioning characterized by increased coping skills, problem-solving capacity, and cognitive mastery. Finally, the fourth level achieved by Input D should be marked by a major increase in the degree of quality of overall morale and life satisfaction commensurate with a general state of ego integrity.

The focus on increased morale, life satisfaction, and even ego integrity as outcomes of the whole intervention process clearly distinguishes the integrative model from the Kuypers and Bengtson model, which does not explicitly identify a morale factor. However, a basic assumption of integrative practice is that increased morale is always the final goal of intervention, even if we are more directly aiming our interventive efforts at such things as improved coping skills, more effective behavior, and so on.[9]

Sherman's Integrative Approach therefore describes the process whereby a person can help himself achieve a sense of integrity as against despair and to integrate the past, present and future in his life in his own unique way.

The principles of integrative practice can be summarized as follows:

1. The belief in the uniqueness of each individual and the intrinsic worth of the client, regardless of attributes or performance, helps the client liberate himself from the functionalistic ethic.
2. The respect for client self-determination recognizes the client's right to fail, accepts the client as the prime problem-solver in the counseling process, and draws on his accumulated life resources for intervention strategies.
3. The focus on the intrinsic value of meaning for the individual's perception of reality encourages assessments that maximize the individuality of approach.
4. The importance of maintaining and enhancing self-esteem to carry out change helps the individual reach the goals of increased morale and integrity in later life.

Sherman explains:

> The implications of this for integrative practice are that we should generally try to support and sustain rather than change such overt areas of functioning as interpersonal relations, lifestyle, and person/ environment transactions. For example, we seek to support and enhance family relations where these have been an essential ingredient in the life of the client. We attempt to sustain a certain level of social interaction through group methods for those clients who, through death of friends, relocation or loss of old work associations, have increased affiliative and emotional support needs. Conversely we tend to work for positive change in covert areas of personality functioning, particularly those areas indicated by the integrative model: enhancement of self-esteem, development of a more internal locus of control, and internalization of more positive self-evaluations.[10]

The Integrative Approach utilizes three basic models of intervention strategies generally discussed in the literature: the behavioral model, exemplified by a stimulus–response approach (S–R); the psychoanalytic approach, which focuses on the unconscious as a mediating factor (S $\rightarrow$ U $\rightarrow$ R); and the cognitive approach, which focuses on the perception or conscious meaning one gives to events (S $\rightarrow$ C $\rightarrow$ R). Cognitive and behavioral techniques can be used alongside psychodynamic and insight-oriented therapies to provide for an integrative approach. *Psychodynamic*, insight-oriented techniques can be applied when working through developmental issues that are likely to arise when dealing with problems of the elderly offender. *Behavior modification* can be applied to decrease certain dysfunctional behaviors and increase functional ones. *Cognitive* techniques can be used in interactional models by helping the person change his perception of the environment to views that are less dysfunctional. Needless to say, no matter which particular theoretical approach one favors, all three types of intervention strategies can be used. This has particular relevance to the elderly offender who finds himself coping with the intertwined problems of being old and having committed a crime.

The Integrative Approach is particularly helpful in treating elderly offenders who are not a homogeneous group and who may have only advanced age in common. As has been discussed by Shichor and by Wilbanks, there are typically few female offenders except for shoplifters, who ordinarily outnumber male shoplifters.[11] Some offenders are frail, are somewhat disabled, or have mental health problems; others function well. Some live below the poverty line, and have no spouses, families, or jobs; others are married, have families, and earn reasonable incomes. In a sense, then, they are no different from any other segment of the population, nor can they be easily stereotyped by the crimes they commit.[12]

Given the diversity of this group, a question arises as to the possibility of common factors that turn individuals to crime as they reach an advanced age. The common-sense approach of the elderly as lonely, depressed, economically desperate, and needing to steal for food has not been borne out by Feinberg's research on elderly shoplifters in Florida.[13] He has offered a hypothesis suggesting that the phenomenon of elderly shoplifting is similar to the antisocial acting out of adolescents as a result of forced idleness and lack of clear role definition. This hypothesis appears to support the thesis that the elderly suffer from the Social Breakdown Syndrome, and thus the Integrative Approach would appear to be an appropriate intervention.

In the Social Breakdown Syndrome, there need not be one traumatic precipitating crisis or stress that "causes" an elderly person to commit a crime; rather, the gradual building of small disappointments, resentments, and sadness can lead to a loosening of ordinarily stable impulse controls. This in combination with the strong temptation and availability of opportunity (such as in shoplifting) can prove too overwhelming for the distressed person. What is interesting about larceny in particular is that the elderly do not view it as a crime, nor do they feel they are in violation of the law.[14] Other misdemeanors, such as drunkenness and vagrancy, can be viewed similarly as unsuccessful attempts to cope with the problems of aging. The younger person who drinks moderately can avoid trouble with the law, but an older jobless individual who has lost his family, and may now also have a more difficult time metabolizing even a small amount of alcohol or wine, can more easily come into conflict with the law and society.

The violent felonies—including assault and murder, which account for 23 percent of the arrests of the elderly—can be understood in terms of an extreme breakdown of impulse control. Whether or not this is due to social breakdown factors, acts of violence against other individuals cannot be condoned. Such elderly people often end up in jails or prisons. The elderly first-time offender's trauma, guilt and anxiety can be debilitating and frightening, and these emotions can set into motion or perpetuate the Social Breakdown Syndrome, which can take another downward turn. Although both groups of first-time offenders, misdemeanants and felons, are intuitively amenable to rehabilitation through diversionary programs, the focus of the few existing programs revolve around misdemeanants, particularly shoplifters, as discussed by Feinberg et al. in Chapter 12 of this book.[15]

Sherman's Integrative Approach takes a dynamic view of the problem and the solution by attacking several areas of functioning through positive social inputs. The problem of the first-time offender will be explored through a modification and application of Sherman's Integrative Approach. The modified approach recognizes the importance of working with elderly first-time offenders who may be particularly vulnerable to the psychosocial problems related to the aging process. Therefore inputs A through D of Sherman's counseling approach are directly applicable to the elderly offender. Accordingly, a modified approach has been developed (Figure 13.1). The purpose of input (A) is to provide maintenance conditions and services and the first objective is to relieve the immediate stress and dependency. Input A is therefore primarily viewed as a beginning point in the counseling process. I suggest, however, that Input A be conceptually expanded to include the beginning point for a complementary or entirely sufficient set of services to include case management, advocacy, referral, provision of hard services, enhancement of formal and informal support, and so on, depending on the client's needs.

This could involve contacting a case manager to work with the elderly person. Ideally, the security officer or policeman would know whom to call to begin to investigate the situation and provide specific services where necessary. This case manager might be from a special division within Adult Protective Services of the Department of Social Services or a senior advocate from private voluntary agencies, the Area Offices of Aging, or the like. The case manager may assess the elderly individual as needing immediate referral in order to receive hard services, and that may close the case. For some offenders, advocacy and referral services are sufficient, while others need formal and informal supports to help carry them through a difficult period.

The formal system of supports include voluntary and government service agencies, which provide medical, income maintenance, and formal social services. Informal support networks are defined as "those groups and individuals in our society who help to sustain vulnerable people in the community and who act to supplement or obviate the use of formalized health, income support and social services. The responsibilities assumed by the informal support network manifests in activities related to information sharing, advocacy, emotional support, personal care and economic assistance."[16] Informal supports are defined as "natural supports consisting of friends, family and neighbors in addition to those mediating structures existing

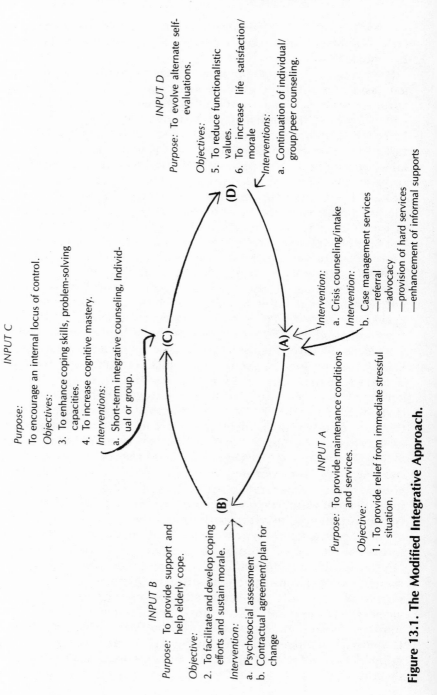

Figure 13.1. The Modified Integrative Approach.

in society."[17] Primary informal supports consist of family, other relatives, friends, and neighbors; their commitment is often long-term as they provide for the daily necessities of life. Secondary informal supports are often the mediating structures in society which we take for granted such as church, fraternal, and other affiliative groups which provide invaluable, ongoing services.

According to the literature review in a recent paper by Goodman and Bok, some authors suggest that informal and formal supports complement one another. Others suggest that there exists a hierarchical ordering of preference of use and that the elderly prefer help from informal services at all levels. Another viewpoint offers that in reality formal supports are considered superior and that the informal system is used only when gaps exist in formal systems.[18]

The conceptual model, used here for purposes of discussion, acknowledges the importance of three types of supports—formal, primary informal, and secondary informal—and suggests that they are probably all underused and at times may interact or overlap. The case manager's role would be to help the elderly offender use the best possible combination of services. For some offenders, a combination of services and/or referral for integrative counseling is necessary. The counselor's task would then be to help the elderly person reduce the stress of a personal problem or situational crisis to manageable proportions and continue the counseling process as indicated by inputs B, C, and D of Sherman's Integrative Approach.

In both Sherman's and the Modified Approach the purpose of input B is to provide support and to help the elderly person cope. The objective(s) is to facilitate coping efforts by helping the individual to stabilize self-esteem, to sustain morale, and to develop coping strategies. The social worker in this instance can be a powerful facilitator among elderly first-time offenders, because given the offeners' options of going to jail and having criminal records or participating in various programs, their motivation for change is apt to be high. At this point a more complete assessment and plan for effective short-term group or individual counseling can have the greatest impact.

The purpose of input C is to encourage an internal locus of control. The objectives are (3) to enhance coping skills and problem-solving capacities, and (4) to increase cognitive mastery. These objectives are operationalized through the counseling process as the offender begins to understand the reasons behind his crime and its consequences, and begins to develop alternative coping mechanisms in order to avoid committing the crime again. Elderly people who commit alcohol- and/or drug-related offenses have the additional task of working through their dependency problem.

The purpose of input D is to help the individual develop an alternate self-evaluation. The objectives are to help the elderly to (5) reduce functionalistic self-evaluations and clarify alternative self- evaluations, and to increase life satisfaction and morale.[19] In the modified model, this is achieved through various forms of continued integrative counseling. Ideally, the individual will function well and will no longer have the need to turn to crime as a means of coping with problems.

APPLICATION OF THE MODIFIED INTEGRATIVE APPROACH TO THE ELDERLY OFFENDER

The Modified Integrative Approach can conceptually be applied to the elderly offender. Whereas Figure 13.1 showed the general purposes, objectives, and intervention strategies of each input point, Figure 13.2 represents a macroscopic view of that process as the elderly offender walks through the system.

The first stage, Crisis Intervention, occurs at the first point of contact, that is, when an elderly person is apprehended and referred prior to adjudication. It is here that a case manager can be called on to assess the situation and refer for counseling and/or advocate services and recommend other appropriate interventions.

When an elderly person gets into trouble with the law, a close relative is notified. Usually the relative has no idea what to do, nor does he understand the cause or corrective actions that might be

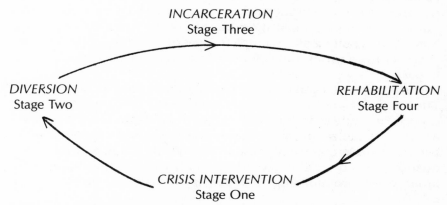

INCARCERATION
Stage Three

DIVERSION
Stage Two

REHABILITATION
Stage Four

CRISIS INTERVENTION
Stage One

Figure 13.2. The modified integrative approach applied to the elderly offender.

taken. Therefore, if an elderly first-time offender is released in custody of a relative to prevent incarceration, it does not particularly address the underlying problem of why the person committed the offense, nor what can be done to prevent future violations. The Integrative Approach specifically applies to the elderly offender in that the case manager plays an important role, not as the social parent who "takes over," but as the one who links or coordinates services and enhances the effectiveness of formal and informal supports. The worker at this point can help the family understand the elderly offender and alleviate some of the pressure that precipitated the acting out. The worker does not usurp the role of the family, but rather works with the family to help them mend the existing problems and to keep the offender out of the formal criminal justice system.

In addition to the family (and particularly when there is no family), friends, neighbors, or volunteers can be marshalled to assist with the elderly offender. This is particularly advantageous because of the reciprocity involved in peer groups. According to Crowe et al., "The concept of reciprocity also provides a means for the receiver to help to feel dignity as a mutual participant in a helping exchange, since he or she possesses the capability of returning favors at a later time"[20] Taking this a step further, beyond family and friends, there often exists a secondary support system of mediating structures. Here too the worker plays the role of coordinator, that is someone who acts as a broker and linker of services combining primary and secondary support systems. Family and friends are able to help cope with certain problems, but others need the use of mediating structures or the use of the formal support system, consisting of the voluntary and government health and social services. After providing the maintenance conditions and services necessary, the case manager can refer the offender for counseling using the Integrative Approach of inputs B, C, and D.

The second stage, Diversion, occurs when the elderly person is arrested, appears in court, pleads guilty, and is not remanded to jail but diverted out of the legal system into the social system. In most instances, the first-time elderly offender is not a pathological criminal nor a danger to society and, unlike elderly recidivists, should be entitled to special help. Diverting the elderly into a social service rather than a law enforcement or punitive system is intrinsically stress reducing, in that such a measure allows the elderly person to be relieved of two worries, the prison itself and the fear of perhaps dying there.

At the present time there are very few diversionary programs which specifically deal with elderly offenders. The Broward Senior Intervention Education (BSIE) Program in Florida for first-time shoplifters is one such program (described more fully in Chapter 12). A formal intervention theory has not been developed as a result of this project. It is clear, however, that the ideas of the Integrative Approach are consonant with the treatment of the BSIE's successful program. The vulnerability of the elderly and precipitating stress contribute to the Social Breakdown Syndrome. BSIE's intervention program provides all four inputs, from the coordinating caseworker who moves from initial involvement at the point of crisis, to diversion from the criminal justice system and to short-term individual counseling.

While the BSIE specifically addresses itself only to first-time elderly shoplifters, the Advocate for Seniors Program—developed in 1978 under the auspices of the Advocate Program, Inc.—in Dade County, Florida, has worked with elderly offenders 60 and over who commit a variety of crimes, 80 percent of which are shoplifting and petty larceny.

The overall Advocate Program is designed to provide an alternative to the traditional criminal justice procedures of jail time, fines, and lengthy probations, regardless of age. The Advocate for Seniors Program has a specific objective to intervene in behalf of elderly clients.

Although there is no formal theoretical model for this program, the ideas of the Modified Approach are consonant with the objectives of the Senior Advocate Program. The objective, to intervene on behalf of the elderly client through the support and involvement of the worker, is similar to Input A in the Modified Approach. The case management functions of advocacy and referral are similar to objectives four and five of the Advocate Program, which are "to serve as a multi-resource center for referral of those with identifiable generic, situational, or emotional problems to appropriate rehabilitative resources" and "to provide clients with volunteer placement settings for job training and creating a greater awareness of community resources."

The third objective is similar to Input B of the Modified Approach in terms of evaluating "the client's general state of health, social resources . . . , in order to prescribe a self-help program . . . " The sixth and seventh objectives are similar to Input C of the Modified Approach in that the interventions provide "a personalized method of accountability while, at the same time, preserving personal integrity and a positive self-image," and the "insight counseling which would bring the circumstances surrounding and leading up to the older person's encounter with the justice system into a comfortable and comprehensible perspective."[21]

The success of the Advocate for Seniors Program has been documented. "Current information on recidivism indicates that senior misdemeanants are not being rearrested. . . . "[22]

In the third stage, Incarceration, the offender serves his time in jail or prison with the expectation, whenever feasible, of eventual release, either to the community on parole or to a halfway house where rehabilitation efforts can be implemented. Although this approach has been developed specifically for the elderly offender, the same concepts can be applied to any first-time offender. Such persons can be worked with successfully since the commission of a crime is a crisis point at which the person's needs and problems forcefully surface and can be more effectively addressed. A successful outcome can be predicted for the elderly first-time offender based on the assumption that a person who has remained law-abiding for fifty-five years or more has many internal strengths that can be mustered to aid in his rehabilitation or reeducation. Any or all of the intervention strategies, from input A through input D, can be used with those in jail. Assessment, planning, and, where indicated, appropriate placement in a detoxification or drug-abuse program can be facilitated by case managers. Comprehensive case management in effect would ensure that inmates receive appropriate services. Rehabilitation and early release to community-based alternatives, when feasible, can become the long-range objectives.

With the goal of systematically linking various elements of the criminal justice system to provide services for inmates, pre-service, in-service, and staff development training of jail personnel can help sensitize them to the problems of elderly inmates. Additionally, mental health care should be provided for all jail inmates.[23]

Braden Walter has described "Project 60," in which workers provided case management as well as counseling services for elderly inmates and parolees.[24] For some the eventual goal was release and Rehabilitation (stage four) in the community; for others who could not be returned to the community, the opportunity for intervention helped enrich their lives in the prison system.

The case manager's task is first to view different aspects of care individually and then to integrate, evaluate, reevaluate, and reintegrate the various components to provide the best level of care for the rehabilitated client. Ideally, each individual should be capable of doing this for himself. The elderly, and particularly the vulnerable elderly offender, may be unable to take the initiative to link these resources, however. The worker's role is to help the elderly explore the alternatives so that each individual can find that combination of services most effective for his particular situation. This coordinative role requires strong case management skills as well as referral for further counseling when necessary.

ISSUES FOR FURTHER RESEARCH AND CLARIFICATION

This conceptual application of the Integrative Approach was developed simply because very few relevant materials were available for working with elderly offenders. The usefulness of the approach, hwoever, is particularly limited by the need for clarification and research of operational hypotheses. First and foremost, as Duffee has pointed out, there is the need to develop methods of accumulating and analyzing data on the nature and extent of the phenomenon of the elderly offender.[25] Second, research needs to focus on why the elderly commit crimes and what are the most effective intervention strategies to help the offender. This leads to the third issue: identifying the best structures to implement those strategies. (1) What agencies will need to be linked? (2) Who will have primary control—criminal justice or social service agencies? (3) How are these programs to be funded? (4) Will legislation be eventually necessary to mandate a new criminal justice system for the elderly as their numbers begin to swell in the next fifty years?

SUMMARY AND CONCLUSIONS

In an era of tightening budgets, it would be difficult to create new systems as old ones are abolished for lack of funding. The challenge is to link and integrate services within existing frameworks effectively and to use those services to provide the best care possible for those in need. A continuum of care for elderly offenders could extend from prevention to diversion to alternative sentencing to incarceration and finally to rehabilitation and release. As service systems and their ports of entry become increasingly complex, the social worker involved in helping this population will need to act as the broker, advocate, and linker of services in addition to providing psychotherapeutic help when necessary.

More often than not, the formal system will have been brought in to assume responsibility for the individual, when harnessing the primary and secondary informal care systems could have served the same purpose. The formal systems may not need to become even minimally involved. More thoughtful use of the informal system can thus free the formal supports to help people who cannot be served in another way.

Second, the informal supports can act to enrich the formal supports. The beauty of the informal support system is that it motivates family, friends, and peers to care for the elderly offender. When attention is initially motivated by care and responsibility for one's loved ones, the level of care has the potential to be far superior than care given by perhaps less interested professionals. In addition, such care has a healing effect on the individual, for he can stay in familiar surroundings with people he knows care for him. Help that is given out of mature love and respect, not as charity or as part of a salaried job, gives the person receiving the help a sense of dignity and sometimes the motivation to reciprocate, which are not inherent in formal support systems. A third factor in developing the full potential of these networks is cost. Escalating institutional costs have forced planners of service to seek alternative means of helping vulnerable populations. Enhancing and sustaining informal supports is one way of keeping costs down.

The question arises, however, as to which agency would have primary responsibility for the client. A senior advocate program, self-supporting and fee-collecting, can possibly be run through local area agencies devoted to aging and through private or voluntary family service agencies or community centers. Case managers should be knowledgeable about the various referral services available in the community and otherwise maintain a good relationship with community prevention and education efforts. A close working relationship with the secular, religious, and voluntary service organizations as well as with courts, public defenders, and probation departments should be developed.

This application of the modified Integrative Treatment Approach has been an attempt to suggest some structure to the treatment of elderly offenders. It is an intervention orientation that has not yet been borne out empirically. There have been very few studies on the treatment of elderly offenders; the few programs that do exist do not follow formal theoretical models, although they are certainly congruent with the ideas presented in this chapter.

This discussion is not meant to provide concrete solutions. Rather, the ideas offered here are meant to serve as only beginning thoughts on an emerging problem. It is now necessary to test some of the ideas in order that operational hypotheses can be formed, tested, and reevaluated in light of hard data. It is hoped that this chapter represents only the beginning of further research into the area of direct practice with the elderly offender. Only time and future research will determine whether this approach has real application for elderly offenders, and perhaps for other first-time offenders as well.

NOTES

1. Edmund Sherman, *Counseling the Aging: An Integrative Approach* (New York: The Free Press, 1981).
2. Max Siporin, *Introduction to Social Work Practice* (New York: Macmillan, 1975), pp. 29–30, 74, 110,116.
3. Ibid., pp. 79,89.
4. Ibid., pp. 116,119.
5. Donald Newman, Chapter 1 of this book, discussion of age definition.
6. Anne Goetting, Chapter 11 of this book, discussion of prison activities.
7. Vern L. Bengtson, *The Social Psychology of Aging* (New York: Bobbs Merrill, 1973).
8. Sherman, *Counseling the Aging*, pp. 24,70.
9. Ibid., p. 170.
10. Ibid., p. 95.
11. David Shichor, Chapter 2, and William Wilbanks, Chapter 6, this book, discussions of female offenders. Also see discussion in Feinberg, Chapter 3, about female shoplifters.
12. Newman, Chapter 1, discussion of types of crime committed by elderly offenders.
13. Feinberg, Chapter 3, description of demographic profile of elderly shoplifters and discussion of emergent role passage.
14. Ibid., p. 43.
15. Gary Feinberg et al., Chapter 12 of this book. See discussion of BSIE program.
16. New York State Health Planning Commission, New York State Health Advisory Council, *Enhancing and Sustaining Informal Support Networks for the Elderly and Disabled: Recommendations* (Albany, 1981), p. 1.
17. Ibid.
18. Nanette Goodman and Marcia Bok, *Aging in New England: Informal and Formal Help for the Elderly, Implications for Social Work Practice*, University of Connecticut, School of Social Work, December 1981, p. 2.
19. Sherman, *Counseling the Aging*, pp. 70, 98.
20. Anne H. Crowe, Elizabeth A. Ferguson, Beth J. Kantrowitz, and Ellen Hogan Biddle, "The Elder Program: An Educational Model for Network Building Among the Elderly," Kent School of Social Work, University of Louisville, Kentucky, 1982, p. 7.
21. Alvin Malley, "The Advocate Program Sees the Elderly Through," *The Florida Bar Journal* (March 1981): 208.
22. Alvin Malley, "When Elderly Turn to Crime, Advocate Sees Them Through," *Aging* (January 1981): 33.
23. Comptroller General, U.S. General Accounting Office, *Report to the Congress of the U.S. Jail Inmates Mental Health Care Neglected. State and Federal Attention Needed* (Washington, D.C.: U.S. Government Printing Office, 1980). See discussion of lack of services and need for state and federal intervention, p. 17.
24. Braden Walter, "Project 60: A Counseling Program for Elderly Inmates," paper presented at the First Annual Conference on Elderly Criminals, Albany. N.Y., March 1982.
25. David Duffee, Chapter 14, this book. See discussion of a research agenda concerning crime committed by the elderly.

PART IV

Research and Policy Implications of Elderly Crime

Crime committed by elderly persons is a new and unfortunately arid field in terms of any sort of respectable research base. Professional literature about elderly criminals is sparse, yet it is clear that this phenomenon is likely to increase simply because our population is aging.

It is a rare opportunity to see a social problem coming with enough lead time to do something about it. This is precisely the case with elderly crime. We are very sure that the demographic balance of our population will shift so that more people will be in the upper age ranges. As this occurs, the elderly crime problem can only assume a more important position on our list of domestic problems. It seems particularly appropriate to begin developing policies of control and prevention right now.

Perhaps more than any other offender groups, elderly criminals are chiefly products of a complex set of relationships, aspirations, and strains on our general social fabric. To this extent, elderly crime is primarily a gerontological problem and only secondarily of concern to criminal justice research. Elderly crime touches criminal justice primarily in terms of control rather than cause. Yet both etiology and control must be studied with more precision and more imagination that has been the case in the past.

The chapters in this last section restate the dual nature of the problem of the elderly offender. David Duffee begins his chapter on research agenda by delineating the gerontological issues of the elderly in American society. He makes the point that dominant societal processes may actually generate deviance among the elderly and stresses the need to examine some of these larger factors rather than focusing on specific elderly deviants, a view that he considers myopic. Instead he raises important gerontological issues about the place of the elderly in our society. He questions the benefits of isolating elderly persons from the main social fabric and asks whether the American welfare system is designed not to help people in need, but rather to maintain an economic system that does not need all members of society. He then turns to the criminal justice aspects of the problem, raising some specific researchable questions about the incidence and causes of crime among the elderly as well as factors that enter into arrest and prosecution decisions. Finally, Duffee discusses the role of research in policy formulation and suggests that researchers in both fields, gerontology and criminal justice, cooperate with each other and with policymakers in undertaking mutual efforts in this new area.

The final chapter, on policy implications, makes some specific recommendations for the processing of elderly offenders in the criminal justice system and the general treatment of the aged in our society. Recognizing that crimes cannot be condoned regardless of the age of the offender, the authors call for immediate action, but the least restrictive action. This involves citations rather than physical custody as in traditional arrest procedures, and alternative sentencing with incarceration used as a last resort.

The final section of the chapter examines some of the specific causes for anxiety among today's older population and concludes that while no public policy statement can order the aged to feel or be honored nor can create in them a sense of personal worth, the resolution of these basic issues is necessary to alleviate the anxieties that often lead to criminal behavior.

Chapter 14

A Research Agenda Concerning Crime Committed by the Elderly

David E. Duffee

CRIME AND AGING

To a degree sufficient to arouse interest in the formulation of public policy, crime by the elderly is a new phenomenon. The age structure of the U.S. population is changing significantly. The baby boom is behind us. Public school populations are shrinking, but people are living longer, and the proportion of the population over 60 is booming. Some policy issues, such as how a shrinking labor force can continue to support a growing retirement force, are already sharply focused although unresolved. Others, such as crime and the elderly, are just emerging.

Victimization of the elderly has received attention first, perhaps because it was more consistent with the stereotype of the elderly as helpless and in need of protection. The aged person as victimizer is more startling, particularly because of the long association of crime and youth. Any prison warden can tell us that if all human interventions fail, the aging process will succeed in reducing the propensity toward crime.

If one passes from lifecycle to cultural and economic explanations of the association between youth and crime, however, then recent trends toward an increase in crime committed by the elderly are less surprising. In the United States, youths have long been segregated from the dominant culture shaped and controlled by adults. So are the aged. To the extent that some crime is associated with the social and political correlates of age, rather than age itself, then an increasingly large class of aged persons may spawn a new group of criminal offenders.

Research in this volume and elsewhere provides tentative support both for the impression that crime committed by the elderly is on the rise and for explanations of that rise rooted in the political, social, and economic aspects of age. But the phenomenon is too new, and too little understood, for us to determine what public policy stance, (if any) may be wise. Research is needed, and we need an orderly approach for research, particularly if it is to be coordinated with potential policy activity.

Research agendas may provide lists of researchable questions, but they need to be more than mere lists. To be agendas, they should provide structure to the progress of inquiry and suggest links between the tasks of seeking information and using it. Hence a major focus of this chapter is on how to order questions rather than on what the questions themselves are. Two different but potentially compatible orders are presented here, one suggested by the structure of the problems of elderly crime and one suggested by the problems of policy relevance.

ELDERLY CRIME AND RESPONSES TO IT

One way to order research on elderly crime seems to be based on the classical behavioral psychology of stimulus and response—or, in this case, problem and response. Some questions concern crime by the elderly and some concern the processing of the elderly offender. Questions about the "problem" would include the incidence of offenses by the elderly, patterns of offense, and types of elderly offenders. Questions about "responses" include processes of arrest or alternatives to arrest, processes of prosecution and defense, decisions about sentence, and treatment of elderly offenders in and out of institutions. Obviously any number of important questions can be raised within this rubric, and the problem/response question-set is clearly relevant to groups concerned with the relationship between elderly offenders and criminal justice systems.

But we should recognize that this focus on crime, criminals, and official response automatically downplays a host of researchable questions, which should not only be underscored but should be actively addressed—if not before, then at least along with, problem and response types of questions. An important set of questions deal with the conditions and processes that give rise to the problems on the one hand and may also push us toward one set of solutions rather than to others. These preconditions to elderly crime are occasionally recognized in the studies presented in this volume, but there has been no single chapter on these research issues themselves.

THE ELDERLY IN AMERICAN SOCIETY

To be specific, research is needed that deals with the infrastructural and structural factors[1] that contribute to the situations the elderly find themselves in and may lead them to commit the types of offenses examined here. For example, a number of writers have said that our society is segregational: that just as it has previously mandated the separation of youth from the mainstream of society now it mandates the separation of the elderly from that mainstream.[2] As previous writers have examined the subcultural and countercultural factors that may give rise to juvenile delinquency,[3] the emerging research on elderly crime suggests parallel sociocultural factors influencing deviance and delinquency by the elderly.[4] The aged feel alienated, powerless, and shut out.

Now subcultures, lack of social control, and anomie can be studied directly as a problem in the problem/response format. But research is also needed on what aspects of the American social structure and economic structure might lead to the creation of subcultures or the loss of social control. For example, are there ways of organizing the production process that would not segregate the elderly from work and family? Can we change our definitions of what is productive? What are the costs as well as the benefits of mandatory retirement? To whom do the costs and benefits fall? Is the American form of welfare structured to help people in need, or to prolong and maintain the economic system, which doesn't need all members of society?[5]

To answer these kinds of questions, cross-cultural and cross-national studies are extremely important. Do all industrialized nations treat their elderly in the same fashion? Are the categorical welfare systems of the United States, and our age-segregated housing patterns, the only available means of dealing with the life cycle? Do the forms of deviance we find among the elderly in the United States exist in other societies? Why or why not?[6]

The reason that these kinds of questions cannot be ignored is that without them one can focus myopically on specific elderly deviants and how they can be most effectively "helped" while ignoring the fact that the very things that generate deviance may be part of our dominant societal processes. Analogously, it has been recognized that problems of unemployment in the United States cannot be addressed by designing retraining programs for the unemployed.[7] A capital-intensive, postindustrial economic system simply doesn't need the work power of all of our potential workers—at least not as we now define work.[8] Likewise, our social system as structured may not need the aged, and finding alternatives to this situation would be far more important than asking only what to do with the aged we do not need.

RESEARCH ON INCIDENCE AND CAUSES OF ELDERLY CRIME

Now we can turn to a variety of questions raised about the "problem" of elderly crime itself. It seems clear for starters that the problem is currently invisible. One of the major research tasks in the near future is simply to shed some light on the dark figure of elderly crime. Since many of our self-report and victimization surveys seem to focus methodologically on uncovering crime unreported about youth or normal criminals, we may need new means of measurement, and certainly new strategies for sampling. Self-reports of delinquency will not uncover crime in the nursing home.

Second, it appears that age itself may confuse our general knowledge about crime and who commits it. As Wilbanks demonstrated, a significant factor in predicting propensity to crime is age.[9] It would seem possible that many crime problems that we have previously associated with race or wealth may be confounded with the probability of living longer. An interesting conceptual problem arises from categorizing offenders by age. Most age groupings are formed by relatively arbitrary cutoff points. These points—such as the voting age, the draft age, the drinking age, and the retirement age—are, to be sure, based on *some* data, or on some assumptions that could be empirically tested. The voting age is based, to some extent, on the point at which the largest number of youths are responsible enough to make political decisions. The retirement age is, presumably, based to some extent on the likelihood of being productive, to some extent on the proportions of the population that can be supported via Social Security by the proportion left working, and to some extent on the proportion of youths who might not be able to obtain jobs if everyone over retirement age did not retire, and so on. But while we are clearly using chronological age in some of these demarcations as a rough and ready proxy for either psychological states or social behavior, it is not clear that the chronological indicators used for Social Security benefits or mandated retirements should also be those used for designating elderly criminals. Professional athletes are old when they turn 30. Would a person committing a first crime at 40 be middle-aged or old, relative to that behavior? Or when he reaches an age above which, say, only 10 percent of prisoners fall? Is there an age difference between the elderly criminal and the elderly victim? The impact of using one cutoff point or another on the policy of controlling crime or processing offenders may be quite important. And we may be better off with different age cutoffs for one part of the problem than another.

Third, it would appear that some interesting research is involved in examining how crime types and crime rates may be affected by age. For example, Shichor demonstrated that murder by the elderly is increasing much more rapidly than the murder rate of the general population, while the aggravated assault rate of the elderly is increasing more slowly.[10] We might conclude that the violent old are more accurate marksmen than their younger counterparts. But it would also seem likely that the aged violent have aged victims who are less likely to survive an assault and more likely to end up as murder victims than assault victims. Likewise, Abrams asserts that we know little about the crime-related effects of medication,[11] and others claim that we need to study the attitudes of the aged vis-à-vis the law and proper behavior.[12] Similarly, from Koss's paper, it seems clear that patterns of drinking and alcoholism by the aged are quite different from the patterns we associate with the young.[13] In other words, our examination of deviance and criminality may be so suffused with the image of the young actor that we need to alter not only our methods and sampling patterns but also our conceptualization to deal adequately with incidence of crime by the elderly.

RESEARCH ON PROCESSING THE ELDERLY OFFENDER

In examining questions about how best to respond to crime by the elderly, it would appear from examining the work of Feinberg, Glugover, and Zwetchkenbaum that we are dealing with multiple problems and thus need multiple responses.[14] Research about program transfer will be very important and must be carefully done. For example, even brief reflection about it might suggest that crime responses designed for a Florida population 30 percent of which is over age 60 may simply be inapplicable for dealing with elderly crime in a community with a smaller proportion—10 or 5 percent—of the population over 60. The motivations for crime committed by the elderly where there is significant elderly in-migration may be quite different from crime committed by the elderly where the old are trapped and left behind. According to Feinberg, one reason the elderly in Broward, Florida, shoplift is that they don't see themselves as criminals.[15] Such first offenders who plead guilty may not reoffend. But will programs designed for these offenders work with the poor and "cold old" of the Northeast?

Another set of research questions would seem to involve distinctions between alternative decision rules on the one hand and alternative processing on the other. For example, both Cohen and Abrams point out that we should be cautious in stripping the elderly of rights in order to provide services to them.[16] Kittrie has previously raised the same issue relative to the mentally ill, and a host of lawyers and social scientists have criticized the handling of juveniles on the same grounds.[17]

But the issues at stake here must be clarified. It is one set of questions whether the elderly should be prosecuted for crimes and found guilty. It is a totally different set of questions whether the elderly criminal should be subject to the same conditions during processing as other criminals. Although we frequently confuse the two sets of questions, we need not. As Gottfredson and Gottfredson have pointed out, an arrest involves two decisions: one concerning the likelihood that a crime was committed and that the suspect committed it, and one concerning the need for custody during the prosecution process.[18] We might decide, for example, that elderly people who commit crimes should be prosecuted. But we need not by the same token decide that they need to be handcuffed and driven to the station house rather than issued a citation. Hence we need to determine separately which decision rules to follow and what processes to adopt while rules are being applied.

In a related sense, we clearly need research on the interaction of policies in different social processing areas. Recently there has been a spate of research examining the relationship between mental health deinstitutionalization and the increase in correctional populations.[19] Similarly, we should be examining whether decisions to deinstitutionalize the elderly have increased their presence in the criminal justice system.

In addition, there is important research on a host of organizational and administrative issues relative to the service delivery and processing structures we have or may establish for the elderly offender. It is much more common in our society to ask deviants about their attitudes toward morality and the law (as in subculture studies) than to ask them about their preferences relative to the organizations that process them. Researchers and policymakers should not assume that the elderly's opinion about whether they prefer mental health to criminal processing or living with other elderly people to living with a mixed age group is irrelevant to what we should do.[20]

A related concern is an examination of the organizations that handle the elderly rather than of the elderly themselves. In social service research, criticism is often raised about the vested interests of the system. In this emerging field, we might want to consider not vested interests but "vestable" interests—will we invent systems for elderly offenders to benefit them, to benefit communities, or to benefit the organizations that run programs? Can we construct organizations with less "vestable" interests, organizations that are more flexible and more open to change?[21]

Finally, if we are to promote change, one research methodology absent in this area is experimentation. It is as we begin to think about the elderly offender that we may be in the best position as researchers, practitioners, and policymakers to insist on systematic rather than accidental reductions in uncertainty. For example, can the Broward program for shoplifters[22] be converted to an experimental design so that we could compare the results for like shoplifters of different forms of processing or compare different sets of decision rules being applied to them? The ethical problems with experimentation are, of course, significant. But the ethical problems with going full speed ahead without experimentation are equally significant, and perhaps in the long run more consequential.[23]

MAKING THE RESEARCH RELEVANT TO POLICY

Having examined some research questions ordered by the nature of the problem, let us now shift gears. Another way of thinking about a research agenda is based on the functions of research. Ilchman and Smith have proposed that in relation to policymaking, research can provide four major functions: (1) generation of information, that is, fact finding; (2) generation of knowledge, that is, linking bits of facts together through "if-then" statements; (3) generations of judgments, that is, helping policymakers consider the appropriateness of alternative solutions or alternative resource expenditures; and (4) legitimation, that is, helping policymakers justify decisions based on information and knowledge by bringing to public attention what a smaller group of policymakers already know.[24]

While it sounds as if we might progress in an orderly fashion from fact finding through knowledge building to decisionmaking and legitimation, the process does not and probably cannot work that way. For example, in this instance we lack many facts about elderly crime. This alone should attune policymakers and research funders to a particular type of research—we need to generate measures and measurement processes. The technology of fact gathering should be important. Until we have some facts, connecting facts with each other will obviously be hard to do. But the kinds of facts we decide to gather are heavily influenced by the kinds of knowledge or fact-connections we want to build. We often ignore some facts because of heavy investments in the presumed connections among others. For example, if our search for facts is guided by the presumption that if there are aged offenders then they should be specially processed, we will not gather the same kinds of facts as if we had started by asking what societies recognize offenses or what societies distinguish social status on the basis of age. In terms of the judgment questions, research can be limited to helping policymakers determine how best to use resources set aside for a particular social problem. But this would inform quite a different set of judgments than if the researchers had investigated what to designate as resources.

Finally, legitimating social policy through research can be either corrupting or ethical depending on how and when legitimacy is sought. For example, researchers in the United States have been used for legitimating responses to crime. They have generally not been sought to legitimate problems.[25] If, in this case, research is used to study how to process elderly offenders rather than how to conceptualize alternative social orders, then questions about whether we should focus on crime or age instead of, say, the division of labor will not be asked.

Setting aside these convolutions among the policy functions of research, we can conclude with some specific questions about each functional area. While policy formation does not always seem to work so, it would seem efficient, if not effective, if we were to have some policy about how to formulate policy. Social science research often follows leads determined in a nonempirical or at least a nonscientific manner. Lyndon Johnson and his advisors determined for political reasons that criminal justice was to become a significant policy area. The political determination of both crime and criminal justice has recently been called to question on scientific grounds,[26] at about the same time that President Carter was declaring that the criminal justice complex created by the federal government could also be disbanded by the federal government. While research on crime and criminal justice will doubtless continue, this flip-flopping on priorities could perhaps be avoided, or at least reduced to the extent that researchers and policymakers can have some initial discussions about the possible shape of the problem area for which policy is being considered.

An important aspect of fact-finding research relative to crime committed by elderly criminals would be some careful discussion about the conceptual rubric guiding the search for facts. The facts, after all, are not out there waiting to be discovered; they are to a large extent determined by the imaginations of those about to seek them. They are discoverable only as they are defined and in the context within which those definitions have meaning. Thus, determinations by policymakers and researchers about the cutoff age for elderly criminals may be crucial to the size of the problem to be discovered. This determination is unavoidably to be influenced by the vested and vestable interests of those making the determinations. This is not the place to attempt a definition of the population of researchers or policymakers, but it is the place to suggest that the net be cast widely—particularly in determining who the relevant policymaker should be. It would seem likely that agencies and legislative committees dealing with the elderly may have quite different vantage points relative to defining the aged criminal population than would agencies and legislators concerned primarily with criminal justice processes and administration. Likewise, experienced gerontologists may approach the measurement of crime or of criminal populations very differently than researchers who have studied crime and criminals—particularly street criminals, who are generally young. Thus the shape and scope of the problem suggested by the facts will depend on definitions shaped not by the problem but by the mix of people seeking the facts. Definitions set by a group with narrow experiences and interests are less likely to be satisfactory than definitions set by a heterogeneous group.

There is, of course, no requirement that such a group arrive at a final definition, or at only one. Indeed, it would probably be wise if policymakers and researchers were to set forth several tentative denotations of the aged offender in order to explore the possible consequences of defining the population narrowly or broadly.

Concerning the function of knowledge building—or making connections among facts—the dialogue between researchers and policymakers is also important. Some connections are policy- relevant and some are not. While social science research often portends policy implications, they are often seen through a glass both darkly and lately. Perhaps the implications would not be so unclear if they were sought earlier in the research process. Researchers are not always very familiar with policy options or constraints. The retort that researchers are of course researchers and not policymakers doesn't really cut it. Not only do researchers not make policy but only infrequently do they do "action research," which is Lewin's term for research done in action settings but formulated as a guide and evaluation of action plans.[27] One example of action research Suchman would call formative evaluation.[28] But the research need not be (or only be) evaluative. Nor does it require experimental design. What is required is that researchers and policymakers agree on research not with policy *implications* but with policy *explications*. Research can be implied in the policy options and the formulation of the research can be used to explicate assumptions and clarify the organization of action. The connections to be sought about crime committed by the elderly can be guided by the possibility of somehow changing the connection by expenditure of public resources. Examining fact connections that are not manipulatable—about which nothing can be done—is not a high-priority investment of public money.

A significant problem is embedded in weighting the fact connections to be sought. Many scientists would appropriately object to research limited to the study of variables for which manipulation is already envisioned. This limitation to what some would call "applied research" can easily degenerate into raw opportunism and incremental policy, which is incapable of keeping pace with the rapidity of societal change. While this caution is warranted, the remedy is not necessarily to commit policymakers to basic research as separate from applied, policy-relevant research. A more productive remedy would be to find knowledge-building activities that advance theory (or new connections) rather than knowledge-based activities that merely adapt present theory to current political possibility.

This kind of remedy asks both researchers and policymakers to adopt some behaviors and value positions they use only infrequently. Policymakers must be willing to seek fact connections that entail programs of research enduring beyond the tenure of particular executives or legislators. At the same time, researchers must be willing to fight for policy and problem areas that are pertinent to the advancement of knowledge. If the definition of "policy-relevant" is limited to mean "consistent with the platform of any existing political regime," it would be inappropriate and self-defeating.

The third function of research involves informing judgments by helping policymakers consider alternative solutions or tradeoffs of alternative expenditures. Probably the most valuable contribution of the researcher here is the commitment to study questions that address the preconditions of particular problems, and particular responses. While value judgments concerning appropriateness are moral or political rather than scientific questions, the policy scientist can be politically moral by pressing continually for alternative conceptualizations of social problems.

Both age and crime are now considered social problems meriting public deliberation and policy responses. But whether these problems should receive higher or lower priority is better known to the extent that we continue to explore competing problems. For example, Wilkins has argued that a concern with social harms should replace a concern with crime.[29] Dealing with some people as aged or criminal may be far less appropriate than finding alternatives to policies that treat persons categorically.

Finally, the justificatory function of research, if invoked in this stage of our knowledge and experience with elderly crime, would probably be unjustified. But the creative marriage of research and policy groups might make future justifications more possible. In many respects, the key to the achievement of this goal would be to consciously seek out as diverse as possible the group of potential researchers and policymakers. Keeping open-ended the population of people who might propose legitimate research or formulate legitimate policy would seem the best guarantee that an elderly crime policy will be justifiable.

THE MANAGEMENT OF RESEARCH ON ELDERLY CRIME

To summarize, the emerging concern about elderly crime presents both an intriguing series of substantive questions and a fresh opportunity to combine research and policy in new ways. Research on elderly crime can be valuable to the criminological community because it presents the occasion to explore incidence and test explanatory theory under new conditons. The usual relationships among person-related and political/social variables will not apply. Measurement techniques and sampling strategies can be modified to new settings and new populations. Likewise, research on elderly crime can provide the gerontologist with new problems to study, which may help both to shake up conceptions of elderliness and to reexamine ethical conflicts between blameworthiness and desert. For policymakers, queries about how to handle elderly offenders are sufficiently new that there is still time for them to relate to researchers in new ways. Perhaps most importantly, they could assign researchers to study the relationship between dominant economic and political processes and to identify deviance and deviants rather than merely investigating options in the processing of troublemakers.

NOTES

1. These terms are used here in the same manner as used by Marvin Harris, *Cultural Materialism* (New York: Random House, 1979).
2. Two important critiques of the American categorical approach to social problems are those by Alfred Kahn and Sheila Kamerman, *Not for the Poor Alone: European Social Services* (New York: Harper, 1977); and by Joe R. Feagin, *Subordinating the Poor: Welfare and American Beliefs* (Englewood Cliffs, N.J.: Prentice-Hall, 1975).
3. Albert K. Cohen, *Delinquent Boys* (Glencoe, Ill.: Free Press, 1955).
4. See Kahn and Kamerman, *Not for the Poor Alone*, pp. 127–152, on the policies that segregate the elderly.
5. See Feagin, *Subordinating the Poor*, and Stephen Rose, *Betrayal of the Poor* (Cambridge, Mass., Schenkman, 1972).
6. Kahn and Kamerman, in *Not for the Poor Alone*, draw interesting contrasts between the United States and northern Europe.
7. Rose, *Betrayal of the Poor*; Peter Marris and Martin Rein, *The Dilemmas of Social Reform* (New York: Basic Books, 1968).
8. For some novel alternatives, see Karl Hess, *Community Technology* (New York: Harper, 1979).
9. William Wilbanks, "Elderly Homicides," presentation at the First Annual Elderly Offender Conference, Albany, N.Y., March 15–16, 1982.
10. David Shichor, "The Extent and Nature of Lawbreaking by the Elderly: A Review of Arrest Statistics," Chapter 2 in this volume.
11. Albert Abrams, foreword to this volume.
12. Jonathan Mandell, "Popular Images and Stereotypes of Elderly Criminals," presentation at the First Elderly Offender Conference, Albany, N.Y., March 15–16, 1982.
13. Sandra Koss, "The Elderly Alcoholic," presentation at the First Annual Elderly Offender Conference, Albany, N.Y.., March 15–16, 1982.
14. Gary Feinberg, Sidney Glugover, and Irene Zwetchenbaum, "The Broward Senior Intervention and Education Program: A Pilot Program," Chapter 12 in this volume; Gary Feinberg, "Profile of the Elderly Shoplifter," Chapter 3 in this volume.
15. Feinberg, ibid.
16. Fred Cohen, "Old Age as a Criminal Defense," Chapter 8 of this volume; Abrams, foreword.
17. Nicholas Kittrie, *The Right to Be Different* (Baltimore: Penguin, 1971). See, for example, Frederic L. Faust and Paul J. Brantingham, *Juvenile Justice Philosophy* (St. Paul, Minn.: West, 1974).
18. Michael R. Gottfredson and Don M. Gottfredson, *Decisionmaking in Criminal Justice: Toward the Rational Exercise of Discretion* (Cambridge, Mass.: Ballinger, 1980), pp. 78–81.

19. The largest and most comprehensive study is that by Henry Steadman and John Monahan, *Incarceration Careers* (National Institute of Justice study to be completed in August 1982).

20. This point is raised by Raymond Broadus in his presentation at the First Annual Elderly Offender Conference, Albany, N.Y., March 15–16, 1982. An important parallel is presented by Irving Pilliavin and Alan E. Gross in "The Effects of Separation of Services and Income Maintenance on AFDC Recipients," *Social Service Review* (September 1977): 389–406.

21. On the problem of human service organizations with vested interests, see Roland Warren, "Comprehensive Planning and Coordination: Some Functional Aspects," *Social Problems* 20, no. 3 (Winter 1973): 355–364.

22. Feinberg, Glugover, and Zwetchenbaum, "Community Alternatives."

23. See Gottfredson and Gottfredson, *Decisionmaking in Criminal Justice*, pp. 329–357.

24. Warren F. Ilchman and Theodore M. Smith, "The Search for the Hyphen in Policy-Relevant Research, Some Notes on the Kinds and Uses of Thought," State University of New York at Albany, mimeo, no date.

25. David E. Duffee, *Explaining Criminal Justice: Community Theory and Criminal Justice Reform* (Cambridge, Mass.: Oelgeschlager, Gunn & Hain, 1980).

26. Leslie Wilkins, "Problems with the Concept of Crime," State University of New York at Albany, mimeo, no date.

27. Wendell L. French and Cecil H. Bell, Jr., *Organization Development* (Englewood Cliffs, N.J.: Prentice-Hall, 1973), pp. 84–96.

28. Edward A. Suchman, *Evaluative Research* (New York: Russell Sage Foundation, 1967), pp. 28–45.

29. Wilkins, "Problems with the Concept of Crime."

Chapter 15

Public Policy Implications of Elderly Crime

Evelyn S. Newman and Donald J. Newman

Both crime and concerns about aging are domestic problems of major significance in our society—problems that require continual reevaluation and new directions. It has been abundantly clear that past policies have been only partially effective in dealing with issues caused by the shift from a youthful to an elderly society; for the most part, our efforts have been dismal failures in addressing the crime problem. Neither the private sector nor the government has developed effective procedures for reducing crime or addressing the problems associated with old age either for the short or for the long range. In looking at the elderly as perpetrators of crime, as in this book, the two make a combination that is atypical of common perceptions of either old age or crime but that is, nevertheless, real and demanding of attention.

In order to suggest some policy issues, it is first necessary to ask whether this combined problem is of such dimensions or of such significance as to necessitate consideration of broad policy choices. We believe this book has clearly demonstrated the significance of the problem. However, given the dearth of research and professional writing and the silence of policy leaders about elderly crime, it is evident that this phenomenon is not yet generally perceived as a significant problem. Until such time as not only the professionals but the public at large recognize that crime by older persons is policy relevant, matters will be handled only by default.

It is a central task of this book to bring to professional and political attention some dimensions of the elderly crime problem. This is only a first and modest step, however. Based on what is already known, sophisticated research in this area appears timely and it is not premature to discuss some broad policy implications of the elderly crime problem.

IS ELDERLY CRIME A SIGNIFICANT ENOUGH SOCIAL ISSUE TO CALL FOR POLICY RESOLUTION?

It is clear from the little research now available that offenses committed by the elderly do not in any sense constitute a "crime wave," the recurrent and dangerous public perception that results when some types of crime or criminals receive extensive media coverage.[1] Even though, as the earlier chapters of this book have demonstrated, the numbers of elderly violators will probably increase as this age segment of our society grows larger, it is unlikely that elderly crime will ever be a large problem requiring emergency measures and quick-fix solutions, as is only too common in criminal justice. Absent great economic deterioration, the *rate* of elderly crimes (i.e., the number of offenses per 100,000 elderly people) probably will remain significantly lower than the criminal rate among younger cohorts. The seriousness of the problem is not in its magnitude, present or projected; the significance of the problem is its uniqueness. The fact that old persons, particularly first offenders who are in the last few years of their lives, commit crimes is anomalous, even incredible. And, of course, these atypical criminals bring confusion to our traditional methods of crime control. Both the goals of our criminal justice system and our techniques of crime control are directed to young criminals. People who commit crimes for the first time when they are elderly (in contrast to habitual criminals simply grown old) present different challenges, not only to our criminal justice system but to our public conscience as well.

In 1980 over 376,000 arrests were made of persons aged 55 and over for crimes ranging from petty misdemeanors to serious felonies.[2] Our common crime control procedures, which are designed for maximum force to halt violence and escape, are generally unnecessary for handling elderly offenders. Aged criminals not only challenge traditional techniques of crime control but raise questions about criminal justice objectives as well. Dealing with elderly violators causes us to consider both means and ends of our system of justice as it is applied to this atypical population and surely raises questions about economic and social policies that can lead life-long law-abiding citizens to engage in law-violating acts. As Wilkins has noted,

> Every person whom we determine as "deviant" is, to some degree, commenting by his actions not only upon himself, but also upon his society. In some deviant acts the degree of comment on society may be the major element, in others it may be a very small element. But even persons adjudged as insane reflect in their insanity something of the culture of their environment. We might try to hear some of the comment, even though we may deprecate the language of theft, assault, drug use, or demonstration in which it is expressed. The message (however encoded) may be important.[3]

GENERAL AWARENESS OF ELDERLY CRIME

Given the assumption that elderly crime is an important issue in our society, either because it challenges our traditional crime control methods or because it tests the boundaries of our ideology, a question remains of how, if at all, general awareness of the significance of this problem can be brought to the attention of the general public, legislators, political executives, and other significant policymaking individuals and groups. Awareness of crime problems usually comes about when the behavior in question is so unusual or threatening and occurs frequently enough across the entire county to enter public consciousness through media coverage. A second way may be when the persons who engage in the particular conduct wish to call attention to themselves, by seeking official approval or condemnation primarily to raise general awareness, as is the case with demonstrators and protestors. The third way to raise general awareness, probably much less efficient than media coverage or riots, is the reporting of research results by social scientists exploring new areas of crime or deviation. This latter method may evoke a much slower response from the general public, but on the other hand it may produce actions that are thought through rather than merely reactive, since presumably the facts are documented rather than merely titillating (as they may be in the media).

At present, elderly crime does not call attention to itself in any way. Except for certain areas of the country having a high concentration of elderly, the problem both in numbers of crimes and in terms of threat or harm is simply not big enough nor pressing enough to receive sustained media attention. In Sunbelt retirement communities, elderly lawbreakers occupy more space in the press and other media; in the rest of the nation, however—in such places as in New York, Chicago, Boston, San Francisco and other major metropolitan areas—elderly crime is a drop in the bucket of the general crime problem.[4]

And, of course, the elderly themselves do not wish to highlight a criminal image. Quite the contrary. A number of lobbying groups for elderly interests resent the linking of "elderly" with "criminal" no matter how factually accurate it may be. In general, the elderly wish to see themselves in quite a different light; in fact, they appear to prefer to be seen as victims deserving to be treated better, not as criminals.[5] In brief, older people have not generated any widespread publicity intended to highlight the crime problem.

Finally, academic research on elderly crime to date has been very sparse; the bulk of what has appeared in the literature has emanated from the criminal justice field rather than from gerontology. This may perhaps be a direct reflection of Gouldner's position that "Still in its early stage, gerontology has itself shown little interest in the social and political components of its developing knowledge base, and it is characterized by non-reflexive approaches that protect and insulate rsearchers from "hostile" information."[6]

Nevertheless, it is most likely that awareness of elderly crime will come from research if careful studies are done in widespread places which highlight dimensions of this problem. Much more fact-finding is essential. The extent and varieties of elderly crime must be measured much more precisely. Any trends in elderly crime patterns must be discovered and described accurately on a national basis. Sophisticated assessment of the problem will depend on empirical research to present a more objective picture and to subject to rigorous scientific measurement the many hypotheses regarding the cause of elderly crime. Duffee has already suggested other possible opportunities for research and its implications for policy.[7] Correlates of elderly crime must be examined that do not necessarily look for "causes" within the individual but that also focus on the social conditions that prompt people to act as they do. If the research is of high quality, of sufficient frequency, and widely disseminated, there is little doubt that issues about elderly crime will begin to be considered at various policymaking levels.[8] Action can then be taken on a rational rather then a *laissez-faire* basis.

PUBLIC POLICY ISSUES RAISED BY ELDERLY CRIME

Although there are policy issues that must be addressed with regard to the criminality of some older citizens, it is generally conceded that criminal justice concerns are ancillary to the drastic and dramatic changes in the economic and social status of the retired and to the public perception and self-concept of older Americans. That is, the root causes of elderly crime are probably no different in principle from the causes of crime committed by persons of any age; they must be found in the complex fabric of the economic and social order.

In considering issues of whether the criminal justice system can, or should, make accommodations in policy specifically for elderly law violators, we must also confront certain fundamental issues related to aging in our society: the complex social issues created by retirement from the work force, changes in economic and social status, health protection, and common public perceptions and stereotypes of the aged. As Estes has noted, "Politics, economics and social structure have far more to do with the role and status of the aged than does the aging process and its effects on the individual."[9] In short, it is necessary to concentrate not only on the criminal acts of old people but on the social conditions that may prompt them to act as they do.

Criminal acts, of necessity, require immediate response. We cannot wait for rehabilitation or punishment policies, for example, to be resolved nor can we wait for dramatic changes in attitudes toward the elderly to occur. Criminal acts cannot be condoned regardless of whether they are, as Wilkins suggests, a comment on society, or whether they are, for some elderly, a plea for attention and help.

THE ELDERLY IN THE CRIMINAL JUSTICE SYSTEM

The fundamental issue raised by elderly persons, perhaps even more than by younger adults, caught in the criminal justice network, apart from what brings them there in the first place, is how they should be treated. Is there something inherently different about older offenders that merits special consideration in criminal processing? In many ways, particularly in that they do not pose a long term continued threat to the social order, elderly offenders differ from yonger adults. In this population the dilemma of punishment or rehabilitation becomes even more real.

As a matter of fact, elderly people are often treated differently, de facto if not de jure, when they commit criminal acts. The reason is that elderly criminals pose many of the same ideological questions as do juvenile delinquents. Apart from culpability, apart from the capacity to comprehend wrongness, it generally seems inappropriate to react against grandparents as vigorously as we react to younger adult violators. It somehow seems wrong that a person who has lived a law-abiding, if not exemplary, life be branded, punished, and perhaps banished in old age for committing a minor crime. We generally attempt to offer in some fashion the same considerations to elderly offenders—particularly those who become first offenders at or near retirement age—as we give to juveniles. The differential treatment of the elderly, however, is unlike that accorded juveniles, in that it is not based on concern for ruining their later life chances or stigmatizing them so that future occupations or professions may be closed to them. Rather, leniency for aged offenders is retrospective, directed toward not dulling an otherwise good record or toward rewarding past "good" behavior by forgiving present indiscretions.

This more lenient attitude is most in evidence in supermarkets that do not bring charges against elderly shoplifters,[10] among police who do not make arrests,[11] and among prosecutors who sometimes do not prosecute[12] even the most extreme acts.[13] Perhaps this common practice of treating the elderly leniently whenever possible should be formalized as policy. Fyfe, for example, calls for increased police discretion in dealing with elderly offenders.[14] This, of course, would serve to enforce the law even more differentially than at present. While this policy appears to be in the older person's best interests, as just noted legal offenses cannot and should not be ignored regardless of the age of the perpetrator. Neither society nor the individual stands to benefit if the incident is not acknowledged by some type of formal action. In short, we cannot allow the differential toleration of crime based on chronological age.[15] Crimes committed by elderly people produce similar consequences as those committed by younger adults, regardless of whether the motives and methods are different. Cold-blooded murder committed by an octogenarian is still cold-blooded murder even though the perpetrator is old.

The case can also be made that non-response only serves to delay amelioration. It serves no useful purpose to simply dismiss elderly violators. Unless and until authorities formally respond to the problem, elderly people will continue to commit crimes. If no formal acknowledgment is made of a crime no intervention will be possible, and the precipitating factors—such as inadequate Social Security checks or lack of meaningful activity—will remain. A preferred policy, therefore, is that the law should be enforced equally for all adults regardless of age. Once that principle is established, the kind and degree of intervention can be examined.

An argument can be made for handling elderly offenders according to the model developed for juvenile delinquents. In some earlier chapters in this book the point was made that the circumstances surrounding elderly crime in our society are often similar to the circumstances surrounding juvenile delinquency. It must be clearly stated at the outset that old people and juveniles are not alike—neither physically, mentally, emotionally, nor in terms of life experiences. They do, however, occupy a similar status in society. Neither the young nor the old are workers in the marketplace. Both are accorded only low prestige, and few occupy dignified and honored roles. Both groups have worries about economic survival, particularly in times when the economy is particularly inflationary. Both have a great deal of leisure time; indeed, the retired old have more, for compulsory school attendance does not occupy their days. To a certain extent, both young and old are often on the fringe of family life, commerce, religion, and education. These factors might mandate treatment comparable to juveniles under the law.

Although chronological age may not be nearly as important as agility, intent, criminal sophistication, or other criteria, it has been U.S. policy to use age as a feasible criterion to separate young offenders from adult offenders and thus to place each of them in different systems for punishment and intervention. Although we allow courts some discretion at "border" ages (16 to 18 years old is common), for nearly a century, chronological age, not mental or emotional age, has been the means of determining who is treated by what system. And it is not always a matter of *mens rea*, the capability of deciding right and wrong. Indeed, *mens rea* may be the pretext for treating minors differently than we treat adults. As a matter of policy, we do not wish to subject young teenagers (until recently, no matter what their violations) to the drastic sanctions provided in criminal statutes. In a very real sense we measure ourselves—perhaps even our degree of civilization—by how we treat young people who deviate prior to maturity.

To a certain extent the juvenile justice system rests on the belief that youngsters should be given another chance, that unfortunate early conduct should not so color their lives that they can never escape from either the physical consequences of having been in jail or the criminal reputation. (In general, this differential treatment holds only for lesser crimes and not for murder, rape, and other atrocious and violent offenses.) The belief is that the bulk of minors who engage in theft or other property crimes should receive differential treatment. Juvenile justice, however, is not simply lenient criminal justice, it is a separate and distinct legal system that differs from the adult system in philosophy, purpose, and technique. Policy for juvenile delinquents and youthful offenders—those minors between the age of reason and of arbitrary adulthood—dictates that they should not be subject to the same sanctions (or, for that matter, to the same degree of proof) as adult offenders. To advocate this position, however, would be to add further indignity to these older persons. In juvenile justice the court acts *in loco parentis*, on the assumption that the child cannot determine what is in his own best interests. Mature individuals generally do not wish to be treated as dependents, or, worse still, to be equated with teenagers.

A better response would be that elderly criminals represent simply a different risk than younger adults do. Thus, less than maximum criminal justice techniques (which already exist) should be used with the elderly, and some leniency should be shown in the use of physical force and restraints. Current research suggests that elderly offenders are different in significant ways from younger ordinary criminals. In the main, elderly criminals are not career criminals. Nor are they likely to abscond if released at pretrial hearings or on post-conviction probation. Whether the differences between elderly criminals and those more youthful are so great as to call for an entirely new geriatric criminal justice system, however, is debatable. Alternatives already existent for younger adults can be used with the aged. Instead of developing new policies and procedures it may simply be necessary to clarify, in policy form, existing practices.

Abrams has called for a special geriatric court in which attention can be given to the elderly's special physical and emotional needs[16] However, it may be undesirable to develop a full-fledged geriatric justice system modeled on the juvenile court. It may be enough to reiterate, as policy, the consistent use of the *least restrictive alternative*,[17] which keeps in mind those special problems of older persons at each stage of criminal processing. For example:

1. *Arrest.* In our system of criminal justice, arrest usually involves taking custody of a suspect, sometimes by the use of force, including threatening the use of deadly force. It is customary to search and handcuff arrestees and to transport them from the point of arrest to a stationhouse for booking, fingerprinting, photographing, and interrogating. However, arrests also may be made by merely issuing the suspect a citation or a summons to appear later at a stationhouse, but not taking immediate physical custody. This is the usual procedure with traffic violations, for example. Under the least- restrictive

doctrine, elderly offenders would be issued citations instead of being taken into immediate physical custody unless there is clear evidence that the arrestee would pose a threat to the community or try to escape. All elderly offenders, whether taken into physical custody or issued citations, would be told of their rights to representation by an attorney. No proceedings would occur until the elderly suspect is represented by counsel, privately retained or court-appointed if the suspect is indigent.

2. *Pretrial release.* There would be a presumption in law that elderly offenders, whether taken into physical custody or arrested by citation, be released without monetary bail prior to further court proceedings. The only exceptions would be elderly offenders who, in the reasonable opinion of the magistrate, are highly likely to flee the jurisdiction. Under such conditions, monetary bail would be set as with all offenders.

3. *Pretrial diversion.* Wherever possible, if an elderly suspect is willing to admit the criminal act, he would be placed in a pretrial diversion program especially developed to supervise and counsel elderly offenders. If the pretrial diversion program proves successful (no recidivism), prosecution for the offense would be dropped. Prosecution would occur only if (a) the elderly person denied guilt and the prosecutor considered it desirable to pursue the case to trial or (b) the offender was found to be so dangerous or so likely to flee that pretrial diversion would be injudicious.

4. *Alternative sentencing.* In the event that the elderly offender is convicted by guilty plea or by trial and comes before the court for sentencing, incarceration should be the last option. If the offense is minor and particularly if it is a first offense, diversionary programs such as the Broward Senior Intervention and Education program[18] should be the treatment of choice. Successful completion of the program should expunge the record.

5. *Probation.* In our first attempts to develop juvenile codes, we used blanket-category exemptions from both liability and punishment. Today, however, juveniles who commit heinous crimes increasingly are being processed as adults. Now in a number of states minors as young as 13 can be tried and convicted for capital crimes (though not executed) in the traditonal criminal justice court system. This pattern of "getting tough" is almost certain to be followed with elderly offenders, particularly if predictions come true that with larger populations of elderly will come more serious crimes committed by this population. For this group of more serious elderly offenders, probation, not diversion into a noncriminal setting, should be the choice. Probation only follows conviction of the crime (in many diversion programs no

conviction record is kept) and involves release of the offender into the community under supervision by specially trained field agents. These probation officers would be specially trained to deal with elderly offenders and be otherwise familiar with gerontological and geriatric issues that might complicate probation supervision. Rules and conditions of probation as fixed by the court would be minimum in number and noninstrusive in content. Probation supervision for elderly offenders should be markedly shorter than for their younger counterparts, for such long-range needs as rehabilitation are probably irrelevant and the life span remaining for elderly offenders is considerably shorter. In effect, shorter terms of probation, as well as any terms of imprisonment, may be *proportionately* as long for elderly offenders. For example, a three-year sentence imposed on a 20-year-old offender may be short, but a similar term may occupy half the probable remaining lifespan of an 80-year-old.

6. *Incarceration*. Elderly offenders would be incarcerated only in the most extreme cases, for instance, if they committed particularly atrocious violent crimes or presented a continuing threat of committing further violent crimes. Incarceration would never be used to punish, to deter others, or to rehabilitate. The sole criterion would be incapacitation to prevent imminent further crimes. Such sentences would be rare. In fixing the length of imprisonment the court should take into account the offender's advanced age and should not impose a term so long as to be a life sentence, unless the particular crime carries a mandatory life sentence. All but the most dangerous elderly inmates should have a realistic chance to earn parole. Parole rules and conditions of supervision would be similar to probation rules and conditions discussed earlier.

It is probably at incarceration that the special needs of elderly persons become most evident. As Golden has pointed out, cellblocks are not designed for the old and infirm.[19] For those who are already incarcerated as well as for those who will be imprisoned, there must be clearly articulated policies addressing their special needs in housing, medical care, diet, and program.

The criminal justice system has not been very effective in controlling our traditional criminal population, not even with current policy to "get tough" through more frequent arrests, prosecutions, convictions, and longer sentences. There is no evidence to indicate that forceful apprehension and continued physical custody of criminals does much to deter others, nor aid in their rehabilitation. Punishment can be achieved by forceful means, of course, and in some cases maximum-security restraint is necessary to prevent individuals from committing more crimes. No one can deny that there are serious violent criminals who pose such a continued threat to our social order and whose acts are so heinous that close-custody incapacitation for life seems appropriate. In general, however, elderly criminals do not commit heinous and atrocious crimes and are not dangerous.

The existence, and the continued growth, of an elderly criminal population gives us an opportunity to experiment with new policies in handling offenders that may indeed be more generalizable than it seems at first. A nonrestrictive approach in processing criminals is a departure from traditional crime control, and it is precisely the opportunity to try this approach that elderly offenders provide for us.

In fact, one contribution elderly offenders may make to the criminal justice system may be to demonstrate that least restrictive methods work just as well as, and perhaps better than, traditional forms of strict prosecution and maximum-security control. It may be that the way we treat elderly criminals can spearhead a return to the structured use of diversion from criminal processing, a development that seemed to be blossoming in our society for the past two decades only to disappear with the end of federal crime control funds and a widespread "get tough" response as fear of crime spread like an epidemic.

It may be that a system of minimum restriction will be effective with elderly criminals and can serve as a model for younger adults. Only time and carefully researched experience will give us the answer. To this end, in addition to the aforementioned policies for processing older offenders, there must be an explicit policy requiring not only the careful measurement of the extent of the problem of elderly crime but careful evaluation of our methods of control. Should our crime control methods with the elderly fail, we can return to the more traditional ways we process younger offenders. But this criminal subpopulation gives us an opportunity to experiment, to try new approaches with minimum risk and with little threat to our social order. Until such time as the elderly in our society can face their post-retirement years with strong, if not absolute, assurance that they will be economically self-sufficient, and have adequate food, clothing, and housing, drastic steps to deal with their shoplifting and other property crimes—necessary though they be—can be only stop-gap measures. Therefore, it will also be necessary to establish policy that discourages those acts in the first place.

THE ELDERLY IN SOCIAL CONTEXT

In spite of such euphemisms as "the golden years," the last decades of the lives of many Americans are frequently not as pleasant as pictured. For many, perhaps most, entrance into old age is a time of uncertainty. And given our culture's long-standing admiration of youth and beauty, impending old age often brings anxiety, depression, and fear, In our fast-changing social order, uncertainty about the future of any aspect of one's life, from wealth to health, makes planning for old age especially risky. Uncertainty not only about the details of individual futures but also about the country's ability to carry out past public policy decisions (such as social security and medicaid) is particularly intense in this time of persistent economic chaos.

Policies for the aged generally have been guided by two conflicting principles. The first of these is that the elderly have not worked hard enough nor saved enough or have lived too long and are therefore responsible for their own plight. The second sees the elderly as victims of an exploitative economic and political system that is beyond their control. Depending on which principle is the guiding force of the moment, official intervention will either protect society from the threat of dependence of the "undeserving" elderly or will provide equity for "deserving" elderly for the hardships generated by society.[20] Moreover, as bad times get worse, and as inflation and depression continue, it is difficult to determine what we really want to do, hope to do, and intend to do about our elderly. It is difficult to determine how much the aged are expected to or can do for themselves or what the society can and should do for them. There is no doubt that the internalization of these uncertainties and fears has a great deal to do with crime by elderly persons.[21]

Some basic issues about the status of the elderly in our society must be addressed and public policies adopted to minimize the negative effects of these conditions on elderly persons. We must generally reduce uncertainty about the future for the increasing numbers of persons who will become old and retire—and, moreover, who will live longer. These general issues have all been discussed elsewhere; they are discussed here as they possibly relate to crimes committed by elderly persons.

1. *Assured income.* A central concern of all elderly is the adequacy of post-retirement income. This is a particularly complex and difficult problem in periods of sustained economic inflation and simultaneously increasing rates of unemployment. Until very recently it was widely believed that this problem had been solved. Out of the ashes

of the Great Depression, increased federal involvement in domestic problems led most people to believe that the Social Security program had settled the problem of assuring at least minimum incomes for most retired elderly. True, a few workers were not covered, but they were expected to have corporate or government retirement plans. In general, however, it was believed that persons who paid into the Social Security retirement system were building a retirement income and providing some insurance coverage for widows (or widowers) and under-age or infirm dependents.

The idea was that the money paid in by employees in the work force would support those retiring until all were so covered and could retire in turn. As we all know, two major problems have surfaced. The first is inflation, which makes the actual value of dollars paid out much lower than the value of earlier dollars paid in. The second is a shift in the ratio of active workers to the number of retired, not only in absolute numbers but in life expectancy as well. Thus, the *quid pro quo* nature of Social Security fell on hard times and is currently in a state of uncertainty as the Social Security Administration faces huge deficits. National political leaders have taken various strict stances, which range from "Social Security at any cost" to "pay-as-you-go" schemes. In any event, even though some form of retirement income is almost certain to remain, the assured income promised by Social Security (and by various private retirement plans as well) has been challenged. This, of course, is having a chilling effect on many who are close to retirement and creates a near panic in those who have retired and are relying on such income. Even those who are convinced that Social Security payments will continue, are concerned about the amount of those payments. For married people, the threat that the death of a spouse may cut income to less than half is devastating, even with the promise of Supplemental Security Income (SSI). Many of the current generation of elderly persons think of SSI as welfare in a new guise.

Although the fear of an uncertain economic future may be an underlying factor in elderly crime, not many of the thefts committed by elderly criminals appear to have been *directly* motivated by economic necessity.[22] In the main, the elderly who steal are adequately supported at present but are deeply (and perhaps accurately) concerned about the near future. Shoplifting can be seen as a way of saving cash for the proverbial "rainy day" or to be spent for other necessary items such as housing and medical care.

2. *Post-retirement housing.* The issue of where a retired person will live is related only in part to predictable retirement income. Of particular policy relevance is the consideration of whether the el-

derly's children (or other younger relatives) have any obligations, legal or moral, to provide housing and emotional support for their parents (or other elderly relatives), and to what extent. Given our nuclear family structure and the usual size of apartments and other housing arrangements, it may be both physically and economically impossible for most families to live with their elderly relatives. Except for some extended families—which, if found at all, are usually located in rural areas with large farms—it may be a physical impossibility for three-, four- (and increasingly five-) generation families to live together. Although recent policy decisions have determined that the children or younger relatives of the elderly are not responsible for their housing nor required to contribute to their support, the decision is still being reviewed and questions remain of what other arrangements are possible and desirable and where the responsibility for these arrangements lies.

Assuming that the *desideratum* is that the aged can be housed in their own dwellings separate from dwellings of their children, how should this housing be arranged, and how financed? The well elderly—that is, those not infirm and not requiring special care—have a variety of options. The availability and cost of these options varies markedly from place to place.

In considering the housing of the elderly apart from their children, one particular policy issue has been given a fair measure of attention by gerontologists: should the elderly be housed in age-segregated or age-integrated housing? Is it more desirable for a heterogeneous collection of elderly people, younger adults, and children to live together, or is it better, safer, and more satisfying to the elderly and to others if the old persons live by themselves? What is best in terms of security and the elderly's fear of crime?

A good deal of the physical and psychological security of retirement has to be do with living arrangements, quite apart from ability to pay. There is some evidence that the elderly have not been abandoned by their families, that visits and telephone calls are frequent, and that families are providing social and emotional support. Feinberg's research, however, has given evidence that, at least subjectively, one of the reasons elderly people shoplift is to provoke additional attention from their families.[23] This finding remains to be substantiated.

It must be remembered, too, that whatever housing arrangements are initially agreed on for the well elderly and the newly retired, needs and requirements may change, and indeed will change, as these "young" elderly age. They will increasingly require greater physical care and assistance, and perhaps special diets or specially equipped physical facilities, as time goes by. The older person typically moves from retirement apartment to nursing home, rarely the reverse. A good deal of the elderly's fear, anxiety, and depression has to do with the uncertainty of appropriate housing and adequate care as physical deterioration and the illnesses of old age set in. Money that has been set aside to provide for the contingencies of old age no longer appears adequate. This is particularly true if one of the partners in a marriage must spend any considerable time in a nursing home and the other must continue to support a lifestyle in the community.

3. *Medical care.* Absent national health insurance, a major concern of the elderly and their families (and indeed of society as a whole) is the quality, availability, and cost of medical care. Medicaid and Medicare, like Social Security, do not relieve financial anxieties. From visits to doctor's offices to intensive hospitalization, the exorbitant costs are as good an indication of inflation as any. The costs of visits to physicians' offices have increased nearly tenfold in the past few years, and expenses for extensive hospitalization are well beyond the economic ability of all but the very rich. Elderly people are well aware that if life expectancy increases as predicted, their medical necessities will also increase in frequency, duration, and cost. The cost of prescription drugs is astronomical, and increasing frailty brings an increased use of such drugs. To prevent theft by the elderly, to prevent anger and frustration leading to assault and to worse offenses, policy decisions to create a predictable, adequate medical environment are essential.

4. *Post-retirement prestige and esteem.* Retirement from the work force in our society is an extremely complex process, both for the people who retire and for the society in which they live. The stress of retirement can be only partially addressed by dealing with financial, housing, and health services. With few exceptions, everyone in our society who has lived long enough will retire from active employment. In a society that stresses youthful values and retains a strong belief that a person is defined by his major employment, people who retire are bound to feel that stepping out is stepping down. There are few role models, except for those in advertising and media stereotyping, of the successfully and happily retired. And more often than not, even the model for a successfully retired person is simply one who has adopted a new occupation that may have been an avocation before retirement. In their efforts to find a meaningful use of newly found time, many people "volunteer" in some new activity, only to find that the major difference between work and retirement is that in retirement one is not paid. Recognition will certainly be given to those with the talent of a Grandma Moses or the energy of an elderly community activist. But the crash of silence, the long,

unfulfilled hours, the fear, the anxiety, and the "nonperson" status of those who leave the world of regular work and regular hours requires complex and fundamental adjustments that, unless carefully planned for, are often traumatic, frightening, and depressing.

All the adjustment, of course, must not be made by those who retire. As a society we are distressed to see old people "doing nothing." They may be happily occupied feeding pigeons in the park, but we do not recognize this as gainful occupation. How much of our guilt produces their anxiety? It might be that if meaningful activities were available for those who wished to pursue such endeavors the rest of society would feel less ill at ease knowing that those in the parks and the shopping malls were there by choice.

The foregoing suggestions have not been offered as any panacea for the prevention of elderly crime, for no simplistic changes in either societal attitudes or economic realities will abolish these acts totally. In fact, several writers have already pointed out that a certain amount of deviance will probably always exist. The point being made here is that elderly people who commit crimes are perhaps influenced more by these external events than are other groups. Altering societal pressures has frequently been offered as one way of decreasing crime statistics for both adults and juveniles. Despite this, we continue to investigate and advocate a reactive rather than a proactive response to crime.

Although it remains to be proved that elderly people begin committing crimes in order to relieve anxiety about the future, research might indeed bear this out. This stance would appear to support the position that redistribution of resources be based on age rather than need, a position quite contrary to current gerontological thought. Such is not the case at all. While calling for remediation of maldistribution for all, we still must point out, at least in terms of crime provocation, that unlike younger people, the elderly will not "outgrow" economic and social neglect. Also unlike younger persons, older persons who are anxious about the future are given no hope that they might eventually grow into something better.

Certainly no public policy statement can simply order us to honor the aged, nor can it create in the elderly a sense of prestige and personal worth. On the other hand, it is increasingly clear that as our population ages and lives longer, the resolution of these basic issues is necessary if old age is ever to be comfortable and attractive and does not precipitate the anxieties described here.

NOTES

1. For an extensive discussion of how crime issues are often turned into media fare, see Dan A. Lewis (ed.), *Reactions to Crime* (Beverly Hills, Calif.: Sage, 1981). See especially the chapters by Fay L. Cook, "Crime and the Elderly: The Emergence of a Policy Issue" and by Margaret T. Gordon and Linda Heath, "The News Business, Crime and Fear."

2. FBI, *Uniform Crime Reports, 1980* (Washington, D.C.: U.S. Government Printing Office, 1980).

3. Leslie T. Wilkins, "Crime in the World of 1980," *Futures* (September 1970): 210.

4. As a result of the First Annual Conference on Elderly Criminals held in Albany, New York, in 1982, publicity was not only nationwide, but international and totally unexpected. This small conference with the reports of participants (many of whom are authors in this book) was given virtually continuous coverage in major American newspapers, on national television, in national news magazines and on radio talk shows, and in newspapers in Europe for most of the year following the conference. Once the stories about elderly crime began, perhaps the major motive perpetuating them was simply competition among media, not an awakening to a pressing problem. However, during the conference and the following year this topic was seized upon by press and other media and widely disseminated. In part, media interest was caught not so much because both elderly and crime are important problems but because the relationship between them seemed exactly contrary to stereotypes of elderly persons and criminals. It is, however, safe to say that awareness of elderly crime in our society is much more widespread now than it was before the Albany conference.

5. The Gray Panthers, for example, distributed a pamphlet at the 1977 annual meeting of the Gerontological Society which read in part, "When persons who are old, poor, and stigmatized by society become objects of gerontological research, they are seen as problems to society, rather than as persons experiencing problems in society. The natural result of such research is to suggest ways in which older people may adjust to society rather than how society might be changed to adjust to the needs of older people."

6. Alvin Gouldner, *The Coming Crisis of Western Sociology* (New York: Basic Books, 1970).

7. David Duffee, "A Research Agenda," Chapter 14, this book.

8. While not specifically addressing the elderly criminal, Edwin M. Schur, *Our Criminal Society* (Englewood Cliffs, N.J.: Prentice-Hall, 1969) and Alfred McClung Lee, *Sociology For Whom?* (New York: Oxford University Press, 1978), have discussed the manner by which sociologists influence social policy in the way they design criminological research. Caroll L. Estes, in *The Aging Enterprise* (San Francisco: Jossey-Bass, 1979), does the same for gerontological research in general.

9. Estes, ibid, p. 28.

10. David Proper, "The Supermarket's Response to the Elderly Shoplifter," paper given at the First Annual Conference on Elderly Criminals, Albany, New York, March 15, 1982.

11. James J. Fyfe, "Police Dilemmas in Processing Elderly Offenders," Chapter 7, this book.

12. Charles Cutshall, "A Preliminary Analysis of the PROMIS Data," unpublished paper, State University of New York at Albany, 1983.

13. Fred Cohen, "Old Age as a Criminal Defense," Chapter 8, this book.

14. Fyfe, "Police Dilemmas."
15. Cohen, "Old Age as a Criminal Defense."
16. Albert J. Abrams, "Foreword," this book.
17. Joseph Goldstein, Anna Freud, and Albert J. Soluit, in *Beyond the Best Interests of the Child* (New York: The Free Press, 1973), proposed "the least detrimental alternative" to convey that the child is already a victim of his environment and that speedy action is necessary to avoid further harm being done (p. 54). We propose the same is true for elderly adults.
18. See Gary Feinberg, Sidney Glugover, and Irene Zwetchkenbaum, "The Broward Senior Intervention and Education Program," Chapter 12, this book.
19. Delores Golden, "Elderly Offenders in Jail," Chapter 9, this book.
20. Estes, *The Aging Enterprise.*
21. This statement is in no way intended to contradict Edelman that acceptances of contradictory myths permit individuals to "play the role society demands while at the same time maintaining a measure of personal integrity by recognizing facts inconsistent with the role....[In this way] people survive by occupying coexisting realities that only rarely disturb each other." M. Edelman, *Words That Succeed and Policies That Fail* (New York: Academic Press, 1977), p. 151. Rather, we are suggesting that the low crime rate of the elderly can be accounted for by the acceptance of this ambiguity by the vast majority. In the small percentage who do find themselves as law breakers, failure to tolerate this ambiguity may be one of the causal factors.
22. Gary Feinberg, "Profile of the Elderly Shoplifter," Chapter 3, this book.
23. Ibid.

Bibliography

Adams, M. E., and C. Vedder. "Age and Crime: Medical and Sociological Characteristics of Prisoners Over 50." *Journal of Geriatrics* 16 (1961): 177–180.

Aday, Ronald H., and Edgar L. Webster. "Aging in Prison: The Development of a Preliminary Model." *Offender Rehabilitation* 3 (Spring 1979): 271–282.

Amir, M., and S. Bergman. "Crime and Delinquency Among Aged in Israel: An Experience Survey." *Israel Annals of Psychiatry and Related Disciplines* 11 (1973): 33–48.

———. "Patterns of Crime Among Aged In Israel: A Second Phase Report." *Israel Annals of Psychiatry and Related Disciplines* 14 (1976): 280–288.

Back, Kurt W., and Kenneth J. Gergen, "Personal Orientation and Morale of the Aged." in Ida H. Simpson and John McKinney, (eds.), *Social Aspects of Aging*. Durham, N.C.: Duke University Press, 1966.

Baier, George F. "The Aged Inmate." *American Journal of Correction* 23 (March–April 1961): 4–6, 30, 34.

Barrett, J. G. "Aging and Delinquency." In *Gerontological Psychology*. Springfield, Ill.: Charles C. Thomas, 1972.

Bengtson, V. L., and David Hàber. "Sociological Approaches to Aging." In D. S. Woodruff and J. E. Birren (eds.), *Aging*. New York: Van Nostrand Reinhold, 1975.

Bergman, S., and M. Amir. "Crime and Delinquency Among the Aged in Israel." *Geriatrics* 28 (January 1973): 149–157.

Bisco, B. "Data on Antisocial Behavior in the Elderly." *Ospedale Psychiatrico* (Napoli) 44 (1973): 219–242.

Bittner, Egon. "The Police on Skid-Row: A Study of Peace Keeping." *American Sociological Review* 32 (1967): 699–715.

Cain, Leonard D. "Aging and the Law." In R. H. Binstock and E. Shanas (eds.), *Handbook of Aging and The Social Sciences*. New York: Van Nostrand Reinhold, 1976.

Cameron, Mary Owen. *The Booster and the Snitch*. New York: The Free Press, 1970.

Carlie, M. K. "The Older Arrestee: Crime in the Later Years of Life." Ph.D. dissertation, Washington University, 1970.

This list is not intended to be exhaustive. In recent months, there has been a marked increase in research about elderly criminals. This bibliography should, however, enable any serious researcher to begin work in this area. Additional specific references are to be found with each chapter.

Casey, Lee, and John L. Shuman. "Police/Probation Shoplifting Reduction Program in San Jose, California: A Synergetic Approach." *Crime Prevention Review* 6 (1970): 1–9.

Chambliss, W. J. *Box Man: A Professional Thief's Journey.* New York: Harper & Row, 1972.

Cohen, Lawrence, and Rodney Stark. "Discriminatory Labeling and the Five Finger Discount: An Empirical Analysis of Differential Shoplifting Dispositions," *Journal of Research in Crime and Delinquency* 11 (1974): 25–39.

Costales, V. E. "Washington—Elderly Offenders, Fiscal Year 1967 through Year 1970." Olympia, Washington Department of Social and Health Services.

Dertke, Max, L. Penner, et al. "Observers Reporting of Shoplifting as a Function of Thief's Race and Sex." *Journal of Social Psychology* 94 (1974): 220.

Dickens, B. M. "Shops, Shoplifting, and Law Enforcement." *Criminal Law Review* (1969): 464–472.

Elwell, F., and Alice D. Maltbie-Crannell. "The Impact of Role Loss upon Coping Resources and Life Satisfaction of the Elderly." *Journal of Gerontology* 36 (March 1981): 223–232.

Epstein, L. J., C. Mills, and A. Simon. "Antisocial Behavior of the Elderly." *Comprehensive Psychiatry* 11 (1970): 36–42.

Etzioni, Amitai, "Old People and Public Policy," *Social Policy* 7 (1976): 21–29.

Fournier, G., et al. "Les Aspects du Vol dans les Grands Magasins." *International Annals of Criminology* 9 (1970): 455–464.

Galiani, I. "Criminological and Medico-Legal Aspects of Sex Crimes Committed by Elderly." *Giornale di Gerontologia* 26 (1978): PO190-0190.

Gillespie, Michael W., and John F. Galliher. "Age, Anomie, and the Inmates' Definition of Aging in Prison: An Exploratory Study." In Donald P. Kent, Robert Kastenbaum, and Sylvia Sherwood (eds.), *Research Planning and Action for the Elderly.* New York: Behavioral Publications, 1972.

Glazer, B., and Anselm Strauss. *Status Passage.* Chicago: Aldine, 1971.

Glueck, Sheldon and Eleanor Glueck. *Later Criminal Careers,* New York: The Commonwealth Fund, 1950.

Ham, J. N. "The Forgotten Minority—An Exploration of Long- Term Institutionalized Aged and Aging Male Prison Inmates." Ph.D. dissertation, University of Michigan, 1976.

Hays, David, and Morris Wisotsky. "The Aged Offender: A Review of the Literature and Two Current Studies from the New York State Division of Parole." *Journal of the American Geriatrics Society.* 17, 11 (1969): 1064–1073.

Jensen, Gary F. "Age and Rule-Breaking in Prison, a Test of Sociocultural Interpretation." *Criminology* 14 (February 1977): 555–568.

Keller, O., and C. Badder. "The Crimes that Old Persons Commit." *Gerontologist* 8 (1968): 43–50.

Knoy, Martha. "Elderly Alcoholics." *Geron Topics,* Vol. II, No. 1, 1978.

Krajick, K. "Growing Old in Prison." *Corrections Magazine* 5 (March 1979): 33–46.

Kunce, Joseph T., Joseph J. Ryan, and C. Cleary Eckelman. "Violent Behavior and Differential WAIS Characteristics." *Journal of Consulting and*

Clinical Psychology 44, 1 (February 1976): 42–45.

Larry, P. "Misuse and Abuse of Drugs by Elderly: Another View." *American Pharmacy* 20, 5 (May 1980): 14.

Lennon, B. E., J. H. Rekosh, V. D. Patch, and L. P. Howe. "Self Reports of Drunkenness Arrests." *Quarterly Journal of Studies on Alcohol* 31 (1970): 90–96.

Lieberman, M. "Institutionalization of the Aged: Effects on Behavior." *Journal of Gerontology* 24 (1969): 330–340.

Lowenthal, Marjorie Fiske. "Social Isolation and Mental Illness in Old Age." *American Sociological Review* 29 (February 1964): 54–70.

McCall, J., W. Christopher, and D. Jurzcak. "Special Problem Patients? Psychotic, Geriatric, Retarded, Sex Offenders." *Mental Health for the Convicted Offender. Patient and Prisoner.* North Carolina Department of Correction, Raleigh, N.C.: (1977), pp. 173–174.

McCarthy, Maureen. "The Health Status of Elderly Inmates." *Corrections Today* (February 1983): 64–74.

McCreary, Charles P., and Ivan N. Mensh. "Personality Differences Associated with Age in Law Offenders." *Journal of Gerontology* 32 (March 1977): 164–167.

Malinchak, Alan A. *Crime and Gerontology.* Englewood Cliffs, N.J.: Prentice-Hall, 1980.

Mandell, Jonathan. "The Unlikely Criminals." *New York Daily News Sunday Magazine,* September 7, 1980.

Markham, G. "The Elderly Offender and the Policy." *Justice of the Peace* 144 (1980): 97–98.

Moberg, David O. "Old Age and Crime." *Journal of Criminal Law, Criminology and Police Science* 43 (1953): 764–776.

Morton, Joann B., and Judy C. Anderson. "Elderly Offenders: The Forgotten Minority." *Corrections Today* (December 1982): 14–20.

Neugarten, Bernice L., Joan W. Moore, and John C. Lowe. "Age Norms, Age Constraints, and Adult Socialization." *American Journal of Sociology* 70 (May 1965): 710–717.

Newman, Donald J., and Evelyn S. Newman. "Senior Citizen Crime." *Justice Reporter* 2, 5 (September–October 1982): 1–8.

North Carolina Department of Corrections. "Characteristics of Aged Inmates." Raleigh, N.C., 1974.

Panton, James H. "Personality Characteristics of Aged Inmates Within a State Prison Population." *Offender Rehabilitation* 1 (Winter 1976–1977): 203–208.

Petersilia, J. "Which Inmates Participate in Prison Treatment Programs?" *Journal of Offender Counseling Services and Rehabilitation* 4, 2 (Winter 1979): 121–135.

Pollak, O. "The Criminality of Old Age." *Journal of Criminal Psychopathology* 3 (1941): 213–235.

Proceedings from the Conference of the German Federal Republic Association for Convicted Offender Assistance, 11th, 1978. Muenster/Westfaler, West Germany, "Convicted Offender Assistance—Yesterday, Today, Tomorrow," available from Bundesausammensehusses, Fuer Straffalligenhilfe, 5300 Bonn-Bad Godesberg, West Germany.

Reed, Monika B., and Francis D. Glamser, "Aging in a Total Institution: The Case of Older Prisoners." *Gerontologist* 19 (August 1979): 354–360.

Rifai, M. A. "Cognitive Aspects of the Older Adult's Attitudes Toward the Legal System." *Applied Systems Research and Development,* Inc., Wilsonville, Or., 1976.

Riley, Matilda White, Ann Foner, et al. *Aging and Society. Volume 1: An Inventory of Research Findings.* New York: Russell Sage Foundation, 1968.

Rodstein, Manuel. "Crime and the Aged." *Journal of the American Medical Association* 234 (November 1975): 639.

Rolph, C. H. *Homeless from Prison.* Dunfermline, Fife, Scotland: Special After-Care Trust.

Rose, Arnold, "The Subculture of Aging: A Framework for Research in Social Gerontology." In Arnold Rose and W. Peterson (eds.), *Older People and Their Social Worlds.* Philadelphia: F. A. Davis, 1965, pp. 3–16.

Rosin, Arnold J., and M. M. Glatt. "Alcohol Excesses in the Elderly." *Quarterly Journal of Studies on Alcohol* 32 (March 1971): 53–59.

Rosow, Irving. *Socialization to Old Age.* Berkeley: University of California Press, 1974.

Roth, M. "Cerebral Disease and Mental Disorders of Old Age as Causes of Antisocial Behavior." In A. DeReuck (ed.), *The Mentally Abnormal Offender.* Boston: Little, Brown, 1968.

Rowe, Alan R., and Charles R. Tuttle. "Life Cycle Changes and Criminal Propensity." *Sociological Quarterly* 18 (Spring 1977): 223–236.

Russell, M. "Programs for Women Who Shoplift." *Canadian Journal of Criminology* 20 (1978): 73–74.

Schroeder, P. L. "Criminal Behavior in the Later Period of Life," *American Journal of Psychiatry* 92 (1936): 915–920.

Schaeffer, H. "Age and Criminality—on the Problem of Breaking Off Criminal Careers." *Kriminologisches Journal* 6, no. 3 (July–September 1974): 209–216.

Shichor, David, and Solomon Kobrin. "Note: Criminal Behavior Among the Elderly." *Gerontologist* 18 (April 1978): 213–218.

Shimzu, M. "A Study on the Crimes of the Aged in Japan," *AETA Criminologue et Medicina-Legalis Japoniza* 39 (1973): 202–213.

Silfen, Peter. "The Adaptation of the Older Prisoner in Israel." *International Journal of Offender Therapy and Comparative Criminology* 21 (1977): 57–65.

Snodgrass, Jon, and The Jack Roller. *The Jack Roller at Seventy.* Lexington, Mass.: Lexington Books, 1982.

Sohier, Jean. "A Rather Ordinary Crime: Shoplifting," *International Criminal Police Review* 229 (1969): 161–166.

Stark, Rodney, and James McEvoy. "Middle-Class Violence." *Psychology Today* 4 (November 1970): 52–54, 110–112.

Steffensmeier, D. J., and R. H. Steffensmeier, "Who Reports Shoplifters? Research Continuities and Further Developments." *International Journal of Criminology and Penology* 5 (1977): 79–95.

Stone, Ken, and Richard A. Kalish. "Of Poker, Roles, and Aging: Description, Discussion, and Data." *International Journal of Aging and Human Development* 4 (1973): 1–13.

Teller, Fran E. "Criminal and Psychological Characteristics of the Older Prisoner." Ph.D. dissertation, Brigham Young University, 1980.

Versele-Severin, C. "A Study of Female Shoplifters in Major Department Stores." *International Police Review* 24 (1969): 66–70.

Wallace, S. E. *Skid Row as a Way of Life.* Lotowa, N.J.: Bedminster Press, 1965.

Wells-Parker, Elizabeth, and Barbara G. Spencer. *Drinking Patterns, Problem Drinking, and Stress in a Sample of Aged Drinking Drivers.* Social Science Research Center, Mississippi State University, 1980.

Whiskin, F. "Delinquency in the Aged." *Journal of Geriatric Psychiatry* 1 (1968): 243–252.

Wiegand, N. D., and J. C. Burger. "Elderly Offender and Parole." *Prison Journal* 59 (Autumn–Winter 1979): 48–57.

Wiltz, C. J. "The Influence of Age on Length of Incarceration." Ph.D. dissertation, University of Iowa, 1978.

Windham, G. O., and E. Posey. "Problem Drinking and the Aged DWI Offender." Paper presented to the Mid-South Sociological Association, Monroe, La., November 1977.

Wixen, Joan. "They Retired to Prison." *Modern Maturity* 18 (February–March 1975): 46–48.

Wooden, Wayne S., and Jay Parker. "Aged Men in a Prison Environment: Life Satisfaction and Coping Strategies." *Gerontologist* 20 (Part II, November 1980): 231.

Won, George, and George Yamamoto. "Social Structure and Deviant Behavior: A Study of Shoplifting," *Sociology and Social Research* 53 (1968): 44–55.

Zax, M., E. A. Gardner, and W. T. Hart. "Public Intoxication in Rochester: A Survey of Individuals Charged During 1961." *Quarterly Journal of Studies on Alcohol* 25 (1964): 669–678.

Zimberg, Sheldon. "Diagnoses and Treatment of the Elderly Alcoholic." *Alcoholism: Clinical and Experimental Research* 2 (January 1978): 27–29.

About the Contributors

Authors and Editors:

Evelyn S. Newman, M.L.S., is Research Associate and former Associate Director of the Ringel Institute of Gerontology, School of Social Welfare, Nelson A. Rockefeller College of Public Affairs and Policy, State University of New York at Albany. She is author of numerous articles in gerontology. Her current research interests, in addition to elderly criminals, are drug use by the elderly and long-term care.

Donald J. Newman, Ph.D., is Dean of the School of Criminal Justice, Nelson A. Rockefeller College of Public Affairs and Policy, State University of New York at Albany. He is author of numerous books, monographs, book chapters, and articles in criminal justice. His current interests are problems of prison overcrowding, long term prisoners, elderly offenders, plea bargaining, and public policy involving major criminal justice issues.

Mindy L. Gewirtz, M.P.S., M.S.W., was Project Coordinator for the First Annual Conference on Elderly Criminals sponsored by the Ringel Institute of Gerontology, School of Social Welfare and the School of Criminal Justice, Nelson A. Rockefeller College of Public Affairs and Policy, State University of New York at Albany. She is currently Coordinator of the Senior Adult Department of Albany Jewish Family Services in Albany, New York. Her research interests include case management and counselling of the elderly.

Contributors:

Albert Abrams, former city manager of Newburgh, New York, and former Secretary of the New York State Senate, was a founder and President of the National Council on the Aging. He now serves as President of the Retired Public Employees Association of New York and President of the Albany Senior Service Centers, Inc.

Fred Cohen, B.S., L.L.B., L.L.M., is Professor of Law and Criminal Justice at the Graduate School of Criminal Justice, Nelson A. Rockefeller College of Public Affairs and Policy, State University of New York at Albany. He is author of numerous books, monographs, and articles in the areas of criminal law and procedure, juvenile justice, and commitment of the mentally incompetent, He is currently editor-in-chief of the *Criminal Law Bulletin.*

David E. Duffee, Ph.D., is Professor of Criminal Justice and Public Policy at the Graduate School of Criminal Justice, Nelson A. Rockefeller College of Public Affairs and Policy, State University of New York at Albany. He has conducted research in schools, courts, and prisons and is currently engaged in community correctional projects in New York and Pennsylvania.

Gary Feinberg, ABD, is Assistant Professor of Sociology and Program Coordinator (Criminal Justice Department) at Biscayne College, Miami, Florida. He has written numerous articles on crime and the elderly and has served public and private agencies as a research consultant on various aspects of elderly criminality. His current areas of interest include: shoplifting by the elderly, victimology, and the impact of criminal justice manpower and budgetary commitment on crime control.

James J. Fyfe, Ph.D., is Associate Professor at The American University School of Justice, College of Public and International Affairs, and is a Senior Fellow at the Police Foundation. A former lieutenant with the New York City Police Department, his research interests focus on police use of deadly force and other police operational practices.

Sidney Glugover, a former sergeant in the New York City Police Department, is counselor at the Broward Senior Intervention and Education Program (Elderly Shoplifters), South East Focal Point Senior Center, Jewish Community Center of South Broward, Hollywood, Florida.

Ann Goetting, Ph.D., is Associate Professor of Sociology at Western Kentucky University, Bowling Green, Kentucky. She is the author of numerous articles on divorce, remarriage, family law, and conjugal association in prison. Her current research interests are women and blacks in prison and recidivism.

Delores Golden is Director of Inmate Services, Albany County Sherriff's Department, Albany County Jail and Penitentiary, Albany, New York. Her current interests are alternatives for the first time offender, program needs for county jail inmates of all ages, and research on the elderly inmate.

Stephen J. Hucker, M.B., B.S., F.R.C.P.(C), M.R.C. Psych, is Chief of Forensic Service at Clarke Institute of Psychiatry and Assistant Professor of Psychiatry at the University of Toronto. He is author or co-author of a number of publications relating to forensic and other aspects of psychiatry. His main interests are teaching of forensic psychiatry and research involved with various types of sex offenders (especially rapists, pedophiles, and those with gender disturbances) in correctional settings.

Allan R. Meyers, Ph.D., is Associate Director of the School of Public Health of the Boston University School of Medicine. His research interests include long-term care, drinking and driving, as well as alcohol use and problem drinking by older adults.

Dennis D. Murphy, Ph.D., is a Research Associate at Academic Computing Services, Florida International University, Miami, Florida. His research interests include analysis of crime statistics.

Daniel I. Rubenstein, Ph.D., A.C.S.W., is Professor of Social Work at the School of Social Work, Syracuse University, Syracuse, New York. As author of studies and articles on the unique elderly, his current study and writing focuses on the incarcerated elderly, the hungry, and the homeless.

David Shichor, Ph.D., is Associate Professor in the Department of Sociology, California State College, San Bernadino. He is author and co-author of two books and numerous articles and book chapters in criminology, juvenile delinquency, penology, and victimology. His current research interests are elderly offenders, corporate crime, and criminal justice policies.

William Wilbanks, Ph.D., is Associate Professor in the Department of Criminal Justice, Florida International University, Miami, Florida. His major research interests and publications are in homicide, women and crime, the elderly offender, and prison riots.

Irene Zwetchkenbaum, B.S., is Counselor/Lecturer for the Broward Senior Intervention and Education Program (Elderly Shoplifters),

South East Focal Point Senior Center, Jewish Community Center of South Broward, Hollywood, Florida. Her current research interests involve mental health and its relation to the behavior patterns of the elderly.